PHILOSOPHY, REVISION, CRITIQUE

DAVID WITTENBERG

Philosophy, Revision, Critique

Rereading Practices in Heidegger, Nietzsche, and Emerson

STANFORD UNIVERSITY PRESS

STANFORD, CALIFORNIA 2001

Stanford University Press
Stanford, California
© 2001 by the Board of Trustees of the
Leland Stanford Junior University

Printed in the United States of America
on acid-free, archival-quality paper

Library of Congress Cataloging-in-Publication Data

Wittenberg, David.
    Philosophy, revision, critique : rereading practices in
Heidegger, Nietzsche, and Emerson / David Wittenberg.
      p. cm.
    Includes bibliographical references and index.
    ISBN 0-8047-3415-1 (alk. paper)
    1. Methodology. 2. Hermeneutics. 3. Philosophy—Historio-
graphy. 4. Heidegger, Martin, 1889–1976. Nietzsche. I. Title.
    BD241.W58 2001
    101—dc21   00-045047

Original Printing 2001
Last figure below indicates year of this printing:
10 09 08 07 06 05 04 03 02 01

Typeset by Robert C. Ehle in 10/13 Janson

For Agnes and Albert Wittenberg

Acknowledgments

For their generosity in reading, criticizing, or otherwise encouraging my work, I thank Jean-Paul Bourdier, Sharon Cameron, Tom Chastain, Renee Chow, Jennifer Culbert, Dennis Deschenes, Tim Duke, Julie Gabrielli, Alex Giardino, Werner Hamacher, Janine Holc, William Huggett, Kathleen James, Debra Keates, Wesley Kisting, David Michael Levin, Ana Lipscomb, Jean McGarry, Lenore Messick, John Srygley, Helen Tartar, Kat Vlahos, Andrzej Warminski, Kate Warne, David Wellbery, and Agnes Wittenberg. I especially thank Timothy Bahti, Lara Trubowitz, Hayden White, and Michael Witmore for their careful and challenging readings of the manuscript. Their responses were invaluable. I thank Jeff Charis-Carlson for his work on the index. I offer my warmest thanks to Judith Butler for her guidance, criticism, and inspiration during all stages of this project. Finally, I am grateful to the members of the academic departments who made possible the research in this book: the Johns Hopkins Humanities Center, the Rhetoric Department at the University of California, Berkeley, and the Departments of Comparative Literature and English at the University of Iowa.

D.W.

Contents

Abbreviations

AI	Bloom, *The Anxiety of Influence*
AR	Jauss, *Toward an Aesthetic of Reception*
BT	Heidegger, *Being and Time*
E	Emerson, *Essays and Lectures*
EP	Heidegger, *The End of Philosophy*
MM	Bloom, *A Map of Misreading*
Ne	Heidegger, *Nietzsche* (in English), volumes 1 through 4
Ng	Heidegger, *Nietzsche* (in German), volumes 1 and 2
S	Nietzsche, *Studienausgabe*, volumes 1 through 15
VA	Heidegger, *Vorträge und Aufsätze*
WP	Nietzsche, *The Will to Power*

PHILOSOPHY, REVISION, CRITIQUE

Oh, Time, Strength, Cash, and Patience!

— MELVILLE, *Moby Dick*

Introduction

This book is a critique of revision in philosophical texts and in the histories formed by those texts. Revision has rarely been considered a problem within the discipline of philosophy, even by thinkers for whom the rhetorical and intertextual characteristics of philosophical thinking are crucial. One of my goals is to help reorient the critique of philosophical textuality around the particular rereading strategies that enable philosophical texts to form, and conform to, canons of inquiry and presentation. This goal allies my study with literary critics concerned with the generic and institutional characteristics of philosophical writing, an alliance which shifts the book away from the disciplinary center at which the traditional philosophical *topoi*—ontology, epistemology, ethics, and so forth—still hold sway. But philosophy, as it confronts us today and as it has for a long time, is such a web of textual affiliations and contraventions that not even a philosopher ought to be surprised if an eccentric analysis of the ways philosophers reread and revise one another ends by proposing a theory of the philosophical itself. It may turn out that the philosophical discipline comprises less a forum for inquiring about the world or the beings within it than a *forum* in the much older sense, a marketplace in which what is produced and traded is not primary or secondary philosophical goods, but instead an elaborate kind of gossip about other philosophers.

My argument will proceed from two premises that, although unsurprising in themselves, together produce implications that have not yet been fully understood either by philosophers or by their critics. The first premise is that philosophical practice is *historical*, not simply in the sense that philosophies belong to varying periods or epochs, but more precisely, in the sense that philosophies develop into and out of canons, and that philosophical thinking within such canons conforms to historically determined forms of inquiry and presentation—in essence, that philosophy is a genre. The second premise, in part following upon the first, is that philosophy is *textual*. The endowment of philosophy consists almost exclusively of a body of written artifacts, constructed and produced through a set of strict protocols according to which such artifacts may be published, disseminated, reread, and criticized, in their minor dialectical divergences from kindred texts. A combination of these two premises gives a starting point for the critique I will conduct here: philosophy is *revision*, a history of textual alterations, or more concisely, a textual historicity.

The immediate consequence of any rigorous application of the notion that philosophy is revision is the obsolescence of any conception of "first philosophy," in the sense of a prior or foundational discourse upon which other philosophical—as well as social, political, or scientific—thinking is grounded. There remain few professional philosophers who would still abide by a first philosophy as a starting point for either scientific or humanistic inquiry. But the residues of first philosophy, and of foundationalist thinking in general, still survive and pervade the practices of actual philosophical writing, a powerful legacy of more or less silent shibboleths concerning the way philosophy is supposed to be done, or the way it is supposed to be represented as having been done.

One of these shibboleths is the figure of the solitary thinker, whose ostensibly antipractical and metasocial vocation sets apart his or her practice of philosophical thinking from worldlier intellectual tasks, and whose ostensible detachment from investment in any particular type of object exempts him or her from the more mundane commitments entailed by other scientific pursuits. The solitary thinker persists as the presumptive source and originator of philosophical "thoughts" or "inquiry" despite our current easy self-consciousness about the invalidity of armchair speculation and the social and psychological debts of authorial subjects. Philosophers continue to behave, by convention, as though the primary vocation of philosophy were the ratiocination of a single inquiring individual, and philosophical writing therefore a sort of documentary report about what that inquiry had accomplished. This is regardless of the fact that in the late professional milieu of philosophy what maintains one as a philosopher is precisely that one does not sit alone and inquire; rather, that one enters the marketplace, writes, and publishes—or at least teaches philosophy at a university, which increasingly verges on the same thing. The available modes of philosophical research still tend to demand at least a stance of de facto speculative autarky, a pretense of solitary "first" thinking, largely aside from the understanding that what we do as philosophical practitioners is primarily reread, react to, and write anew about what is already written down, for the benefit of narrow professional audiences.

If we take seriously, and combine rigorously, the premises that the practice of philosophy is essentially historical and textual, then there can be neither any first philosophy nor any solitary thinking, perhaps not even in a form critics of philosophy could comfortably challenge and negate. The denial of the primacy of any given philosophical position entailed by a truly strict historicism must occur not for the relatively exalted theoretical reason that philosophy has now arrived at a vantage from which it is able to reject the quest for absolute foundations or standpoints, but for the more mundane, and therefore more critically formidable, reason that there is no philosophical thinking without a published (in the broadest sense) collection of prior philosophical forms, along with the prescription and circumscription of procedures that such a collection dictates. In the shadow of the published philosophical record, there are always conventions of argumentation and categories of institutional deference within which even an aggressively "first" or "solitary" inquiry must tow the line and become acceptable to its professional audiences—precisely in order not to offend, in order to be publishable. In this sense, there is no primary thought or work in philosophy. All philosophy is secondary work, a revision of other philosophical positions and, more precisely, of other texts.

As an example of both the persistence and the problem of first or solitary thinking, here is the opening of the text that will occupy the largest part of the present book, Martin Heidegger's lectures on Nietzsche. The following is from Heidegger's "Forward to All Volumes," added to the collected 1961 publication:

> It consists of lectures, which were held during the years 1936 to 1940 at the University of Freiburg-im-Breisgau. Attached are *treatises*, which originated during the years 1940–1946. The treatises build up or support [*ausbauen*] the way [*Weg*] by which the lectures, which were then still underway [*unterwegs*], paved the way for the confrontation [*die Aus-einander-setzung anbahnen*]. (*Ne*, 1:xxxix; *Ng*, 1:9, Heidegger's emphasis)

The statement anticipates the fact that throughout the *Nietzsche* lectures Heidegger will be concerned with the "way [*Weg*]" or "path [*Gang*]" or "train of thought [*Gedanken-Gang*; literally, 'thought-path']" (*Ne*, 3:14; *Ng*, 1:487) of philosophy, and with the proper "way" generally to think philosophical history through a reinterpretation of Nietzsche. In the "Forward," Heidegger calls upon the reader him- or herself to follow that way, and such a following will be cast explicitly as the pursuit of a set of "thoughts" that originally comprised, and still comprise, the content of the lectures themselves. This is the case even though, as Heidegger says, the new edition "lacks the advantages of an oral presentation [*mündlichen Vortrags*]" (*Ne*, 1:xl; *Ng*, 1:10), advantages which presumably were palpable only because speaking, traditionally, is a more direct evocation of thought than the written word. In short, the lectures are reoffered not as themselves a specific philosophical practice—a writing practice—but only as the secondary depiction or representation of practice, a "*view of* the way of thinking [*Denkweg*] that I followed from 1930 to . . . 1947" (*Ne*, 1:xl; *Ng*, 1:10, my emphasis), and which the reader is now politely invited also to pursue: "From where the confrontation [*Aus-einander-setzung*] with the matter of Nietzsche comes, and to where it goes, may become manifest to the reader when he himself sets off along the way [*Weg*] the following texts have taken" (*Ne*, 1:xl; *Ng*, 1:10). But what is such a "way" or "path," which the lectures have taken and which the reader may now take? That way is precisely to compose texts—for instance, the 1961 republication of the lectures, or more generally, the written record of the thought-paths that supposedly comprised the lectures before they became *lectionis*—and to spawn further such textual productions. In fact, the texts of the lectures themselves *are* the way or path they purport to depict, at least because there is unlikely to be any following way or path that will not eventuate in the production of yet other texts. These texts may be produced through critical and philosophical responses to the reading of Nietzsche, or through the medium of other works of Nietzsche scholarship compelled to react to this encounter. Or they may be produced through other textual constructions of "metaphysics," including Heidegger's own, or even through student papers written in university courses. There remain few, if any, environments for the reception of these lectures not organized or even founded upon the continuous reproduction, rereading, and revision of texts.

Let us then say—and perhaps no one but a philosopher would disagree with such a claim—that the way of the lectures Heidegger is about to re-present in 1961 is at least as much a "train of writing" as a "train of thought," a *Schrift-Gang* as much as a *Gedanken-Gang*, and that what philosophers, readers, and critics will do by following these lectures is not primarily to pursue a thought-path, but to think only insofar as such thinking eventuates in more writing, in more published or otherwise public calls to think, which in turn must be reread. This is not to imply some utilitarian or mercenary interpretation of philosophical thinking—that it somehow promotes itself, and perhaps debases itself, by arming for publicity or material gain. Rather, the claim for philosophy's materiality here, and against its ideality, is a structural claim. If philosophy is "thought," then this is true only in the same sense that a novel is a "world"—by virtue of representing itself as such in a more or less accepted generic language, therefore suppressing the more immediate world in which it exists materially as text.[1]

Texts

Heidegger's *Nietzsche* is an edited version of four lecture courses he gave at the University of Freiburg-im-Breisgau from approximately 1936 to 1940, edited and published under Heidegger's own supervision, along with several supplementary texts composed during the 1940s.[2] The two volumes of the *Nietzsche* comprise the lengthiest and arguably the most important of Heidegger's writings after *Being and Time*, as well as one of the most influential works of twentieth-century European philosophy. Aside from their massive, sometimes not fully acknowledged influence on Nietzsche studies, they lay much of the groundwork for criticism of the specific canon we tend to call, following Heidegger himself, "Western metaphysics," the hegemony of which has become a commonplace within philosophy, literary studies, and cultural studies. Despite their importance, there exists no full-length study of the Nietzsche lectures, even as the shadow of this text haunts the work of nearly all writers concerned with Nietzsche specifically or with the theme of the "end of metaphysics" generally.[3] Part of the reason for this dearth of attention is precisely the fact that the *Nietzsche* is secondary material, an interpretation and revision of another philosopher's thinking and, therefore, ostensibly not an "original" or "primary" work of philosophy. Any study of the lectures must therefore propose itself as "tertiary" interpretation, a mode not common on publishers' lists. For reasons I have already begun to outline here, the present book is unembarrassed to offer itself as a tertiary reading, and presents, among other things, a rare full-length analysis of a secondary work of philosophy. Moreover, I continue to assume that the central interest of Heidegger's *Nietzsche* is precisely that it *is* secondary work, and that it deliberately perceives itself as a rereading instead of an origin.

Heidegger is unusual among major philosophers for the proportion of his philosophical production devoted to other figures in the tradition.[4] In part, this devotion arises from an abiding theoretical equivalence within his work between the topics of specific philosophical inquiries and the history of those inquiries. It is precisely this rigorous historicist tendency that makes the *Nietzsche* lectures essential not only as an example of philosophical revision but also as a theoretical source for a historiography of philosophy itself. Through his ruminations on Nietzsche's "position" within philosophical history, Heidegger constructs a model of the history of philosophy as "recollection" and "overcoming," a stringent historicism in which philosophy's central concern, the question of the "meaning of Being" itself, cannot be separated from a strict historicist theorization of the forms of philosophical presentation in which Being "appears" within Western philosophical history.

There are, however, certain serious limitations to the theoretical terms Heidegger provides for a historiography of philosophy. In particular, Heidegger's model of philosophical historicity seriously underplays the rhetorical characteristics that make rereadings and revisions of philosophy into effective agents of philosophical canon formation, and by which conceptual revisions are formally transmitted to, and through, philosophical audiences. While Heidegger is quite content to impose topical and methodological canons upon the future history of philosophical thought, he does not begin to theorize the rhetorical processes necessary for him or any other writer to establish such canons as historical artifacts and influences. This apparent duplicity is an entirely conventional stance within the discipline of philosophy. Heidegger, like most philosophers, does not theorize his own practice of writing and publishing, a failure which, in part because of its very normalcy, serves to reinforce the power or historical "greatness" of his own thought, its ostensible originality or indispensability.

In order to complete the theoretical apparatus I am developing, I turn away from Heidegger in the second half of the book and chiefly toward two other theorists of textual historicality, Ralph Waldo Emerson, especially in his *First Series* of essays, and Harold Bloom, in his early theoretical work on poetry. This turn represents, as well, a shift away from European hermeneutical models of historiography to what I perceive as an Emersonian-American rhetorical tradition. Bloom's model of textual historicity, and to a greater extent Emerson's model of history reading, are beneficial for understanding philosophy precisely as a kind of writing *praxis*, an attempt to influence, through published rhetorical mechanisms, both the past and future histories of philosophical ideas. I use Bloom and Emerson to argue for a view that treats philosophy less as a document of thought or inquiry, than as a rhetorical solicitation to professional audiences, whose rules of rigor and acceptability implicitly govern the form that philosophical interpretations can take. This swerve toward literary theory and rhetoric, and away from hermeneutics, initiates a darker, but hopefully more productive view of philosophical interpretation as persuasion, manipulation of protocol, concealed influence, and historical constructivism—essentially, the "paralipsis," or sideways-speaking, of intellectual power.

A philosophical text does not get read after it is finished—it begins to be finished only in being read. No model of the philosophical text or intertext that does not take full and careful account of the *reception* of philosophical textuality and revision can account for the structure of the philosophical text itself in its full historicity. Starting in the Interlude, I consider the potential for a "reception aesthetics" of philosophy, beginning with an interpretation of the literary historiography of Hans Robert Jauss and ending, after the discussion of Bloom, Emerson, and (again) Heidegger, with brief analyses of two later inheritors of a rhetorical tradition of historiography and interpretive revisionism, Stanley Fish and Richard Rorty. The issue of revision, as the book proceeds toward its end, becomes increasingly an issue of canon formation, another provocation to the disciplinary center of philosophy. But one wants precisely to exceed philosophy's own time-honored disciplinary self-understanding, the topical prejudice separating philosophy from literature, quarantining it from the critique of canon formation which, within literary studies, is already canonical.

Background and Methodology

Where the category of revision arises for philosophy, it is usually the tool of the philosopher writing in the capacity of a critic, evaluating and distinguishing between respective thinkers or schools, or between two or more phases of a single thinker's work. In such a quasi-literary-critical context, revision belongs to the scholarly apparatus that conventionally precedes philosophical argumentation "proper." For instance, Kant's reader finds out quickly in the prefaces to the *Critique of Pure Reason* how the author will revise Hume or the Scholastics, but this knowledge is ostensibly not the final aim of reading the *Critique*.[5]

Similarly, the Preface of the *Philosophical Investigations* tells the reader
how the later Wittgenstein has reacted against the earlier one of the
Tractatus, but here, too, knowledge about Wittgenstein's self-revision-
ist stance is probably not the reader's main reason for opening either
book.[6] More often than not, the label "revision" insinuates an interpreter's inaccuracy or distortion, as when Heidegger complains that
Schopenhauer's botched reading of Kant's aesthetics also leads Nietzsche astray (*Ne*, 1:107–14; *Ng*, 1:126–35), or when Sartre laments that
Husserl's reversion to a notion of "the transcendental ego" in the *Ideas*
and *Cartesian Meditations* renders his theory of consciousness inadequate.[7] But in such cases, the issue of revision tends to remain subordinate to topics assumed to be more centrally philosophical, and this
subordination is the norm even where interpretation and intertextual-
ity have become critical watchwords.[8] Within the present critique, I
commit to a methodological shift away from such conventional usage
of the term "revision," a usage which still supports the notion of an
essential distinction between primary and secondary philosophical
texts.[9] Instead, for the model of philosophy I wish to develop here,
revision is a structural category, which also means that issues about the
forms of revisionist reading and rereading become philosophical contents in their own right, and move to center stage. I am primarily concerned neither with the accuracy or fidelity of, for instance, Heidegger's interpretation of Nietzsche, nor with its actual or potential
effects on scholarship, nor with its impact on more ostensibly philosophical topics spawned by the work of either thinker. Rather, I
attempt to describe as fully as possible the specificity of the revisionist
gesture itself, the peculiarly constructed space that simultaneously
connects and distinguishes the two thinkers. Such an approach is "phenomenological," but in the older Hegelian sense, permitting the phenomenon at hand to carry out its own self-evaluation, eschewing any
external critical standard which would only prejudice and delay the
inquiry's self-development by virtue of the phenomenon's own inner
tension or restlessness. A phenomenological approach is by nature

comprehensive and theoretical: "the method," to emulate Hegel's ambition if not his confidence, "is nothing other than the structure of the whole [*der Bau des Ganzen*] set forth in its pure essentiality,"[10] alongside which criticisms of specific philosophical positions such as Nietzsche's or Heidegger's would be a distraction. In general, I accept Hegel's objections to particular criticism of philosophies, as well as to any simple historicist conception of philosophical systems as merely competing for truth in their respective manners. Against these particularities, Hegel proposes a systematic structural model of the developing forms of philosophy and their relation to a historical whole:

> The more that [conventional] opinion fixes upon the opposition of truth and falsity, the more it tends to expect either agreement with or contradiction of [*entweder Beistimmung oder Widerspruch gegen*] a given philosophical system, and in explaining such a system it sees only one or the other. It does not so much comprehend the diversity of philosophical systems as the progressive unfolding [*fortschreitende Entwicklung*] of truth, as it sees in that diversity merely contradictions. . . . The contradict[ing] of a philosophical system does not itself tend to comprehend what it is doing in this way. Nor does the comprehending consciousness generally know how to free [the system] from its one-sidedness, or to maintain it in its freedom, and to recognize, in the shape of [its] conflictual and self-contradicting appearances [*streitend und sich zuwider Scheinenden*], reciprocally necessary moments.[11]

For the critique of revision, the "necessary moments" of the "whole" may be reconstrued as the structurally inherent "corrective" stances of philosophies with respect to one another, which I will present in the form of a general description of philosophical production, in contrast to any "one-sided" criticism of particular systems such as Nietzsche's or Heidegger's.

Hegel's *Phenomenology of Spirit*, which analyzes and presents the historico-logical relations between "configurations [*Gestaltungen*] of consciousness," may itself be described as a phenomenology of the successive revisions of consciousness, figured as the unfolding self-revision of *Geist* in the form of "experience." Furthermore, since philosophical systems are themselves among the "configurations of consciousness,"[12] Hegel's phenomenology offers the first detailed terms to account for the dialectical structure of change between philosophical texts. But the basic conditions for such an inquiry are established even earlier, in Hegel's so-called *Differenzschrift*, where he states the following two propositions within a few pages of one another: "Every philosophical system is able to be treated historically. As every living form belongs at the same time to appearance [*Erscheinung*], so too does philosophy"; "Every philosophy is in itself complete, and, like an authentic [*echtes*] work of art, has totality within itself."[13] Taken together, the propositions imply a self-contradiction or delusion on the part of philosophers. If every philosophical system belongs to a history in which many philosophies "appear" or "step out [*auftreten*]," then no one system can in good faith claim to be "complete": "Each is only *one* philosophy," as Hegel imagines such a contradiction in the later *Encyclopedia Logic*, "none is *the* philosophy."[14] Hegel himself resolves such a dilemma in advance by claiming that either the different systems are "just *one* philosophy at various stages of development," or that "the particular *principle*, which lies at the ground of each system, is only a *branch* of one and the same whole."[15] A "phenomenology" of this difference-in-sameness—that is, a critique of philosophical revision—would then seek the mechanisms by which philosophies continue to revise the conditions of "*the* philosophy" in order to permit their own "completions" to stand, without fully realizing that they do so within the horizon of the *self*-alteration of "*the* philosophy."

Philosophy's need to "step out" upon the scene of history should already suggest that Hegel's second proposition, which affirms the completeness of particular philosophies, is subject to conditions not available to a phenomenology of philosophical *thinking* alone, for it is not thoughts, but rather *texts* that "step out" into history, in the form of published revisions of other thoughts and texts. The very fact that a philosophy is compelled to step out in the form of a text automatically—indeed, on the level of structure—contests any aspiration a given philosophy might have to absolute completion. For precisely insofar as it steps out, philosophy, for which it is "a principle to include all particular principles in itself,"[16] is fated spontaneously to create that one particular principle most resilient to its machinations of sublation, namely, the occasion of its own appearance in the here and now, the *ergo sum* of philosophical *writing*.[17] This unavoidable and irrescindable act of appearing is philosophy's entry into real history, into *experience*, its subjecting itself to being reread and revised. But philosophy's appearance for revision must not be mistaken for an aesthetic phenomenon, as though it were a sensory experience. Writing is not seen, but read, or rather, reread, and thus the "here and now" of the text is never a present, but instead a future. Rereading and revision are not "experiences" of a consciousness per se, even a reading consciousness, but only a kind of textual and intertextual *work*. The analysis of revision is therefore distinguished from any immanent mapping of philosophical or metaphysical "thinking," for instance in an intellectual history, and is closer to the type of literary interpretation commonly referred to as deconstruction.[18] For my purposes, such labels simply help to indicate that the critique of revision entails searching for something more radically exterior to a given philosophical system than whatever it itself views as improper or mistaken either within its own pages or within some other philosophical system. What I seek are precisely the textual conditions that permit the comprehensibility of any such distinction between the proper and the improper to be made at all. These conditions comprise an ongoing process of rereading in which no text "stands" except by persuading other readers that it is doing so. The phenomenology of philosophical thinking must ultimately give way to the rhetoric of philosophical writing and rereading.

As a rhetoric of intertextual structure, and more importantly as an analysis of the structure of reception and rereading, the critique of revision is related to poetics or aesthetics of reception, and seeks what Roman Ingarden has called the "essential anatomy" or "skeleton" of the text as read.[19] However, my term "structure" is meant less in Ingarden's sense of "the basic structure that is common to all [literary] works," than in Thomas Kuhn's sense of "the structure of scientific revolutions." What I examine, to employ more of Kuhn's terms, is not the structure of the "normal"[20] philosophical work, even where it may imply its reader, but strictly the anatomy of the region in-between works, the space in which they "revolutionize"[21] one another. Such a "region" is always constructed *by* particular textual readings, but the activity of construction never ends with the work of reading itself. It necessarily involves other readers to whom the reading is passed on, and who, in turn, reread and revise it with more or less fidelity (the negotiation of this "more or less" being itself the effect of further readings, and so on). Revision is a historical or historicizing *movement*, an ongoing process of positioning and repositioning texts and textual implications with respect to one another. Therefore no strictly formal analysis of the philosophical *work*, even one that treats the work as "intentional" toward its reader, can ever account fully for what I will eventually call the "revision-encounter" between thinkers.[22] That is also why, finally, a merely critical approach to philosophical revision is bound to fail, as Hegel already understood: any analysis of philosophical interpretation that attempts to distinguish critically between what is proper and what is improper within the interpretation of a text (whether propriety is ascribed to the original text as against the revision, or to the revision as against the original) simply participates in the same process of demarcation and evaluation that structures the act of revision in the first place. My goal is to *describe* this process, in all the details of its phenomenological structure and rhetorical logic, and therefore not to reduplicate it.

On a more practical level, the descriptive discipline I propose requires that I eschew particular claims about, for instance, what Nietzsche's text "says" outside of the context of Heidegger's reading, or more exactly, about what it "*really* says," as if the content of the text could be examined independent of any reading, including my own. All such claims for the text's "true voice" belong to the immanent language of revisionist interpretations and are therefore subject to analysis. Indeed, the discourse of "saying" and "speaking" itself—for instance, when Heidegger claims that Nietzsche says something different from what his philosophy truly signifies, or when he declares that a thinker "always *thinks* one more leap more originally than he directly *speaks*" (*Ne*, 1:134; *Ng*, 1:158, Heidegger's emphasis)—indicates that a revision-encounter is already under way. Any explicit discourse about the voice of a text implies an (at least) implicit discourse about that text's intention, and therefore also a basic decision about whether or not what is explicitly said corresponds to what the text "properly" intends or connotes. Within this book, any locution that identifies texts as the "voice" or the "speech" of a subject is always an immanent locution and, in the context of my discussions of Heidegger, generally comes from his own usage. In the end, I will argue that texts "speak" only *through* readings, never simply *to* them. Therefore they "speak" in the particular tropes that compose revisionist rereading: in a revision's own peculiarly orchestrated ways. The text's voice has no determined temporal presence, but remains ongoing, an anticipation of its own ex post facto reconstruction—structurally, historically, and practically not-yet-itself.

Politics

I offer one final comment on the texts of Heidegger that I will be using, texts which originate during the tenure of the mid-1930s to the early 1940s. These works belong to the tenure of Heidegger's membership in the Nazi Party, following his term as rector of the University of Freiburg. Heidegger joined the party on May 1, 1933, and maintained this membership by paying dues through the end of the war (and the end of the party) in 1945, despite resigning the Freiburg Rectorate in 1934.[23] Moreover, Heidegger declined at any time afterward to recant his collusion with Nazi politics. His notorious interview with the magazine *Der Spiegel* was merely the most public of the settings within which he was invited to do so, and would have been a conveniently sympathetic setting.[24] Anyone perusing Heidegger's political texts, from his well-known *Rektoratsrede* of 1933 to less-known later retrospective narratives, cannot help but be impressed by the self-serving tone of his account of life and work under the Nazis.[25] That Heidegger was at times an enthusiastic supporter of Nazism, at other times an evasive and dishonest witness, is abundantly clear, and to suggest that a postwar silence about his Nazism somehow represents an honest political engagement with the past, as critics as scrupulous as Hans-Georg Gadamer and Jacques Derrida have at times done, verges on interpretive travesty.[26]

The prolific stir caused by the work of Victor Farias and Hugo Ott in the late 1980s, whether or not the material they disclosed was new or surprising (the stir itself is proof that it was), confirms at least one thing: it would be a serious mistake to believe Heidegger's own assertions that his political activities under the Nazis were reluctant and ambivalent, even critical of the regime. It is worth citing at least one brief document in full to show the enthusiastic tone of Heidegger's (relatively) early fascism, and his ease with propagandistic rhetoric. Here is an article he published on November 3, 1933, in the *Freiburger Studentenzeitung*, the university's student newspaper, on the occasion of Hitler's impending plebiscite to support withdrawal from the League of Nations:

German Students

The National Socialist revolution brings about the complete revolution [*Umwälzung*] of our German *Dasein*.

It falls to you, in these events, to remain those who always push on and are ready, who always stand tough and grow.

Your will to knowledge seeks to experience what is essential, simple and great.

You yearn to be exposed to what afflicts you from nearby and what obligates you from afar.

Be hard and true [*echt*] in your demands

Remain clear and sure in your refusal.

Do not turn the knowledge you have acquired into a vain possession. Preserve it as the necessary original possession of the person who leads [*des führerischen Menschen*] the popular [*völkisch*] professions of the state. You can no longer be those who merely "listen" [*die nur "Hörenden"*]. You are obligated to know together and act together in the creation of the future university [*hohe Schule*] of the German spirit. Each of you must first of all test and justify each of your endowments and privileges. This will happen through the power of [your] militant engagement [*die Macht des kämpferischen Einsatzes*] in the struggle of the whole people for itself.

Daily and hourly let your will to follow [*Gefolgschaftswillens*] be strengthened. Unceasingly develop your courage for the sacrifice [necessary] for the salvation of the essence of our people, and the elevation of its innermost strength, in its State.

Do not let axioms and "ideas" [*Lehrsätze und "Ideen"*] be the rules of your Being [*Sein*].

The *Führer* himself, and alone, *is* the present and future German reality and its law. Learn to know ever more deeply: from now on each and every thing demands decision, and all actions responsibility.

Heil Hitler!

Martin Heidegger, Rector[27]

This exhortation to the university student body appeared two years before the lecture courses on Nietzsche began at Freiburg. The style of the text is disturbingly familiar as Heidegger's own, and a number of its terms are borrowed from the traditional philosophical vocabulary with which Heidegger constructs his better-known work. In any case, these stylistic parallels, notable or not, are irrelevant to the central political issue raised by the text: its author is the same as the author of *Being and Time*, the lectures on Nietzsche and Hölderlin, the essay on the "Origin of the Work of Art," the "Letter on Humanism," and so on. This equivalence in itself is sufficient basis for a moral decision

about the "political thought" of Martin Heidegger. Further hypothe-
sizing about the precise speculative links between Heidegger's politics
and philosophy dilutes such a decision, whatever other merits it may
offer for criticism.

The facts of Heidegger's collusion with Nazi politics—his leader-
ship of the university under, and in cooperation with, the Hitler government, his continued support or tolerance for Nazism, his postwar
nonchalance about his wartime activities—are not especially dis-
putable, and constitute more than enough ground for healthy suspicion toward any reinterpretation or explanation of Heidegger's political claims, whether proffered by himself, his students, or his critics.
Such suspicion ought to come into play, for instance, when we read the
claim of Philippe Lacoue-Labarthe, one of the most careful and
exhaustive thinkers on this topic, that "[Heidegger's] first political
choice is philosophical through and through; it is not *first* a political
choice, it is not even a *political* choice, because the first choice, if it is a
choice, is a *philosophical* choice."[28] Could such a claim be made of any
other professional in European or other society? For instance, would
one claim that Albert Speer's Nazism was an architectural choice, or
Henry Ford's anti-Semitism an automotive one? Is it because Heidegger was not so much an influential Nazi as a *philosopher* that we should
examine his political activities primarily through the lens of their connections to his philosophical thinking and production? Or are we to
assume that the discipline of philosophy somehow essentially or automatically undergirds politics, such that the philosopher is better posi-
tioned to act or think politically than another professional? Even while
Lacoue-Labarthe wishes to underscore and criticize precisely "the
unconditional valorization or, if you will, overvalorization of the philosophical" within Heidegger's habits of thinking,[29] his approach exemplifies an unfortunate apologistic tendency to examine the political
activities of the philosopher as first a philosophical, only then a political, matter.

The problem can be seen again in the highly limited choices

Lacoue-Labarthe offers us for "thinking" Heidegger's political stance. For instance, he writes:

> Heidegger's political commitment is undeniably "metaphysical," in the strictest and most powerful sense of the term. He repeats or means to repeat the initial gesture of Nietzsche (no doubt overlooked), that is to say, taking due account of an irreparable historical break, the founding gesture—for the West—of Plato. And in this light it was no doubt one of the last possible grand philosophic-political gestures.[30]

The notion that the case against Heidegger will be made either better or worse, or just clearer, through a reading of his relation to philosophy relies on a view of the influence of philosophy on the polis borrowed nearly verbatim from Plato's infamous overestimation of the philosopher's role in advising kings and other policymakers. More crucially, it colludes with the very strategies Heidegger himself uses to evade the responsibility of his own political acts, as when he suggests, in his 1945 request for reinstatement at Freiburg, that his writing and lectures after 1934 constituted a "spiritual resistance" to Nazism.[31] Any such suggestion concedes to the philosopher a status different from that of any other producer or consumer in the society, as if philosophers really did create the foundations of the society in which they, like everyone else, participate—as if they, too, were not produced within and by that society.

The debate over the connection between politics and philosophy in the Heidegger case has produced responses ranging from the sublimely hyperbolic—"any deduction, even a mediated one, of Heidegger's 'Nazism' from the text of *Sein und Zeit* is impossible"—to the ridiculously elliptical—"When Heidegger summarizes his discussion of *Entschlossenheit* by observing that, 'When *Dasein* is resolute it can become the conscience of others,' it requires no special talent for political forecasting to divine the philosopher's future party loyalties."[32]

Neither of these caricatures is likely to produce a persuasive explanation of Heidegger's political actions, let alone of whether or not his work is "Nazi philosophy." But hyperbole aside, even the basic critical tendencies overdrawn by these critics—to *explain* Heidegger's party loyalties, and to *theorize* the political content of his work—are highly problematic, suggesting an unreasonable faith in the ability of philosophers to influence politics. It is as if, wholly in agreement with Heidegger's own ironic Platonism in this vein, one should first assume the philosopher has a special, "spiritual" opportunity either to resist the Führer or to lead him, and only then ask whether or not the philosopher has succeeded.

While one may easily agree that "there would be no affair if this were not Heidegger: this was no 'normal Nazi,'"[33] such an observation in no way implies that Heidegger's political stance was not a perfectly normal Nazism and could not have conformed precisely to the most craven norms of political behavior available to him. Hans Sluga's book *Heidegger's Crisis* remains the most valuable analytical work to date on Heidegger's politics, precisely because of Sluga's self-consciously historicist approach to the political collusion of a variety of philosophers in the German academy during the Weimar and Nazi periods. Sluga demonstrates that Heidegger's Nazism was *precisely* a normal mode of political participation—if not of the average citizen, for no one with Heidegger's institutional status and celebrity could be called that—at least of the average philosopher and academician, a demonstration which certainly makes Heidegger's conformity no less disgusting. Above all, let us not mistake metaphysical subtlety for political savvy. To act straightforwardly, in a "crudely decisive moment of vision,"[34] may at times be precisely the essence of a subtle politics, and there are also times when it would be lacking in subtlety to think less crudely. A truly subtle understanding of politics ought to see a philosophical subtlety such as Heidegger's, under such circumstances, for the political crudeness it is. In turn, any seriously radical critique of a philosopher's politics must acknowledge that philosophy, too, is a mode of citizenry, and its writing and teaching practices a mere profession. The gulf between the reprehensibility of Heidegger's political activities and the extreme critical interest and subtlety of his philosophical productions should neither surprise nor deter us from simultaneously analyzing the latter and condemning the former.

In the remainder of the present book I neither make nor intend any specific political prescriptions, any more than my readings of the texts of Heidegger and Nietzsche make specific critical evaluations. The political stance of a critique such as mine is no less dependent upon its actual reception by a practical—that is, a political—readership than is any critical negotiation of a philosophical text. Politics is the domain of effects, not of intentions. Nonetheless, I do both offer and analyze claims about the practical—and therefore, by some extension, political—assumptions philosophers make, and the stances we take, in our philosophical reading practices. Even the analysis of the structural and formal characteristics of philosophical interpretation has potential political implications for the institutional disposition of the philosophical discipline, precisely because the discipline itself remains invested in its own disciplinary forms and boundaries.

ONE

The Art of Reading Properly, Part 1:
The Discordance of Art and Truth

The best insights are arrived at last. But the best insights are methods!

— NIETZSCHE, *The Will to Power*

In a fragment dated 1888 and published after his death, Nietzsche writes, "Very early in my life I became serious about the relation of *art* to *truth*: and even now I stand in a holy terror before this discordance" (*Ne*, 1:74; *Ng*, 1:88).[1] Heidegger, in his lecture course for the winter term of 1936–1937, sets out to rethink Nietzsche's philosophy in such a way that art and truth will no longer stand in this "*Entsetzen erregender Zwiespalt*," or "terror arousing discordance" (*Ne*, 1:142; *Ng*, 1:167).[2] Instead, what Heidegger's interpretation will expose is an underlying "concordance [*Einklang*]" or "unity [*Einheit*]" between the concepts of art and truth. On the face of it, then, Heidegger's first revision of Nietzsche proceeds by means of a simple reversal, a tactic ostensibly borrowed from Nietzsche himself, whose characteristic "procedure," Heidegger writes, "is a constant reversing" (*Ne*, 1:29; *Ng*, 1:38).

Ultimately, Heidegger will not follow this procedure, although, as I will discuss, he will recast the relationship between art and truth in a number of more complicated ways. The full character of his engagement with Nietzsche's discordance can only be understood by pursuing his references to the underlying and overarching context of Nietzsche's essential "thinking," with respect to which reversals and revisions in Heidegger's reading acquire consequences far beyond those of any straightforward correction of Nietzsche's understanding of two concepts. Heidegger offers his entire analysis of Nietzsche in the light of a general concern with "Western metaphysics," a term which names an epoch of thought both he and Nietzsche also characterize as "Platonism," conceptions I will analyze in more detail. For Heidegger, the dispute between himself and Nietzsche over the relation of art and truth signifies a profound divergence in their respective interpretations of the character of Platonism and its influence on Western thinking. The discordance of art and truth within Nietzsche's thinking is symptomatic of his "failure" properly to understand this broader context and to understand his own immanence within it. Thus, quite in contrast to a reversal of Nietzsche's thoughts on art and truth, Heidegger's interpretation attempts to contextualize and "ground" Nietzsche's faulty stance with respect to Platonism overall, an essential revision not only of Nietzsche's position on truth and art, but of the entire metaphysics his position represents. And through this broader understanding of Nietzsche, and of the context of his thinking, Heidegger's reading aims, or at least begins to aim, at an overcoming of metaphysics itself.[3]

The reading of Nietzsche that Heidegger offers is therefore revisionist in a quite fundamental sense, for in his effort to make Nietzsche "understood," Heidegger presumes to say what is most crucially implicit in the underground of Nietzsche's thinking, but often directly against what Nietzsche explicitly states. Heidegger's reading will expose meanings within Nietzsche's thinking truer than any Nietzsche would or could have thought of himself: indeed, he identifies such implicit meanings as Nietzsche's "fundamental metaphysical position [*metaphysische Grundstellung*]." So, for instance, although the discordance of art and truth is manifest and even obvious in Nietzsche's writing, the putatively more basic concordance that Heidegger uncovers and interprets out of the context of Nietzsche's thinking is a facet of Nietzsche's *metaphysische Grundstellung*, despite what the *text* says, and despite what Nietzsche might have thought it says. With the identification of such a basic divergence between Nietzsche's explicit statement and his underlying position, we have a first indication of the shape of Heidegger's revision, beyond simple reversal: the revision forms itself around a distinction between, and an evaluation of, at least two different *levels* of Nietzsche's thinking.

The big picture that will allow us to distinguish Nietzsche's immanent Platonism from its historical ground can emerge only in a historical epoch after Nietzsche, an emergence in contrast with which Nietzsche's own philosophy appears essentially nascent. Heidegger names this epoch with terms peculiar to his own historical self-description: for instance, he calls it the "epoch of the question of Being." Under such a hermeneutical umbrella Heidegger finds himself at a vantage from which to perceive a general economy of unity or belonging-together not only between art and truth but also between any number of Nietzsche's most adamant discordances and antipathies, indeed within his very tone of discordance. In general, Heidegger declares with respect to Nietzsche's texts, "only those [things] which are related to one another can be opposed to one another" (*Ne*, 1:189; *Ng*, 1:219).[4] Or, more elaborately: "Discordance is present only where [the elements] which sever the unity of their belonging-together must diverge from one another by virtue of that very unity. . . . While truth and art belong to the essence of reality with equal originality [*gleichursprünglich*], they [must] diverge from one another and go against one another [*gehen sie auseinander und gegeneinander*]" (*Ne*, 1:217; *Ng*, 1:250).[5] The discordance of art and truth, and indeed the typical (and strategic) discordant tone of Nietzsche's polemical conceptualizations generally, are viewed by Heidegger as an epochal prolepsis; they are the historically determined anticipations of their own unifications in a concordant reading such as Heidegger's own. Thus Nietzsche's own procedures are placed quite in a passive position by Heidegger's reading, as though the discordance of art and truth were something that happened *to* Nietzsche by virtue of a certain metaphysical predicament. Heidegger calls his own more advantageous viewpoint upon this predicament simply "understanding Nietzsche's philosophy," but at times he also calls it "confrontation [*Auseinandersetzung*]," to be distinguished from argument or simple interpretation, and of course, from mere disagreement or reversal:

> Confrontation is genuine criticism [*echte Kritik*]. It is the highest and only way to the true estimation of a thinker. For [confrontation] undertakes to reflect on his thinking and to trace it in its effective power [*wirkende Kraft*], not in its weakness. To what end? So that through the confrontation we ourselves may become free for the highest exertion of thinking. (*Ne*, 1:4–5; *Ng*, 1:13)[6]

When we are "freed" through the hermeneutical or quasi-therapeutical standpoint of a confrontation, a "genuine criticism," art and truth will belong together in Nietzsche's text all the more because they discord. Hence the imperative tone of the passage cited above: "art and truth . . . [must] diverge." Or, as Heidegger asserts in a formulation not paradoxical but thoroughly dialectical, a discordance such as that of art and truth, far from contradicting the unity of these concepts, may be "proof for it."[7] Because of the historical context to which it constantly refers, Heidegger's rereading of art and truth in Nietzsche's philosophy is neither a critical substitution of relatedness for nonrelatedness, nor even a step in the evolution of the truer relation between art and truth. It is rather a basic revision in the perspective from which such a relation must be viewed, the opening up of the more grounded and grounding position and level of argumentation. With this, we arrive at a second preliminary description of the shape of Heidegger's revision of Nietzsche, and a more subtle one: Heidegger reinterprets Nietzsche's discordance *as* a concordance, precisely because he interprets Nietzsche's text as having first asserted concordance *as*, or *in the form of*, discordance.

This double "as" is the linchpin of Heidegger's entire interpretation of Nietzsche, and even in the later years of the lectures, when Heidegger's emphasis has shifted away from the topics of art and truth, the structure of this basic dialectical move will remain intact: to read the text's x *as* y, because from the viewpoint of a broader context, the text already connotes y *in the form of* x. In the first lecture course, the revision entailed by this "as" develops particularly around Nietzsche's and Heidegger's differing definitions and interpretations of the concept of "the true," and I will look closely at that particular difference. Heidegger claims that the definition of truth that Nietzsche holds, along with the discordance that follows from that definition, is inherited from a tradition of Platonic thinking by which Heidegger believes Nietzsche, along with "all other philosophy before him," to be constrained. Despite Nietzsche's efforts to overturn the Platonic tradition, he remains its last full subscriber, and therefore also its most conspicuous signifier. However, to follow Heidegger's own general formulation of the "as-structure [*Als-Struktur*]" in *Being and Time*, to make something explicit is to disclose its "as" for the understanding: "the 'as' makes up the structure of the explicitness [*Ausdrücklichkeit*] of that which is understood; it constitutes the interpretation" (*BT*, 140 [149]).[8] When Nietzsche's immanence in Platonism is made explicit by Heidegger's reading, "we" ourselves will be in a position to "understand," and then revise—essentially, to "appropriate [*zueignen*]"—what has so far remained only implicit in whatever Nietzsche actually wrote; we will be able to view Nietzsche's explicit statements about truth *as* his *metaphysische Grundstellung*, and Platonism itself *as* the prolepsis of the grounding Origin.

Art and Truth

If the concepts of art and truth relate to one another at all, then it is not because a work of art is similar to a logical proposition or a truth claim (although this is sometimes the case), but rather because art and truth are rubrics for a family of working oppositions familiar to Western philosophy at least since Plato. To speak with the extremely broad vocabulary Heidegger himself offers us at such moments, these oppositions are collected, or collectively signified, by the term "metaphysical distinction [*metaphysische Unterscheidung*]," and, in a manner which will require more explanation, point to the "older" and more basic, but still concealed, "ontological difference [*ontologische Differenz*]," out of a response to which metaphysics in the West has developed throughout its history since the pre-Socratics.[9] The metaphysical distinction takes particular conceptual forms in its emergence within philosophical discourses, for instance, physical versus metaphysical, material versus spiritual, or sensuous versus ideal. Heidegger evokes the latter pairing when he states bluntly that for Nietzsche "art is the will to semblance as the sensuous" whereas "'truth' means the 'true world' of the super-sensuous" (*Ne*, 1:74; *Ng*, 1:88),[10] an opposition borrowed from Plato, although Nietzsche of course ironizes and reverses its respective valuations. While truth is not as obviously related to art as it is, say, to falsehood or semblance, the fact that for Plato the inherent sensuousness of art is prejudged precisely as falsehood or semblance makes its discordance with truth virtually automatic within any thinking structured by Platonism. Part of Heidegger's task in the lectures is to question the spontaneity with which associations such as the one between art and "mere semblance" are made within a type of thinking that remains, still with Nietzsche, bound up in Platonic preconceptions, even as these preconceptions come to critical attention within Nietzsche's work.

The variety of distinctions that the opposition art/truth collects has also, indeed more often, been collected or signified by the pair of terms "Being" and "becoming." Truth—and here we refer to the Platonic interpretation—is *Being*, and art is *becoming*.[11] To be sure, we are dealing in vagaries here, as well as invoking a copula that has not yet been carefully defined—truth "is" Being, art "is" becoming. But the vagueness of these words, and indeed the vagueness generally under which Heidegger conducts his argument with Nietzsche, and Nietzsche in turn with the Platonic tradition, are not incidental to the dispute itself, nor do they represent some failure on the part of the disputants to get down to brass tacks.[12] Vagueness itself signifies the historical scope under which the argument is designed to take shape, the breadth of its intended effects, and the variousness of the phenomena it is designed to explain. This breadth and variousness are themselves subjects and contents, not merely attributes, of Heidegger's rereading of Platonism.[13]

During the first lecture course, Heidegger gives more or less equal time to each term of Nietzsche's discordance, art and truth—that is to say, he addresses matters of aesthetics approximately as much as he analyzes "the true." Nonetheless, it is clearly the concept of truth that is his primary concern, and from the outset his chief interest in aesthetics is to discover "that which in the essence of art calls forth the question concerning truth" (*Ne*, 1:142; *Ng*, 1:167). To this end, Heidegger offers, in the form of a paraphrase, five "statements" about art culled from Nietzsche's *Nachlaß*.[14] The final of the five statements, which Heidegger identifies as the most important, is, "art is more valuable than 'truth.'" But what makes this the most important of Nietzsche's statements on art is that through it one arrives at a very particular set of follow-up questions: "Everything hangs on the clarification and grounding of the *fifth* statement; art is more valuable than truth. What is truth? In what does its essence consist?" (*Ne*, 1:141; *Ng*, 1:166). This pair of questions about the essence of truth— or rather, the implicit basic question of truth to which the two questions point—comprises, for Heidegger, the "preliminary question of philosophy," and therefore Heidegger concludes that "the question about art leads us directly to the question preliminary to all questions" (*Ne*, 1:142; *Ng*, 1:166). I want to ask, not whether Heidegger's perhaps antithetical interpretation of Nietzsche's statements on art—that they lead us not to art, but rather to truth—are valid or legitimate, but how this gesture on Heidegger's part illuminates what I have been calling the shape of Heidegger's revision, or how it may begin to suggest a mechanism or terminology that we can use to describe that shape more fully.

With his gesture toward a "question preliminary to all questions," Heidegger has already departed from whatever specific emphases Nietzsche himself places on his own interpretations of the problem of truth. This departure is justified because Heidegger's "sole concern is to know Nietzsche's basic position as thinker" (*Ne*, 1:131; *Ng*, 1:154), or in other words, to grasp the proleptic "as" that Nietzsche himself only "indirectly" understood, and which continued to remain essentially "beyond" him (see *Ne*, 1:68; *Ng*, 1:81). What Heidegger seeks is a "direction" in Nietzsche's thinking, a "path [*Weg*]" or "bypath [*Seitenweg*]," and along such a path an access to metaphysics as a whole (see *Ne*, 1:163; *Ng*, 1:190, and *Ne*, 1:143; *Ng*, 1:168). Nietzsche, calling into question for the first time the *value* of truth by linking it to its apotheosis and antithesis, art, even if only to devalue or destroy it through art, culminates Western philosophy's inquiry into its most "preliminary question." Thus, for Heidegger, Nietzsche's devaluation of truth is ironically equivalent to the highest valuation of truth so far—the first inquiry into truth *as such*, the first *absolute* inquiry, and thus metaphysics' own special synecdoche.

Nietzsche's epochal valuation of truth is said to be at the same time both the very center of his thinking, the matter that gives Nietzsche's philosophy its full historical value, and yet still something about which Nietzsche fails to achieve a proper self-understanding. Truth is "manifestly the point where all the bypaths of Nietzsche's metaphysical thought converge. It is one thing if Nietzsche himself, under the burden of his destiny, did not achieve sufficient perspicuity [*Durch-*

sichtigkeit] here; it is another if we ourselves, who come after him, give up the task of a penetrating [*durchdringenden*] reflection" (*Ne*, 1:143; *Ng*, 1:167–68). Heidegger is forceful here: Nietzsche's own metaphysical "convergence" point remains unknown to him, and therefore Heidegger's revision should be able, where Nietzsche's own thinking is not yet able, to see through to the philosophical and historical core of Nietzsche's thinking.[15] Of course, nothing is surprising in Heidegger's claim to know the essence of these matters better than Nietzsche himself; philosophers constantly claim to know an issue better—else why write? What is odd is that this essence is figured not at all as Heidegger's production or reinterpretation, but rather as the center of Nietzsche's *own* thinking, troped therefore as a proleptic commencement of Heidegger's subsequent rereading—the reading precisely of Nietzsche's center. What Heidegger offers us is Nietzsche's anticipatory para-practice of preceding and anticipating Heidegger's own interpretation *of Nietzsche himself*. Here, then, is a third preliminary description of the shape of Heidegger's reading: Nietzsche's thought is *as* the prolepsis of Heidegger's reading of that same thought. To put it even more bluntly: Nietzsche's thought *is* Heidegger's rereading of it.

"The True" in Platonism and Positivism

In citing the fifth of Nietzsche's five statements on art, "art is more valuable than 'truth,'" Heidegger sometimes maintains the quotation marks around "truth," and sometimes not. It will, however, be crucially important to understand how Nietzsche's use of the phrase "*die Wahrheit*" is marked, and how Heidegger quotes it as marked in order to distinguish the revision of the concept of truth which his reading undertakes. When Nietzsche refers to truth, according to Heidegger's interpretation, he means not truth (*die Wahrheit*) as such, but "the true" (*das Wahre*). The essence of "the true" is that which has being, that which is "in truth" actual (*wirklich*). What is truly actual (or truly *not* actual, false) is a matter of knowledge, a matter of what we know or can know to be the case. Such an interpretation of "the true" allows Heidegger to explain how "the *problem* of truth" as such does not properly arise for Nietzsche, despite Nietzsche's clear emphasis on the topic of truth throughout his writing. Because, for Heidegger, the epistemological understanding of truth as "the true" must be considered derived and secondary, opposed to other notions more originary and basic, he concludes that what Nietzsche takes to be an acceptable definition of truth is precisely not the basic or originary one.[16] Nietzsche therefore fails to understand what is true about his own notion of truth, and in turn fails to question truth as such. As I suggested above, however, for Heidegger Nietzsche's thought is proleptically the first absolute inquiry into truth. We therefore need to understand where, exactly, for Heidegger's reading, Nietzsche's failure occurs—where his questioning of the truth arrives at its historical and metaphysical limit.

Platonism is the development of the epistemological notion of "the true," a development which culminates in its own distinctive overturning, identified as positivism; these are the two historical "ends" between which Nietzsche will be shown to fit by Heidegger's reading. The historical phenomenon of Platonism does not correspond exactly to the philosophy of Plato himself, but rather is a certain reinterpretation of that philosophy, a trend in thinking originating roughly with the translation of Platonic thinking into Christian-Latin categories and based on an interpretation of the basic character of Being as the transcendence of the *eidos* or *idea*.[17] Indeed, Heidegger's own critique of both Plato and Nietzsche positions itself as an understanding of Plato antithetical to what has passed for a standard interpretation in Western philosophy, an interpretation integral to the tradition that Nietzsche, too, follows even in his overturning of it:

> We say Platonism and not Plato, because here we are dealing with the conception of knowledge that corresponds to that term, not

through an original and detailed examination of Plato's works, but only by setting out roughly one particular aspect of his work. Knowing is approximation to what is to be known. What is to be known? The being [*das Seiende*] itself. Of what does it consist? From where is its Being [*Sein*] determined? From the ideas and *as* the *ideai*. (*Ne*, 1:151; *Ng*, 1:177)

Platonism is not Plato, and just the same positivism is not Nietzsche—it does not precisely correspond to Nietzsche's own position toward Platonism, although the divergence is subtle. Nietzsche's philosophy is positivism with a "twist,"[18] such that he gives a slight but revolutionary turn to the general opposition to Platonism already prevalent during the late epoch of philosophical thought to which he belongs. This twist—difficult to locate and highly ambiguous—is the specific difference that Heidegger's reading locates between Nietzsche's thought and other anti-Platonic critiques, but it is therefore also the difference that Heidegger's own reading brings into being by interpreting Nietzsche, or by reinterpreting what Heidegger will take to be Nietzsche's prophetic and proleptically divergent direction. Thus Nietzsche's difference from positivism—and therefore ultimately from Platonism—does not, strictly speaking, occur within Nietzsche's thinking itself, but only within a certain perspective on that thinking. Nonetheless, the difference is consistently *troped* by Heidegger's reading as though still within Nietzsche's thinking, and we must account for this fact in any full description of Heidegger's interpretation. This is to get slightly ahead of Heidegger: from the point of view of the first lecture course, the task at hand is to understand precisely where, within Nietzsche's thought, the twisting out of positivism, and therefore out of positivism's own specific and inadequate divergence from Platonism, takes place—in essence, where Nietzsche anticipates what we might call, polemically, a proto-Heideggerian, and therefore post-Nietzschean, overcoming of Platonic metaphysics.

While Heidegger admits that "it is indisputable that prior to the time of his work on the planned magnum opus, *The Will to Power* . . . Nietzsche went through a period of extreme positivism," he qualifies this assertion by adding that Nietzsche's positivism, "though of course transformed, also became a part of his later fundamental position" (*Ne*, 1:154; *Ng*, 1:181). Moreover, "what matters is precisely the transformation; this is especially the case in relation to the overturning of Platonism as a whole" (*Ne*, 1:154; *Ng*, 1:181). Nietzsche's thinking is positivistic in his reversal of the Platonic assumption that "the idea, the supersensuous, is the true" (*Ne*, 1:154; *Ng*, 1:180). But Nietzsche subtly transcends the positivist critique in his interpretation of Christian-Platonic history as nihilism, with respect to which even positivism itself may be seen as a negative idealism, "the evaluation [*abschätzen*] . . . of beings [on the basis of] what they should or ought to be [*was sein soll und sein darf*]" (*Ne*, 1:160; *Ng*, 1:187). Because positivism is basically a reaction to doctrines of Being as ideal or supersensuous, it, too, generally accepts the basic opposition of sensuous versus ideal that characterizes Platonism. Positivism reverses Platonism only on its own terms, merely inserting another content (the sensuous) into the categorical position of "true being," which position retains both its Platonic configuration and its essential nihilism. It is Nietzsche's advance on this positioning itself, upon this basic categorization, that must be identified in order to distinguish him from a merely routine positivist, to distinguish not the divergent content of the thought per se, but its "direction."

The structural affinity of positivism with Platonism means that positivism shares with Platonism a basic schema in which "the true," as a knowledge of what actually is, is essentially a correspondence of the object with something else, and therefore not fully proper to the object itself. In every case, as Heidegger explains, knowledge of the true requires some kind of standard [*etwas Maßstäbliches*] with which to compare [*anmessen*] what is known to the actual [*das Wirkliche*]. Knowledge here is always a matter of adequacy, of approximation [*Angleichung*] to a perfect accounting of what actually exists, what "has being." In Platonism, where the standard is *idea*, the object of knowledge is always, in its true essence, something nonsensuous, a description Heidegger invokes in its originally paradoxical emphasis on the quite sensory faculty of sight: "What makes a table a table, table-being, lets itself be seen [or learned—*läßt sich ersehen*]; to be sure, not with the sensory eye of the body, but with that of the soul. Such sight is apprehension of what a thing is, its idea [*Idee*]" (*Ne*, 1:151; *Ng*, 1:177). Therefore the sensuous instance of a being, for instance the famous craftsman's bed in Plato's *Republic*, Book X, is merely the occasion of our seeing, or more properly, re-collecting, the formal *idea*, which determines our ability to view the sensory object in the first place.[19] This type of knowledge, which compares itself to the transcendent idea, and which must present or bring forward (*vorstellen*) the idea as "the true," is a theoretical knowledge, *theoreia* (see *Ne*, 1:152; *Ng*, 1:178), or, in other words, a metaphysical knowledge. Indeed, this knowledge invokes an implicit interpretation of all of being (*das Seiende*) as the supersensuous, a *meta*physics at large. Thus, within Platonism, truth is metaphysical on two distinct but related levels: its standard of actuality is ideal, and it entails a theory or doctrine of the *ideai* as its ground.

If Platonism is essentially metaphysical, positivism differs[20] from this position by virtue of its reversal of the particular metaphysical doctrine at the core of Platonism. Within positivism, precisely the sensuous instance, or *positum*, is the standard of knowledge, that which is actual or has being (*Ne*, 1:152; *Ng*, 1:178). Positivism is manifestly antimetaphysical in both of the senses in which Platonism was metaphysical: it denies simultaneously the actuality of the *idea* and the applicability or coherence of any general doctrine of ideality.[21] Yet, again, in the basic scheme through which they approach the object of knowing, the two historically opposed doctrines are the same: where Platonism compares or approximates knowledge of the sensuous object to the *idea*, positivism, too, effects a comparison, but the standard of knowledge is "what lies before us from the outset, what is constantly placed before us, the *positum*. As such, the latter is what is given in sensation, the sensuous" (*Ne*, 1:152; *Ng*, 1:178). Crucially, at the epistemological ground of both doctrines, the notion of approximation to some standard remains intact, even where the precise character of the standard shifts: both Platonism and positivism assume a knowledge approximated to the true being or being-in-itself interpreted as the actual, and each merely negotiates the specific content of whatever constitutes actuality.

Positivism, therefore, cannot effect any fundamental critique of Platonism, since it shares Platonism's basic epistemological assumption about the essence of the true, leaving the opposition of sensuous/ideal intact while merely valorizing a new one of its poles. What is required instead, by the time of Nietzsche, is a critique of opposition itself, a destruction of the correspondent model of "true being" and its structuring binarism, the "metaphysical distinction." Unless a positivistic inversion can achieve this profoundly structural level of (self-)critique, it remains merely "formal [*formal*]" (*Ne*, 1:161; *Ng*, 1:188), incapable of a "shattering of the preeminence of the supersensuous as the ideal" (*Ne*, 1:160; *Ng*, 1:187). Such a shattering would require not another new doctrine of "the true," but rather an antitruth, a mode of attack on the very notion of the truth as comparison or approximation or opposition to ideality—a reconsideration of the full set of relationships between the sensuous and the ideal. Both Heidegger and Nietzsche will posit art as this means of attacking truth, a weapon uncannily both near and far from truth, and therefore for Platonism (if not precisely for Plato)[22] the antitruth *par excellence*. More precisely, art is that affirmation of the sensuous which comprises the "specific countermovement [*bestimmte Gegenbewegung*]" (*WP*, par. 794) to the true:

> Within the horizon of the meditation on nihilism, "overturning [*Umdrehung*]" of Platonism takes on another meaning. It is not the simple, almost mechanical exchange of one epistemological standpoint for another, that of positivism. Overturning Platonism

means, above all, shattering the preeminence of the supersensuous as the ideal. *Das Seiende*, [being] what it is, may not be despised on the basis of what should and ought to be [the case]. . . .

Against Platonism, the question must be asked: "What is true being?" The answer is: "The true is the sensuous." Against nihilism, the creative life—which means, first of all, art—must be set to work. But art creates out of the sensuous. . . . Art and truth, creating and knowing, meet each other in the single guiding perspective [*Hinsicht*] of the rescue and configuring [*Rettung und Gestaltung*] of the sensuous. (*Ne*, 1:161; *Ng*, 1:188–89)

That which positivism already posits, ostensibly against Platonism, as its own version of "the true," namely, the sensuous particular, can be reconstrued as a type or instance of artwork, just as the form or the universal is a type or instance of truth. In the end this art is allied *with truth* against the true, whenever the latter is construed as the transcendent, the ideal, or the supersensuous. But positivism on its own is not yet capable of such an artistic vision of truth. This incapacity will in turn allow space for Nietzsche's subtle divergence from positivism. More precisely, it will allow for his own more perspicacious positivism as a transcendence of the still-immanent positivist critique: a more truthful use of art directly against "the true."

Nevertheless, it remains no simple matter to determine the precise difference between Nietzsche's polemical and destructive *art*, as a rubric for the sensuous, and the *positum* of the positivists, as a doctrine of the sense object as the true. So far, Nietzsche's "artistic" critique of Platonism's notion of truth would seem to be just a subspecies of positivism. But if this were simply the case, several aspects of Nietzsche's thinking would still beg to be explained. Foremost, as Heidegger continually asks, why should art, or sensuousness, be in a "raging discordance" with truth, for Nietzsche, if within Platonism art is simply an inferior sort of truth-claim, and if for positivism the sensuous *positum* simply replaces the Platonic *idea* as the true? I have already mentioned how, for Heidegger, the explanation of Nietzsche's "raging discordance" entails an understanding of the basic concordance or belonging-together (*Zusammenhang*) of truth and art which first grounds the opposition between them. Art, within Nietzsche's thinking and elsewhere, must be something quite different than a mere *positum*, for it does not simply replace the particular standard for true knowledge of beings, but instead relates to it at some more essential level, in such a way as to cause raging at the heart of truth, and to be potentially an attack on the structural binarism of metaphysics at large.

Art in Platonism

What does the "artistic" mean within the Platonic epistemology such that for Nietzsche it can eventually come altogether to "rage," as Heidegger claims, against Platonism itself? For Platonic metaphysics, an artwork is a certain benighted species of true thing, something essentially *un*true, or more precisely, something distant from truth. For instance, for Plato, the artist's rendering of the bed, already once removed from the bed made by a craftsman, is thereby twice removed from the true form.[23] While the artist indeed reproduces the form, he does so in a manner that exhibits only one view or *phantasma* of its true being. Art is a subordinate, and therefore for Plato an inferior, manner of truth-production.[24] But for Nietzsche's brand of positivism, which reverses the respective Platonic valuation of the supersensuous ideal, it is *truth* that is a subordinate or inferior manner of *artistic* production—which latter is perspectival, creative interpretation. What has been traditionally called truth—the constant, the fixed, the substantive, the categorizable, and so on—is, according to Nietzsche's new reversed way of looking at the matter, the invention or interpretation of a particular organism, a particular kind of art-work.

For Nietzsche, "what[ever] lives [*Das Lebendige*]" (*Ne*, 1:212; *Ng*, 1:244), based on its own particular desires and from its own perspective, constructs limitations to the sensuous manifold of the "organic world" (*Ne*, 1:214; *Ng*, 1:246).[25] These limitations, carved out in accommodation to the pressures of the surrounding environment, but also in response to pressures exerted by the organism's own will, define a set of "things that are true." In negotiation with these pressures, by virtue of a reciprocal accommodation, the organism creatively organizes its environment into a reality:

> What lives [*das Lebendige*] is exposed to other forces, but in such a way that, striving against them, it deals with them at the same time according to their form and rhythm, in order to estimate them in relation to possible incorporation or elimination. According to this angle of vision [*Sehwinkel*] everything that is encountered is interpreted in terms of the living creature's capacity for life. (*Ne*, 1:212; *Ng*, 1:244)

"Angle of vision [*Sehwinkel*]" is the crucial term here, for it indicates that the doctrine of perspectivism is fully entailed by Nietzsche's "new interpretation of sensuousness," as much for Heidegger as for Nietzsche himself:[26]

> The angle of vision, and the realm it opens to view, themselves draw the borderlines around what it is that creatures can or cannot encounter. For example, a lizard hears the slightest rustling in the grass but it does not hear a pistol shot fired quite close by. Accordingly, the creature develops a kind of interpretation of its surroundings and thereby of all occurrence, not incidentally, but as the fundamental process of life itself: "The *perspectival* [is] the basic condition of life." (*Ne*, 1:212; *Ng*, 1:244)[27]

In short, the truth of things is always an interpretation of something's or someone's situation, a creative delimitation (*Begrenzung*) of the sensuous manifold. For Nietzsche, truth is a certain artistic perspective, and therefore precisely not "the true" by Platonic standards: "*Truth is the kind of error* without which a certain kind of living being could not live. The value for life ultimately decides" (*WP*, par. 493, qtd. in *Ne*, 1:214; *Ng*, 1:247, Heidegger's emphasis). Here it is clear why Nietzsche's philosophy, by his own description, is an "inverted Platonism." Whereas within Platonism art signifies an inferior or devalued production of truth, for Nietzsche just the opposite is the case: truth is an inferior species of art.

With this inversion in mind, we can move to the crux of Heidegger's reading of art and truth in Nietzsche, as well as to the specific moment in which Heidegger attempts to expose Nietzsche's divergence from, and advance upon, positivism's critical position toward Platonism. This moment occurs for Heidegger in a terse and even simplistic passage from Nietzsche's *Twilight of the Idols*, entitled "How the True World Finally Became a Fable." Heidegger describes this text in characteristically hyperbolic tones that cannot help but indicate that whatever climax in Nietzsche's thinking this text signifies also corresponds to a climax in Heidegger's own reading of Western metaphysics through Nietzsche. Heidegger identifies the text "as Nietzsche's final step [*als letzten Schritt Nietzsches*]" (*Ne*, 1:202; *Ng*, 1:233), a "decisive questioning [*entscheidenden Fragen*]" (*Ne*, 1:203; *Ng*, 1:234) and a "great moment of vision [in which] the entire realm of Nietzsche's thought is permeated by a new and singular brilliance" (*Ne*, 1:202; *Ng*, 1:234). Nor does Heidegger fail to exploit the coincidental melodrama of Nietzsche's late biography to sensationalize his own discussion: "During the time in which the overturning [*Umdrehung*] of Platonism became for Nietzsche a twisting free [*Herausdrehung*] of it, madness befell him. Until now no one at all has recognized this reversal as Nietzsche's final step; neither has anyone perceived that only in his final year (1888) is the step clearly taken" (*Ne*, 1:202; *Ng*, 1:233). It becomes quickly apparent that the "brilliance" of this particular passage in Nietzsche consists in the fact that it perfectly anticipates what Heidegger himself construes as Nietzsche's "fundamental metaphysical position." The text is "brilliant" because its "final step" is *almost* Heidegger's thinking itself—almost, except for a just-sufficient divergence in style, a certain aphoristic, discordant, fragmentary quality, nonetheless recuperable, for Heidegger, through a systematic reconsideration of Nietzsche's text in its "proper" context. This revision will eventually constitute something like Heidegger's own position, to the degree that this position may be distilled from a reading ostensibly focused entirely on Nietzsche. In short, from the angle of vision of Heidegger's reading, Nietzsche writes just barely *as* himself, so that he may then be reread as writing not quite *as* Heidegger.

TWO

The Art of Reading Properly, Part 2:
Nietzsche's Philosophy Proper

In identifying history as a process in linear time, we tacitly assume that our knowledge of the moment at which an event emerges from the flow of time will help us to account for its occurrence. The date of the event is a value-laden fact.   —KRACAUER, *History: The Last Things Before the Last*

How the "True World" Finally Became a Fable

The History of an Error

1. The true world attainable for the sage, the pious, the virtuous one—he lives in it, *he is it*.
   (oldest form of the idea, relatively sensible, simple and persuasive. Circumlocution for the sentence, "I, Plato, *am* the truth.")
2. The true world, unattainable for now, but promised for the sage, the pious, the virtuous one ("for the sinner who repents"). (Progress of the idea: it becomes more subtle, insidious, incomprehensible—*it becomes female*, it becomes Christian [. . .])
3. The true world, unattainable, unprovable, unpromisable; but the very thought of it a consolation, an obligation, an imperative.

(At bottom, the old sun, but through mist and skepticism. The idea has become elusive, pale, Nordic, Königsbergian.)

4. The true world—unattainable? In any case unattained. And as unattained, also *unknown*. Consequently also not consoling, redeeming, or obligating: how could something unknown obligate us? [...]
(Gray morning. The first yawn of reason. Cockcrow of positivism.)

5. The "true world"—an idea which is no longer useful for anything, no longer even obligating—an idea which has become useless and superfluous, *therefore* a refuted idea: let us abolish it! (Bright day; breakfast; return of *bons sens* and cheerfulness; Plato's embarrassed blush; pandemonium of all free spirits.)

6. The true world we have abolished; what world has remained? the apparent one perhaps? [...] But no! *With the true world we have also abolished the apparent one!*
(Noon; moment of the briefest shadow; end of the longest error; high point of humanity; INCIPIT ZARATHUSTRA.)[1]

In the first chapter, I suggested some tentative descriptions of the shape of Heidegger's reading of Nietzsche, each of which successively replaced the simple impression with which one necessarily begins, that Heidegger's reading reverses Nietzsche's "discordance of art and truth," making it a concordance. The third and most complex of my descriptions proposes something quite far from a reversal, that in fact Nietzsche's thought *is* (as) the prolepsis of Heidegger's reading—or in short, that Nietzsche's "philosophy proper" *is* Heidegger's rereading of it. What sense can be made of such an aggressive equivalence between two thinkers who are separated not only by whatever circumstances normally make one philosopher different from another, but in addition by the fact that one thinker sets out in particular to reread and revise the other? Why should revision, of all things, be a making-equivalent?

I turn now to the centerpiece of Heidegger's first lecture course, his reading of Nietzsche's brief text from *Twilight of the Idols* entitled "How the True World Finally Became a Fable." This text presents a schematic history of Western thought divided into six polemically abbreviated sections, which, Heidegger asserts perhaps even more polemically, "can easily [*leicht*] be recognized as the most important epochs of Western thought" (*Ne*, 1:202; *Ng*, 1:234).[2] The six stages refer to basic philosophical positions on the definition of truth or of a "true world." The first three positions are familiar enough: Platonism, Christianity, and Kantianism. The next two less clearly correspond to particular doctrines. Plainly, however, section four presents some version of a positivist critique of Kantian transcendentalism, a refutation of the concept of a *Ding an sich*. In section five, positivism is in full swing, in the form of an active rejection of the metaphysical as such. Here, as Heidegger points out, Nietzsche's own thought is anticipated by the characteristic terms "free spirit," "bright day," and "cheerfulness." The sixth division is the crucial one for Heidegger, for although the first five ostensibly achieve the overturning of Platonism and the abolition of the Platonic "true world," only in the sixth is Nietzsche's unique revision of the positivistic critique first apparent. Heidegger states: "That Nietzsche appends a sixth division here shows that, and how, he must advance beyond himself and beyond sheer abolition of the supersensuous. . . . [Hence] the onset of the final division of his own philosophy" (*Ne*, 1:208; *Ng*, 1:240). Here, then, for Heidegger, Nietzsche's whole thought is expressed in its most compact resolution.

When the "true world" is abolished by positivism, a reversal of valuation occurs such that what had previously been called mere "semblance [*Schein*]" according to the standard of the *idea* may now be seen as reality itself. Semblance is more real than that which it was supposed to resemble; indeed for the positivist it is the only reality. In turn, any "true world" is reduced to mere illusion. But the sensuous being of things in the world was called semblance only by virtue of its reciprocal relationship with the nonsensuous "true world" of Platonism. When the "true world" is abolished, sensuousness no longer warrants the pejorative attribute of "appearance"; it simply *is*. The sensory is now *the true*, and therefore "the true (world)" is no longer . . . true.

Yet even such a revaluation and destruction of the value of truth cannot be Nietzsche's final step beyond Platonism, since in order for Nietzsche to call truth itself untrue, or "error," and to call sensuousness ("art") truer to life, a standard of the true as adequation or correspondence to reality must still hold sway. In Nietzsche's explicit philosophy, "truth is untrue" still precisely by Platonic standards, and therefore even his arguments with Platonism remain a refutation of Platonism on Platonism's own ground.[3] For Heidegger, the positing of truth *as* art (or of art *as* the true) is not what twists Nietzsche's thinking free of Platonism. Rather, the twist is effected by something still implicit in the character of art itself as radically perspectival, a latent implication of art that hints at a more essential understanding of truth (*alētheia*) to which Nietzsche himself is not yet privy. Whereas Nietzsche, pursuing as his "metaphysical task" the implications of the end of Platonism, takes his postpositivist (and hence post-Platonist) "final step" in the sixth division of "How the True World . . . ," he nonetheless cannot take this step on his own. The step requires a further reading, and with it a more *gründlich* understanding of the step's own significance, from the proper, but still not yet fully possible, perspective. The step must be reviewed—must therefore be reread—properly *as.* . . . To understand how and why this is the case will be tantamount to understanding how the discordance that permits Nietzsche to use art against Platonism can signify, for Heidegger, a more basic concordance underlying and transcending the entire history of Platonism up through Nietzsche's just-anticipated twisting free of it. We must see how Nietzsche's discordant thinking is interpreted by Heidegger as the storm before the calm, so as to reveal the calm *as* having been before the storm.

Everything that characterizes truth when Nietzsche polemically redefines it as a perspective of "organic" life is also already characteristic of art. Heidegger writes that "creation, as forming and shaping, [*das Schaffen als Formen und Gestalten*] [and] likewise the aesthetic pleasures related to such shaping, are grounded in the essence of life. Hence art, too, and precisely it, must cohere most inherently with perspectival appearance and letting-appear [*mit dem pespektivischen Scheinen und Scheinenlassen*]" (*Ne*, 1:216; *Ng*, 1:248–49). Truth and art, once Nietzsche has destroyed the fixed ideal standard that governed the true within Platonism, are both seen to be perspectival interpretations. For Nietzsche, then, or for Heidegger's reading of Nietzsche, truth and art emerge as similar occurrences of "appearance," of "perspectival shining [*Scheinen*]." Both are creative acts in accordance with the pressures and desires of life. But the will to truth, driving to fix and immobilize the essential flux of the sensuous manifold, is a bad faith toward the sensuous, an antivitalism. By contrast, "art in the proper sense" is an enhancement of life, a "liberating for expansion" or a "[transfiguring] clarifying [*verklären*]" (*Ne*, 1:216; *Ng*, 1:249).

Nietzsche identifies the experience of artistry as "*Rausch*," or "rapture."[4] *Rausch* is a feeling of power experienced in the presence of form, and, as Nietzsche defines it, is fundamentally the experience of a creator and not of an audience; it is the affect attendant upon the experience of a "form-creating force [*formschaffende Kraft*]" (*Ne*, 1:115; *Ng*, 1:135).[5] The creation of form is "idealization," which is "the sweeping emphasis upon the main features [*ungeheuren Heraustreiben der Hauptzüge*]" (qtd. in *Ne*, 1:116; *Ng*, 1:137). *Rausch* is therefore the sensation of pleasure arising from the activity of idealization, a pleasure in imposing or reducing to form. Of course, reduction to "the true" is also an act of idealization, inasmuch as it sets up the object to conform to the *idea*. Thus it becomes crucial for Heidegger to determine in what sense idealization as an artistic activity is akin to, and in what sense different from, the idealization accompanying the making of truth within Platonism. Heidegger writes, referring to the artist's kind of idealization:

The fuller, simpler, stronger vision in creation Nietzsche calls "idealizing." . . . But to idealize is not, as one might believe, merely to omit, strike, or otherwise discount what is insignificant and ancillary. Idealization is not a defensive action. Rather, its essence consists in a "*sweeping emphasis* upon the main features." What is decisive therefore lies in an anticipatory discernment [*vorgreifenden Heraussehen*] of these traits, in a reaching out [*Ausgreifen*] toward what we believe we are barely ready for, barely able to survive. . . .[6]

Creation is an emphasizing [*Heraustreiben*] of major features, a seeing more simply and strongly. It is bare survival before the court of last resort. (*Ne*, 1:116–17; *Ng*, 1:137)

Whereas truth limits and circumscribes, art "sweeps," "reaches out," and "expands," striving not for the fixation of sensuous life but for its outermost domains and risks. Rapturous idealization is "ascent-beyond-oneself [*über-sich-hinaus-Steigen*]" (*Ne*, 1:116; *Ng*, 1:136). Once again, the extreme hyperbole and vagueness of these formulations is not gratuitous. In a strong sense, the extremity of such rhetorical tension or antagonism is the only thing that can establish the difference between the two types of idealization represented respectively by truth and art. One can justifiably revert to broad formal descriptions here: truth-idealization, speaking in the hyperbolic style of an epochal rubric, is a "shrinking," whereas art-idealization is an "expanding to the outermost. . . . " Indeed, inasmuch as both art and truth idealize, particular conceptual distinctions between them are sufficiently indistinguishable to allow Nietzsche consistently and usefully to interchange them, for instance when he proposes that "it is the powerful who made the names of things into law, and among the powerful it is the greatest artists in abstraction who created the categories" (*WP*, par. 513).[7] Similarly, but for his own purposes, Heidegger is able to gloss several passages from Nietzsche's text as follows: "By way of a commentary on Nietzsche's definition [of the artist] let us say only this: 'Form,' *forma*, corresponds to the Greek *morphe*. It is the enclosing limit and delimitation, that which brings and places a being in[to] that which it is, so that it stands in itself: its form or configuration [*die Gestalt*]" (*Ne*, 1:118–19; *Ng*, 1:139). The identification of art as the specific antitruth, the secret subversive *life* of truth within the self-deluded formalism of Platonic thought, of course gives Nietzsche the polemical thrust needed to destroy the pretension of Platonism, which, as a will to truth, must be viewed not merely as an error but as nihilism. Positivism, as still a Platonistic will to truth, is also nihilistic. Thus, for Nietzsche, art becomes an entirely general "countermovement [*Gegenbewegung*]" against a culture that has grown decadent or exhausted within the moralistic categories of knowledge it inherits from the Christian-Platonic tradition. The need that engenders the overcoming of Platonism and its accoutrements is the will toward self-overcoming of "man" himself:

> Consequently, the overturning of Platonism and the ultimate twist out of it imply a transformation [*Verwandlung*] of man. At the end of Platonism stands the decision about the transformation [*Wandlung*] of man. That is how the phrase "high point of humanity" [from the sixth division of Nietzsche's "How the True World . . ."] is to be understood, as the peak of decision, namely, as to whether now, with the end of Platonism, man as he has hitherto been ought to come to an end, whether he is to become that kind of man Nietzsche characterizes as the "last man"; or whether that type of man can be overcome and the "overman" begin. (*Ne*, 1:208; *Ng*, 1:240–41)

"Man," by definition, will overcome himself one way or another, whether in self-denial, for instance by positing a true world against the sensuous realm in which he actually lives, or by affirmatively overcoming that very temptation to deny the sensuous. For this reason, in light of Nietzsche's desire to overcome nihilism and in light of the human tendency toward overcoming generally, "art is more valuable than truth"—art is more valuable to sensuous *life* than truth, because truth is antisensuous. In sum: *"Art, as [transfiguring] clarification* [Verk-lärung], *is more enhancing to life than truth, as fixation of an impression* [Anscheins]" (*Ne*, 1:217; *Ng*, 1:250, Heidegger's emphasis). Finally, therefore, art, as the action of the "artist-philosopher," can become the historic enterprise of abolishing truth.

We now are in a position to understand more fully why Nietzsche's discordance of art and truth is *Entsetzen erregender*, why it rages or arouses terror; at the same time we will understand Heidegger's inter-pretation of that discordance *as* a more fundamental concordance. Within Heidegger's reading of Nietzsche, art and truth eventually dis-cord because art represents the particular perspective on truth from which truth is seen to *destroy itself*, once Platonism achieves its apothe-osis in positivism. But the reason that art can serve this historical func-tion is that the concept "art" is extremely close to "truth"; indeed it is the rubric for truth's own secret self-negating essence. Art, the essence of the perspectival or the sensuous, is the will or willfulness at the for-gotten root of truth's own merely apparent presence and placidity.

Of course even when they are critically opposed, for instance within the conceptual schematics of Nietzsche's positivism, art and truth "belong together" precisely to the degree that truth is construed as an inferior type of artwork or artistry. As the specific *reductio ad absurdum* of a true world, art belongs more essentially to the realm of truth than anything else, for truth *is* precisely a species of art, of form-creating force. But—and this is the point that opens the way to Heidegger's revision—Nietzsche fails to arrive at this concordant *form* of a conclu-sion, because he still has no category to describe the truth of art other than the Platonic-epistemological category of "the true," a category which still ragingly discords with art.

Art and truth must always be in a raging discordance for Nietzsche so long as he is still tied to the Platonic "true world" as the definition of "the true," and that means *even when he criticizes it*, and even in his most stringent attacks upon positivism, for instance in "How the True World Finally Became a Fable." The discordance rages in Nietzsche because he simultaneously uses art against Platonism and yet remains formally Platonistic, failing, from Heidegger's vantage, to gain the perspective, the particular angle of vision, from which these terms could be reconciled. Nonetheless, beneath the symptoms of the lack of such a concordant viewpoint, Nietzsche's *thought* itself concords, as it were, with a life of its own. The fact that art and truth are brought into proximity at all in Nietzsche's thought is troped by Heidegger as the anticipation of the eventual concordance that his own reading will posit at the ground of Nietzsche's raging discordance. And it is this proleptic value of Nietzsche's text—seen, however, only from the historically advantageous point of view of Heidegger's lectures—that Heidegger is able to name the "fundamental position" or "direction" of Nietzsche's thinking, the grounding concordance of art and truth that underlies the merely apparent discordance within Platonism, as first brought forward by Nietzsche some four or five decades before.

Rereading Truth

Clearly, for Heidegger to be able to demonstrate Nietzsche's unwitting complicity with a historic failure to overcome Platonism, it must really be the case that within Nietzsche's written production he is constrained by a definition of "the true" in its traditional Platonic form. In other words, the concept of truth that Nietzsche overturns, and which he devalues alongside art, must be precisely the Platonic notion of truth and nothing more, even if, proleptically, it is more than what positivism can muster. For it is constitutive of Nietzsche's position, as Heidegger reconstructs it, and in turn of Heidegger's position in relation to that reconstruction, that Nietzsche fails to understand what is really true about truth, an understanding which only becomes possible radically *after* positivism. Such an "after" names for Heidegger a historical context in which truth can be examined in its most basic signification, a signification prior to and more originary than the one invoked by Platonism. Heidegger calls this context the epoch of the "grounding question [*Grundfrage*] of Being," a phrase I will analyze in detail in the following two chapters. For now I want to turn to Heidegger's attempt, still in the first lecture course, to outline the basic features of this historical context and its relevance to the reading of Western philosophy through Nietzsche—the context of "philosophy proper" beyond or despite Nietzsche's own particular limited self-understanding.

For Heidegger's reading, as I have remarked, Nietzsche's meditation on art is always already a meditation on truth. But now, it is absolutely crucial to indicate that the "truth" referred to in this statement is no longer that of Platonism, but a more basic and original conception of which Nietzsche's awareness is, as Heidegger claims, only "obscure and amorphous [*dunkle und ungestaltete*]" (*Ne*, 1:122; *Ng*, 1:144). In short, for Heidegger's reading, Nietzsche's meditation on art is always already, proleptically, a meditation upon *Heidegger's understanding of truth*—and therefore not upon Nietzsche's own self-understanding. The effect of Heidegger's rereading, then, is to make Nietzsche essentially a revisor of himself—when reread "properly." Heidegger's interpretation of Nietzsche *is* Nietzsche's *self*-revision, and only thereby its putative improvement and completion.[8] Thus we would do more violence to Nietzsche's text by straightforwardly accepting what it manifestly says, than by "simplifying" and "clarifying" its content into a basically Heideggerian form. The apparent reductionism of such a simplifying and clarifying is precisely, and ironically, what allows Nietzsche's "questioning *to go its own way*":

> The less we do violence to Nietzsche's "aesthetics" by building it up as an edifice of seemingly obvious doctrines, [and] the more we allow his searching and questioning to go its own way, the more surely do we hit upon those outlooks [*Ausblicke*] and basic ideas [*Grundvorstellungen*] within which the whole for Nietzsche possesses a mature, albeit obscure and amorphous, unity. (*Ne*, 1:122; *Ng*, 1:144)

What is most striking here is the nonchalance with which Heidegger insinuates that his own reading—a reading which imputes a failure of self-understanding to Nietzsche—is precisely what is "basic" to Nietzsche's thinking, its very "own way," while Nietzsche's self-understanding, what would comprise his "seemingly obvious doctrines," is what is extrinsic or imposed. The passage continues, "The ideas need to be clarified if we want to grasp the basic metaphysical position of Nietzsche's thought. Therefore we must now attempt to simplify Nietzsche's explanations about art to what is essential, without relinquishing the multiplicity of perspectives, yet neither by imposing some questionable schema from the outside" (*Ne*, 1:122–23; *Ng*, 1:144). But the "questionable schema from the outside" is easily seen to be Nietzsche's *own* schema, that is, the discordance of art and truth. Nietzsche is quite essentially outside himself here, outside his own basic position or unity. I have spoken of the formal need for Heidegger's interpretation to establish a context in which Nietzsche's "failure" properly to understand the content of his own thinking may be reviewed for its more essential proleptic position or direction. The above passage confirms that the discordance of art and truth in Nietzsche's work is, for Heidegger, the result of just such a previously absent or latent context, a hyperbolic historical purview that encompasses both Platonism and Nietzsche's own thinking, and is able to see the mutual origin of both, to see it properly *as. . . .*

To be sure, Nietzsche's "sixth and final step" in "How the True World Finally Became a Fable," in which the very opposition of sensuous/supersensuous (art/truth) is abolished, is in a formal way the prototype of Heidegger's reading—as is only proper, since Heidegger's reading after all claims to uncover no more than the basic, intrinsic direction of Nietzsche's own thinking. But the difference Heidegger's reading posits is a perspective that permits a gesture toward grounds that Nietzsche never makes in anything but a parodic form. And as much as this gesture is, or would have been, the clarification and simplification of Nietzsche's own written material, it is also the clarification and simplification of the Western tradition as such, for which Nietzsche is consistently, for Heidegger, the penultimate exemplar, most especially where he remains trapped within discordances and ambiguities. Thus Heidegger, identifying Nietzsche's difficulties in completing his "meditation on truth," claims generally that

> it was not the extrinsic question of finding a suitable connection or link among the handwritten materials available; it was, *without Nietzsche coming properly to know of it or stumbling across it*, the question of *philosophy's self-grounding.* . . . [Philosophy's] *proper essence turns ever [up] against itself [immer gegen sie selbst]*, and the more original a philosophy is, the more purely it swings in this turn about [or inverting of] itself [*in dieser Kehre um sich selbst*]. (*Ne*, 1:16; *Ng*, 1:24, my emphasis)

Nietzsche's destruction of Platonism is thus more properly seen as a grounding, or at least as an implicit gesture toward grounding, a concordant rather than discordant gesture toward the tradition of metaphysics, although, of course, Nietzsche would not have seen it this way. Nietzsche is logically correct to define and criticize Platonic philosophy as an inquiry into "the true." But because he fails, for Heidegger, to come to any further understanding of what historically grounds "the true" than the self-understanding that Platonism itself first posits—namely, that the true is what is adequate to reality, what corresponds—he naturally holds truth to discord with art and art to be the potential destruction of all inquiry into truth. Hence Heidegger can summarize his reading of Nietzsche's criticism of truth as follows:

> We must first ask: upon which route of meaning [*Bedeutungsbahn*] does the word "truth" move for Nietzsche in the context of his discussions of the relationship between art and truth? The answer is that it moves along the route which deviates from the essence [*auf der dem Wesen abgekehrten Bahn*]. That indicates [*besagt*] that

in the fundamental question which arouses terror Nietzsche nevertheless does not arrive at the proper [*eigentlichen*] question of truth, in the sense of a discussion of the essence of the true. . . . It is of decisive importance to know that Nietzsche does not pose the question of truth proper [*die eigentliche Wahrheitsfrage*], the question concerning the essence of the true and the truth of essence, and with it the question of the necessary possibility of its essential transformation; nor does he ever stake out the domain of the question. (*Ne*, 1:148–49; *Ng*, 1:174–75)

And of course, this omission in Nietzsche is characteristic of the entire history of thinking in the West: "That in Nietzsche's thought the question of the essence of truth is left out, is an oversight of a peculiar sort [*eigener Art*]; it cannot be blamed on him alone, or him first of all, if [it can be blamed on] anyone. This 'oversight' runs through the entire history of Western philosophy since Plato and Aristotle" (*Ne*, 1:149; *Ng*, 1:175).

While truth is "[the point at which] all the bypaths of Nietzsche's metaphysical thought obviously converge" (*Ne*, 1:143; *Ng*, 1:167–68), this convergence, like the concordance of truth with art, is *first* made manifest only by and through Heidegger's reading; Nietzsche himself "did not achieve sufficient perspicuity [*Durchsichtigkeit*] here" (*Ne*, 1:143; *Ng*, 1:168). Such blindness is absolutely decisive: Nietzsche fails to achieve perspicuity or insight (*Einsicht*) into precisely the core of his entire philosophy, so that what *we*, Heidegger and the lecture audience, may now see as the essence of Nietzsche's metaphysics, Nietzsche himself essentially cannot see. In short, Heidegger's reading is itself *Nietzsches eigentliches Philosophie*, "Nietzsche's philosophy proper."

With respect only to the structure and form of his revision, Heidegger adds nothing to "Nietzsche's philosophy proper," even while he necessarily adds much to what Nietzsche's text explicitly states. By the logic of the rereading, it is no violence to Nietzsche's text for Heidegger to impute what he comprehends to be the proper meaning of

Nietzsche's thought. It would be violence precisely *not* to impute it, for by failing to execute the proper imputation we would fail also to receive and follow Nietzsche's thinking in the proper—the "metaphysically true"—direction.

Basic Words

To conclude this discussion of Heidegger's reading of the discordance of art and truth, I will look briefly at Heidegger's own interpretation of truth within the *Nietzsche* lectures, to show precisely how he positions it as the now unconcealed implicit meaning of Nietzsche's thinking. I continue to aim toward an understanding of how truth and art can be said to concord in Heidegger's reading in a way not yet to be found in Nietzsche's explicit text.

Heidegger identifies "truth" as a *Grundwort*, a basic or fundamental word, akin to such words as "beauty, Being, art, knowledge, history, and freedom" (*Ne*, 1:143; *Ng*, 1:168). What does the word's basic-ness or grounded-ness consist in? Among the various significations of the word truth—scientific truths, mathematical or axiomatic truths, daily commonplaces, or simply the set of facts that are the case according to these various other significations—we may discern, still vaguely, an essence that ties together and relates these various meanings. This "common ground" is something of which we are normally aware only in the background of our everyday assertions, and which "is always only previewed and implied" (*Ne*, 1:146; *Ng*, 1:172). Here Heidegger describes the experience of a preunderstanding entailed generally by our using or connoting a *Grundwort*. What he presents is a phenomenological description, not of a particular writer or reader per se, but rather of *Dasein* itself in its use of language:

> If we mean something true, we of course understand the essence
> of truth along with it. We must understand the latter if, whenever

we intend something true, we are to know what we have in front of us. Although the essence itself is not expressly [*eigens*] and especially named, . . . the word "truth," which names the essence, is nevertheless used for true things themselves. The name for the essence glides unobtrusively into our naming such things that participate in that essence. (*Ne*, 1:146; *Ng*, 1:172).

Such a phenomenology of "us" and of our experience of the word truth is grounded first in the ontological structure of *Dasein*: "truth, understood in the most primordial sense, belongs to the basic constitution of *Dasein*" (*BT*, 208 [226]). But *Dasein*'s constitution is equally primordially historical.[9] When we utter the word truth in its various meanings we take a stance in relation to the historicality of truth, that is, we adopt and adapt to a particular thought-system, a metaphysics. No basic word would have a meaning for us without such an understanding. Furthermore, as Heidegger argues, the historicality of a "stance" is not the simple relativity of passing historical periods: "*Basic words are historical* [*geschichtlich*]. This does not mean simply that they have various meanings for various ages, which, because they are past, we can survey historically [*historisch*]" (*Ne*, 1:144; *Ng*, 1:169, Heidegger's emphasis). *Dasein*'s experience of such words, and its being in relation to them, is an essential relatedness to the historical ground and source of their meaning: "Here all the meanings, and likewise their differences, are historical [*geschichtlich*] and therefore necessary" (*Ne*, 1:144; *Ng*, 1:169). The past and present uses of a basic word are not available to us as a series of choices, as in a lexicon, because *Dasein* is always already too closely related to the object of any such survey: "[Basic words] are now and futurally [*künftig*] history-grounding [*geschichte-gründend*], in accordance with the interpretation of them that comes to prevail" (*Ne*, 1:144; *Ng*, 1:169). Even a mere survey of word usages would be itself a quite particular use (or misuse) of the basis of words, for every invocation is also a relation to the essence of the *Grundwort*.

Thus, even if our experience of such words can seem arbitrary or "extrinsic [*äußerlich*]"—a choice from a dictionary—in this extrinsic usage we still take a stance toward the essence of the word. Our stance might be a negative one, a relinquishing of essence: "The manner in which we examine the basic words therefore moves along two principal routes [*Hauptbahnen*]: the route of the essence [*der Wesensbahn*], and that which veers away from the essence and yet is related back to it [*der dem Wesen abgekehrten und doch darauf rückbezogenen Bahn*]" (*Ne*, 1:146; *Ng*, 1:172). We already know that Nietzsche takes the "veering-away route" with regard to the *Grundwort* truth, a route which results in the discordance of his conceptualization of truth with that of art. It remains only to determine the precise sense in which Nietzsche's route, for Heidegger's interpretation, is nonetheless "related back" to the essence, and therefore at bottom a concordance.

When Heidegger casts his discussion of truth in the essentialist context of the basic words, we have before us a circular argument. The word truth, in both its essence and its "veering away from the essence," is historically necessary and determined,[10] because it stands in essential relation to *Dasein*. But *Dasein* is that type of being which constructs its own historical position based on the use of, and the relation to, such basic words. In short, *Dasein* understands a basic word a certain way because that word itself defines just how *Dasein* understands. For Heidegger, this circularity is precisely the proper uncovering and illumination of the understanding of *Dasein* in its world. The circle, as we examine it phenomenologically, discloses the preunderstanding that constitutes *Dasein*'s relation to its metaphysical inheritance, whether a particular *Dasein* realizes it in a given situation (such as a given use of the word truth) or not: "human *Dasein*, insofar as it is—[insofar as it is] itself—is steered directly toward that which is named in such basic words and is bound up in relations with it" (*Ne*, 1:143; *Ng*, 1:168).

This sort of argumentative circularity—essentially appropriate to the hermeneutical circularity of *Dasein* itself[11]—"shows itself [*zeigt sich*]" (*Ne*, 1:143; *Ng*, 1:168)[12] whenever *Dasein* becomes aware of itself as essentially "historical," that is, "whenever it comes to a confrontation with being [*dem Seienden*] as such, in order to adopt a stance in its midst and to ground the site of that stance definitively" (*Ne*, 1:143; *Ng*, 1:168). Among other such situations, it can show itself when "we" the lecture audience are able, thanks to a particular rereading of Nietzsche, to anticipate a proper review of Platonic metaphysics as a whole, in its completed form. For now we begin to see both the veering away of truth and the basis back to which that veering away is related, the *Grund* of veering away. Hermeneutical circularity, and clarity regarding truth, *follow* Nietzsche's critique of Platonism and nihilism in more than just a *historisch* manner. The reading of Nietzsche, which is the reading of all of Platonism in its ultimatum, is the event of this disclosure or "unconcealment [*Unverborgenheit*]" of the essence, the event of its truth ["*alētheia*"].

With Nietzsche's concept of truth, which encapsulates or expresses in a proleptic form the essence understood by all Western philosophy since Plato, and with the advent of Heidegger's "clarification" of that essence, we have before us two contrasting perspectives that Heidegger posits as equally necessary and determined by the concept of truth itself and by its history. For the negativity of a basic word's history—its decline into obscurity and reification—even into "death," "petrifaction [*Vereisung*]," and "devastation [*Verödung*]" (*Ne*, 1:144; *Ng*, 1:168–69)—belongs integrally to the historicity of the word itself and is therefore only apparently, or phenomenologically, negative:

> That a clarification is necessary here has its grounds in the concealment [*Verborgenheit*] of the essence of that which is named in such words. Such clarification becomes unavoidable from the moment we experience [the fact] that human *Dasein*, insofar as it is—[insofar as] it is itself—is steered directly toward that which is

named in such basic words and is bound up in relations with it.
(*Ne*, 1:143; *Ng*, 1:168)

From the perspective granted by an insight into the basic words of the
text, the essential meaning of truth necessarily remains concealed for
Nietzsche, but is unconcealed for Heidegger. Or rather, Heidegger's
interpretive work, following Nietzsche's lead, begins to unconceal it *as*
. . . , therefore to bring about its disclosure [*Eröffnung*]. Nietzsche's
quasi-positivistic overturning of Platonism exposes the Platonic
notion of truth as bankrupt and nihilistic, and in place of this *nihil*
Nietzsche posits art, the perspectival creation of form. Truth itself,
under this definition, is merely a species of art, and a species of a lesser
value, because it is too much fixed, limited, restricted. But for Heidegger this truth is, in its unconcealment, . . . *unconcealment itself*,
"*Unverborgenheit*," "*alētheia*." And as such truth is, and was, perspectival, always already tied to the emergence or "presencing [*Anwesen*]" of
Being, and hence always already in concordance with art:[13] "The unity
of their belonging together is granted by the *one* reality, perspectival
appearance. To it belong both semblance [*Anschein*] and scintillating
appearance [*Aufscheinen*] as [transfiguring] clarification [*Verklärung*]"
(*Ne*, 1:217; *Ng*, 1:250). What does such a unity signify, finally, for our
understanding of the relation between Heidegger and Nietzsche, for
the shape of Heidegger's revision of Nietzsche? If Nietzsche had been
able to see the limitation of truth inherent in Platonism, and the
derivative quality of the Platonic definition of truth, then its overturning would not have exposed a discordant *nihil*, to be overturned or
replaced by art. From Heidegger's angle of vision, "art and truth
belong to the essence of reality with equal originality" (*Ne*, 1:217; *Ng*,
1:250), and "as *equally necessary* they stand in severance" (*Ne*, 1:217;
Ng, 1:251, my emphasis). "Severance [*Entzweiung*]" is essentially
already a unity [*Einheit*], unity-that-severs-itself, a movement which
Nietzsche stops just short of seeing at the ground of his discordance of

art and truth. But he nevertheless "says" that ground proleptically—it is his "philosophy proper" in Heidegger's reading, his true "final step." And only thus, *within the framework of a revision*, is Heidegger able to state, for instance, that "[Nietzsche's philosophy] proper can never be arrived at if we have not in our questioning conceived of Nietzsche as the end of Western metaphysics and proceeded on to the entirely different question about the truth of Being" (*Ne*, 1:10; *Ng*, 1:18–19).

Let me propose one more version of the shape of Heidegger's revision of Nietzsche on art and truth: *If Nietzsche had been Heidegger, he would have seen the "proper" direction of his own philosophy, and his own fundamental metaphysical position.* If such a thing *were* possible. My proposal here provides a fuller content for my earlier statement that Heidegger's reading *is* "Nietzsche's philosophy proper," a somewhat more concrete rendering of the moment entailed by that speculative copula, and of the "as . . ." that constitutes the essence of Nietzsche's text when that text is interpretively reread. Nietzsche *is* essentially, proleptically, perhaps prophetically, Heidegger. And Heidegger is thus more essentially Nietzschean than Nietzsche himself, through or because of Heidegger's own reading. It thereby becomes Heidegger's privilege to claim that "in spite of everything, we must try to make more explicit what is essential in and for Nietzsche, going beyond him" (*Ne*, 1:123; *Ng*, 1:145), and more generally, that "every great thinker always *thinks* one leap more originally than he directly *speaks*. The interpretation must therefore try to say what is unsaid by him [*sein Ungesagtes*—'his unsaid']" (*Ne*, 1:134; *Ng*, 1:158, Heidegger's emphasis). One is accustomed to conventional critical formulations such as "Heidegger's reading of Nietzsche," or "Nietzsche's influence on Heidegger," or even "Heidegger's influence on Nietzsche-readings." But within the structure of the revision I have outlined there is little sense to any historical chronology unless "history" itself is interpreted in an extremely strong way, as theoretically and metaphysically deterministic, according to a powerful hermeneutic of textual interpositioning that Heidegger's work itself prepares:

> Every true thinking lets itself be determined by that which itself is to be thought. In philosophy the Being of beings is to be thought; there is no loftier or stricter commitment for thinking and questioning in [philosophy]. All the sciences, by contrast, think always only of *one* being among others, *one* particular region of being. They are committed by this region of being only in an immediate manner, [and yet] never straightforwardly so. However, because in philosophical thought the highest possible commitment prevails, *all great thinkers think the same.* Yet this "same" is so essential and so rich that no single thinker exhausts it; rather, each commits the others to it all the more strictly. (*Ne*, 1:35–36; *Ng*, 1:45–46)

In the thinking of "the same" that comprises the imputation of Heidegger's reading (back) into Nietzsche's text, the "prior" thinker, Nietzsche, properly thinks "Heidegger's" thought in the form of an "*as* . . . ," at least as explicitly as Heidegger can be said to rethink Nietzsche's thought. The names, the chronology, the directions of influence—all are potentially reversible within this peculiar curved space of revision. Indeed there is far more sense to the claim that Heidegger *is* Nietzsche, Nietzsche *proper*, than to the truism that he merely succeeds him. In any case, the better description of the revision is that Nietzsche bespeaks Heidegger's reading of him in a veiled, "unthought" manner, and we may add, this bespeaking is of course peculiarly the effect of Heidegger's reading itself and of our own encounter with it.

In essence, Heidegger acts as a pure middleman—a sort of excluded middleman—between a Nietzsche not yet aware of his "own" philosophical ground, who is made to "speak" that ground in the form of an interpreted "*as* . . . ," and a Nietzsche who, recuperated through a rereading practice, now expresses fully "his" fundamental metaphysical position. Thus there is no "Heidegger's reading proper" within Heidegger's lectures, rather only Nietzsche's self-understanding and, opposed to it as ground to figure, "Nietzsche's philosophy proper." At least, this remains true until "we," the other readers, unconceal the implicit direction of, for instance, Heidegger's text. The validity or propriety of readings is determinable only in light of the thinking, or the thinkers, or the reading, that each of them, through the other, becomes *next*. Philosophers are one another's revisions, and, through revision, are their "own" concealed anticipations.

THREE

Paralipsis, Part 1: A Rhetoric of Rereading

The essence of a thing never appears at the outset, but in the middle, in the
course of its development, when its strength is assured.

— D E L E U Z E , *Cinema I*

My question about the shape of revision has not asked whether Heidegger reads Nietzsche accurately or faithfully, or whether, by contrast, he distorts or "reads into" Nietzsche's texts. Presumably any critical approach must eventually encounter these or similar issues of
accuracy or of the degree of a reader's revisionism. My own reading
will do so, to some extent, in the final chapter, which is about Heidegger's interpretation of *Thus Spoke Zarathustra* and *Ecce Homo*. But to
assume a critical perspective toward a philosophical reading too
quickly would be to risk overlooking the self-consciously revisionist
attitude that a reader such as Heidegger himself adopts toward a text
such as Nietzsche's. Heidegger deliberately flouts straightforward
meanings in his pursuit of what is "essential" in Nietzsche's thinking,

positioning Nietzsche's own explicit statements as distortions of that essence, as the "veering-away route" from what is true within the text. Accuracy is not a useful criterion for gauging the character or power of such a reading except with respect to minute exegetical points.

Nevertheless, reflecting upon the limits of a critical attack on Heidegger's *Nietzsche* can give an indication of just how the reading's own basic critical structure might be more usefully described. Heidegger relativizes Nietzsche's explicit statements, evoking a context against which Nietzsche's text appears to be a restricted understanding of precisely that same context. So, for instance, from the perspective of Heidegger's reading, Nietzsche does not, properly speaking, think the discordance of art and truth, per se, despite the fact that this is what he actually writes, but rather is seen to think, as it were proleptically, the underlying concordance of art and truth that grounds the relation between art and truth *as*, or in the form of, discordance. As Heidegger suggests, Nietzsche "thinks one leap more 'originally' than he speaks," and thinking in leaps will be precisely the thought-style that sanctions the revisionist gestures Heidegger's reading undertakes, even on the basis of a fidelity to Nietzsche's thinking "proper."

To start with, then, Heidegger's reading comprises two basic gestures: a limiting of the value of Nietzsche's statement with respect to a broader or more "original" understanding of the thought, and an overstepping of that same limit. But Heidegger clearly does not perceive himself as actively limit*ing* Nietzsche, only as disclosing a limitation already present, albeit concealed, within Nietzsche's text: Nietzsche's limitation, once exposed, should exhibit itself as determined by the peculiar metaphysical immanence of his *own* thinking. Thus, although the exposure of Nietzsche's limit is in any case an effect of Heidegger's reading, from Heidegger's vantage the effect results not from any action on his part, but simply from a divergence of historical perspective on the relation of art and truth that Nietzsche was unable to summon. The limitation of Nietzsche's thinking, within Heidegger's scenario, does not signify, strictly speaking, any oversight or deficiency in

Nietzsche's self-understanding, putatively exposed by its contrast with Heidegger's own more enlightened view. The limitation is the positive presence of the tradition *in the text*, despite Nietzsche's cognition of it, or lack thereof.

In short, Heidegger does not present his reading as a revision of Nietzsche at all, but rather as the elaboration of an "angle of vision" from which a "proper" Nietzsche may be seen, as it were, to *revise himself*. Such a perspective could arise only within a "more clarified domain [*geklärteren Bereich*]" (*Ne*, 3:102; *Ng*, 1:592), or a "grounding domain [*gründenden Bereich*]" (*Ne*, 2:156; *Ng*, 1:418)[1] that Nietzsche himself anticipates and for which he even establishes the conditions. Ironically, then, by Heidegger's own standards, the loyalty or accuracy of a reading of Nietzsche resides in the degree to which it permits precisely the antithetical self-divergence of Nietzsche's text properly to emerge, even the degree to which it permits of Nietzsche's self-contradiction. Heidegger writes, "We must grasp what Nietzsche *properly wanted to think* [*den eigentlichen Denkwillen Nietzsches*]," but presumably could not yet directly say (*Ne*, 1:65; *Ng*, 1:78, my emphasis).[2] In order to hear "Nietzsche himself," Heidegger asserts, we must "inquire with him and through him *and therefore at the same time against him* [*mit ihm, durch ihn hindurch und so zugleich gegen ihn . . . zu fragen*]" (*Ne*, 1:24; *Ng*, 1:33, Heidegger's emphasis).

To account for this crucial *anti*revisionist stance within Heidegger's reading, by which Heidegger constructs himself as a middleman negotiating between Nietzsche's explicit statement and his implicit proper thought, I will continue to exercise what might be called a bracketing or *epochē* of critical questions about revision or revisionism in the reading. This bracketing suspends any adjudication between Heidegger's and Nietzsche's texts, or between the philosophical positions they putatively embody, so as more fully to depict the peculiar space between them constructed by Heidegger's reading. Within the *epochē* I will refer to the rereading not as Heidegger's "revision," per se, but as the "revision-encounter" between the two thinkers. What this terminology should allow to emerge is the structure of the rereading encounter itself, as something other than a genealogy or mere contrast of the two competing texts at hand—the space *between* the two thinkers, as free as possible from any critical evaluation implied by the term "revision" alone. More specifically, the "revision-encounter" encompasses both revision—a gesture by virtue of perspectival difference—and essentialization—an antirevisionist instantiation of that difference in the form of a truth about the text—each of which is a crucial moment in Heidegger's encounter with Nietzsche. Finally, "revision-encounter" signifies that while we are analyzing a reading that posits an essential alteration of the prior text, we bracket decisions as to the source of that alteration: whether it is Heidegger's delimiting action or Nietzsche's "intrinsic" metaphysical limitation. Only by such a bracketing do we avoid merely repeating, instead of analyzing, Heidegger's revisionist gestures: a decision about what is proper within Nietzsche's text itself and a negotiation of the proper as against the improper.

To reformulate, then, my question of the first two chapters: What is the shape of the revision-*encounter* between Heidegger and Nietzsche? Within the revision-encounter, a self-difference within Nietzsche's own text emerges, albeit perceived only from the domain granted to a posterior reading. Nietzsche's written work, from this perspective, is "[mere] words" (*Ne*, 2:156; *Ng*, 1:418) or "extrinsic calculations [*äußerlichen Verrechnen*]" (*Ne*, 2:156; *Ng*, 1:418) about what is ultimately his "proper [*eigentlich*]" thought. As Heidegger states in one context, a statement which describes his whole practice of rereading: "Nietzsche means something other than would appear" (*Ne*, 3:102; *Ng*, 1:592).[3] Figuratively or tropologically speaking—and this way of speaking is appropriate because the revision-encounter posits a divergence or "turn" away, at the core of Nietzsche's own language, from what is literally said within his text—Nietzsche's "saying [*Spruch*]" or "uttering [*Aussprechen*]" (*Ne*, 3:35; *Ng*, 1:513)[4] is ironic. There is a gap or contradiction between what the text "would appear" to say and what it truly means: "In oratorical discourse there frequently occurs a figure of speech which bears the name of irony and whose characteristic is this: to say the opposite of what is meant. With this we already have a determination present in all forms of irony, namely, the phenomenon is not the essence but the opposite of the essence."[5] Calling Nietzsche's text ironic identifies as a characteristic of the text itself what might conventionally have been identified simply as the difference between Heidegger's and Nietzsche's philosophical views: Heidegger's "says" concordance whereas Nietzsche's "says" discordance. In terms of the revision-encounter we can be more precise: invoking irony as a genus of communication in which meaning diverges from statement,[6] Nietzsche "speaks"—but ironically—the concordance of art and truth. Specifically, the concordance is bespoken by Nietzsche in the veiled form of its own denial or self-recantation, a *dis*cordance, which is the particular dissimulation of the concordance arising through Nietzsche's (ironic) immanence in the very metaphysics he attempts to destroy. Thus Heidegger's reading, from its "no longer metaphysical" (*Ne*, 3:138; *Ng*, 1:633) vantage, shows Nietzsche's text to have, more particularly, the structure of the ironic figure the classical rhetorical theorists call *occultatio* or *paralipsis*, a figure that occurs, in Cicero's words, "when we say that we are passing by, or do not know, or refuse to say that which precisely now we are saying."[7] The lawyer Cicero seems especially to enjoy citing the figure of paralipsis, which for obvious reasons is useful in the courts:

> Your boyhood, indeed, which you dedicated to intemperance of all kinds, I would discuss, if I thought this the right time. But at present I advisedly leave that aside. This too I pass by, that the tribunes have reported you as irregular in military service. Also that you have given satisfaction to Lucius Labeo for injuries done him I regard as irrelevant to the present matter. Of these things I say nothing, but return to the issue in this trial.[8]

The advocate speaks here as though he were not speaking, or more precisely, what he says is said in the *form* of something unsaid. From the perspective opened by our description of the revision-encounter, Nietzsche speaks just this sort of self-recantation to Heidegger's rereading. He utters his essential or proper intention paraliptically, in the veiled form of its own metaphysically bounded self-exclusion: concordance *as* the lack or failure of concordance, *as* discordance.

Of course, there is a difference in the way paralipsis is used by the speaker in Cicero's example and the way it is putatively used by the contextual bespeaker within Nietzsche's text. Nietzsche does not, indeed he could not, deliberately "*say* that [he is] passing by or do[es] not know, or refuse[s] to say that which precisely now [he is] saying." The content expressed paraliptically by Nietzsche's text is precisely not included, even negatively, *by* Nietzsche himself—only, perhaps, *through* him, and only then through the perspective "granted" by Heidegger's interpretation. At every moment of rereading Heidegger's reading, we remain potentially or actually aware that it is Heidegger who says concordance, while he declares that Nietzsche means it—but never Nietzsche himself. Nevertheless, neither for Cicero nor for us is the speaker's intention the crux of the matter. A paraliptical utterance, like any irony, need not be intended as such. Just as a speaker may unwittingly express to the hearer the opposite of what the speaker intends to say, so, too, a speech may be unwittingly paraliptical, implicitly expressing precisely the meaning being denied. In such a case, the underlying intention of speech, its duplicitous content, is perceived, for instance, as an unconscious slip, the connotation of an unknown implication within what is said, or simply as an (ironic) artifact of language itself. The crucial aspect of the trope's usage is always that the utterance is received *as* paraliptical, that a voice other than the speaker's is heard through the utterance, and construed as an intention that diverges from the one directly expressed.[9] Regardless of the subjective coherence or motive of the duplicity, the utterance *as* ironic or paraliptical is determined only in its reception, and this kind of reception entails that both literal and underlying meaning be simultaneously conveyed.[10] Thus Kierkegaard writes, "The ironic figure of speech cancels itself. . . . It is like a riddle and its solution possessed simultaneously."[11] In Kierkegaard, but more generally as well, irony shifts from a particular oratorical device to a general structural relation between expression and reception, or what Kierkegaard calls a "standpoint." Quintilian describes this expansion of the ironic attitude, analogous to the better-known broadening of metaphor into allegory,[12] as the move from the "concise" trope of irony to a more general figure. To illustrate the broader attitude entailed by ironic figures, Quintilian cites examples of *antiphrasis*, a trope identical to Cicero's *occultatio*[13] except for a slightly less blatant admission of its own duplicity. In the general figurative form of irony characteristic of such tropological usages, Quintilian writes, "the speaker disguises his entire meaning, the disguise being apparent rather than confessed. For in the *trope* the conflict is purely verbal, while in the *figure* the meaning, and sometimes the whole aspect of our case, conflicts with the language and the tone of voice adopted."[14] Irony's duplicity is only understood—for even here it is quite crucial that the advocate be understood—in an encounter within which "the disguise is apparent," and within which both "voices" of the speaker are hermeneutically interrelated in and by the ear of the receiver.[15]

I rehearse this tropology in such detail because it points to a crucial facet of Heidegger's rereading of Nietzsche that might otherwise remain obscured. Within the revision-encounter, Nietzsche's literal statements are understood—just as any ironic or paraliptical speech must be understood—only as an ancillary and subordinate manifestation of a second voice, by virtue of which a meaning is bespoken and indirectly received. In this light, the question of the shape of the revision-encounter now becomes: Whence the second voice, the voice that grounds but then bespeaks Nietzsche's text? I have discussed already how Nietzsche's immanence in Platonism provides, for Heidegger, the necessary background for Nietzsche's "failure" to think through the proper relation of art and truth, a limitation overcome only in a context in which the ground of Platonism, the "question of Being" in the form of a "grounding question [*Grundfrage*]," first arises. The limitation of Nietzsche's essentially paraliptical thinking is always relative to this context, which in turn makes the proper center of that thinking a matter for the revisionist clarification that is able to expose the grounding voice, or "soundless voice [*lautlosen Stimme*]" (*EP*, 77; *Ng*, 2:484), and which thereby lends the literal text its paraliptical *as*. Thus:

> The presupposition and guide of our procedure remains a historical reflection that, by asking the grounding question of philosophy, grasps the beginning and the end of Western metaphysics in their oppositional historical unity. This more original reflection thinks no longer metaphysically, but instead asks and transforms the guiding question of metaphysics, What is a being?, on the basis of the (no longer metaphysical) grounding question about the truth of Being. . . .
>
> Here Nietzsche fails to give us any help, because he was unable to see through [to] the historical roots of the metaphysical question of truth in general, and those of his own decisions in particular. (*Ne*, 3:138; *Ng*, 1:633–34)

"Help" in reading Nietzsche properly, in reading him properly *as* . . . , cannot come from Nietzsche himself, whose own self-reading is by definition not the proper *as* of the revision-encounter. Axiomatically, Nietzsche "is unable to see through [to] the historical roots" of his own thought; if he were able to do so, as I suggested at the end of the previous chapter, he would already have been Heidegger. To be sure, expressing the "as" in this way makes it the pivot of a tautology: Nietzsche does not understand himself in the same way as Heidegger because he *is* merely himself, not Heidegger. Heidegger's revision-encounter with Nietzsche cannot avoid a certain circularity in its construction of Nietzsche's limit, for of course Heidegger, like any critic, finds at the core of Nietzsche's thinking only what he himself is able to see. Is the limitation of the texts he rereads therefore an inherent aspect of all such reading, which qua reading necessarily and even automatically posits the given text as other-than-itself, and yet within the rereading's own parameters? To give this question anything but a truistic answer—to expose this circle as properly or fully hermeneutical or, in the end, as not quite only hermeneutical—I must move beyond Heidegger's reading of art and truth, where Nietzsche's limited thought is construed as the result of the historical conditions of late Platonism, and toward interpretations where these conditions themselves are more fully theorized as inherent facets of (metaphysical) thinking as such.

Will to Power and Eternal Recurrence

In the beginning of the first lecture course, even before turning to the question of the relation between art and truth, Heidegger offers an extended preface that introduces "Nietzsche's metaphysics" as a specific revision of a traditional German philosophy of the will and willing [*Willen*]. The preface sets up the task of the lecture course overall as the unification of Nietzsche's two "basic doctrines [*Grundlehren*]," will to power and eternal return of the same.[16] The problem of art and truth, which occupies the remainder of the first course, is then situated as a paradigmatic instance for understanding Nietzsche's conception of will to power, for reasons connected to the Nietzschean definition of art as a rubric for "becoming," which I outlined in the first chapter. Only in the second lecture course does Heidegger return explicitly to the "unification of will to power and eternal recurrence," after the discussion of art and truth has been concluded.

By the time he does return, Heidegger's views on Nietzsche's thinking have shifted, and the question of art and truth will never again occupy the exemplary position it was given in the first course. There are a number of possible reasons for this shift. The reason with which I am particularly concerned is that, for the reading of art and truth, Nietzsche's "failure" to understand the nature of truth is the result of an inherited oversight with respect to the definition of truth.

However historically embedded and determined Heidegger may regard that oversight, it is still essentially a specific doctrinal failure, redressable at the present historical juncture by the substitution of a different, more proper, understanding of truth. However, for the reading of will to power and eternal return, Nietzsche's limitation, which is still, as always, attributable to his immanence in metaphysics, begins to take on the aspect of an inherent attribute of metaphysical thinking as such, of which Nietzsche is now less a strong example than the prime exemplar. The failure of Nietzsche's thinking, and therefore also the necessity of revising him, now become structural entailments of "the metaphysical" itself within the history of thought, not merely attributes of particular metaphysical speculations or particular conceptual rereadings.

To "grasp in a unified way [*einheitlich . . . zu begreifen*]" Nietzsche's two "teachings" or "doctrines" [*Lehren*] (*Ne*, 1:17; *Ng*, 1:25), Heidegger is required to use texts where the interrelation of the doctrines is suggested by little more than proximity, for Nietzsche never makes any systematic effort to connect them.[17] One text Heidegger finds suggestive is an aphorism Nietzsche's editors titled "Recapitulation [*Rekapitulation*]" (*WP*, par. 617),[17] which Heidegger cites several times. His first gloss is as follows: "[Nietzsche states:] '*Recapitulation*: To *stamp* becoming with the character of Being—that is the *supreme will to power*.' This suggests that becoming only *is* if it is grounded in Being as Being: 'That *everything recurs* is the closest *approximation* of a world of becoming to one of Being:—peak of the meditation'" (*Ne*, 1:19; *Ng*, 1:27). Heidegger's tendency to view Nietzsche's thought as the synecdoche for all of Western philosophy rests increasingly on this passage, which he claims is "expressly formulated to provide an encompassing overview" (*Ne*, 1:19; *Ng*, 1:27). Nevertheless, the passage diverges significantly from Nietzsche's more common quasi-Heraclitean critique that "the expression 'will to power' names the basic character of *das Seiende*" (*Ne*, 1:18; *Ng*, 1:26). In this aphorism, will to power, as Heidegger reads it, is only to be thought as a doctrine about *das Sein*, which in Nietzsche's text belongs under the dominion of eternal recurrence. Thus, Heidegger claims, "Whoever does not think the thought of eternal recurrence, as what is philosophically proper to thinking, along with will to power, also cannot adequately grasp the metaphysical content of the doctrine of will to power in the scope of all its implications" (*Ne*, 1:21; *Ng*, 1:29). The confluence of will to power and eternal recurrence, viewed with respect to its full "metaphysical content," "reverts to the beginning of Western philosophy" (*Ne*, 1:19; *Ng*, 1:27–28).[18] This beginning is characterized by the competing yet complementary doctrines of Parmenides (*das Seiende* is— that is, in Nietzsche's language, it is "eternally" present), and Heraclitus (*das Seiende* becomes—that is, it is "will to power"),[19] which together connote the grounding but concealed unity of Being and becoming at the origin of Western thinking. This unity-in-ground is "the most difficult thought of philosophy, because it is simultaneously its innermost and uttermost thought, the one with which it stands and falls" (*Ne*, 1:19; *Ng*, 1:27). The fact that Nietzsche himself did not proceed far enough in Heidegger's direction to have recuperated the "pristine form" of the question of Being in the pre-Platonic origins of Western philosophy is yet another sign, for Heidegger, of Nietzsche's metaphysical immanence. For it is precisely within metaphysics that the original coherence of Being with becoming, and therefore the most basic form of the question of "the meaning of Being as such," has become lost:

> Neither Nietzsche nor any thinker before him—even and especially not the one who before Nietzsche first thought the *history* of philosophy philosophically, namely, Hegel—comes [back] upon the incipient beginning [*kommen in den anfänglichen Anfang*]. Rather, they invariably see the beginning already and only in light of a philosophy which is already a decline from the beginning, and the arresting [*Stillstellung*] of the beginning—[that is,] in light of Platonic philosophy. (*Ne*, 2:205; *Ng*, 1:469)

Nietzsche, once again, remains too much the Platonist. Even in the act of destroying the concept of Being, he fails to transcend the essentially Platonic milieu in which the destruction takes place, and in which critique becomes for him a matter of choosing a falsely hypostatic Platonic "Being" or nothing at all. Yet from the paraliptically bespoken perspective of the *Grundfrage*, from which perspective Heidegger can see the "innermost will of Nietzsche's thought [*dem innersten Denkwillen Nietzsches*], things are altogether different."[20] What appears to be Nietzsche's absolute destruction of Being is rather its ultimate recuperation. For what is preserved in the destruction, albeit in a veiled, paraliptical form, is the very character of Being *as becoming* that was concealed by the Platonic devaluation of the sensuous. Therefore, for Heidegger, when Nietzsche overturns Platonism by reducing it absolutely to the Heraclitean diagnosis of pure becoming or flux, this means that Being, precisely in its most original form, has returned— but obscurely, paraliptically. Hence will to power is (obscurely or paraliptically) posited by Nietzsche *as* eternal recurrence, that is, as ultimate and permanent Being.[21] In terms of the paralipsis which structures Nietzsche's appearance within Heidegger's interpretation, Nietzsche *says* "flux" and "nothing," but *means* "presence" and "Being."

To demonstrate Nietzsche's implicit or veiled "recollection" of the unified prehistory of Being and becoming, Heidegger again cites the "Recapitulation" aphorism: "'to *stamp* becoming with the character of Being—that is the supreme *will to power* . . .'" (*Ne*, 2:202; *Ng*, 1:466). Here he glosses the passage as follows: "Nietzsche joins into one [*schließt . . . in Eins zusammen*], in his most essential thought of the eternal recurrence of the same, both of the basic determinations [*Grundbestimmungen*] of being that emerge from the beginning of Western philosophy: *das Seiende* as becoming and *das Seiende* as permanence" (*Ne*, 2:204; *Ng*, 1:468). The two doctrines, as "joined together" or "made one," comprise a paralipsis of the true reversion to the beginning, and therefore of the overcoming of Western philosophy as a whole, for in the history of philosophy "Being and becoming are only seemingly [*treten nur scheinbar*] in opposition" (*Ne*, 3:212–13; *Ng*, 2:288).[22] Nietzsche exposes this semblance, albeit still paraliptically and therefore only as the prolepsis of Heidegger's own rereading, by showing that "the character of becoming in will to power is in its innermost essence eternal recurrence of the same, and thus the constant permanentizing of the impermanent [*die beständige Beständigung des Bestandlosen*]" (*Ne*, 3:213; *Ng*, 2:288).

Heidegger considers his interpretation of Nietzsche's will to power *as* eternal recurrence both original and, not surprisingly, perfectly in line with the spirit and tendency of his own philosophical thought.[23] Indeed here, even more explicitly than usual, he positions Nietzsche's thinking as the anticipation of his own distinctive revision of the history of philosophy:

> To think Being [*Sein*], will to power, as eternal return, to think the most difficult thought of philosophy, means to think Being as time. Nietzsche thought this thought but did not yet think it as the *question* of Being and time. Plato and Aristotle also thought this thought when they conceived Being as *ousia* (presence), but just as little as Nietzsche did they think it as a question. (*Ne*, 1:20; *Ng*, 1:28)

This bold assertion uncharacteristically alludes to Heidegger's own earlier thinking in *Being and Time*, where usually at such moments he would tend to appeal more objectively to a general metaphysical context.[24] But especially with respect to eternal return, Heidegger's own positing of the paraliptical intentionality of Nietzsche's text, from the "clarified realm" in which he (Heidegger) alone (for the moment) stands, becomes increasingly vehement. In the previous citation, when Heidegger writes that Nietzsche thinks through these matters "in his way," this of course means, just as it did with respect to the discordance of art and truth, precisely that Nietzsche does *not* yet think them through in Heidegger's way. And with the straightforward acknowledgment of these differing ways of thinking, Heidegger brings his own revising and essentializing gestures, *as* gestures, closer to the foreground: "Will to power is never the willing of a particular, actual entity. It concerns the Being and essence of beings; it is this itself. Therefore we can say that will to power is always essential will. Although Nietzsche does not formulate it expressly in this way, at bottom [*im Grunde*] that is what he means" (*Ne*, 1:61; *Ng*, 1:73). At other moments, which, perhaps incongruously (in light of the above passage), name the "innermost will [*innersten . . . (W)illen*]" (*Ne*, 1:93; *Ng*, 1:111) of Nietzsche's text *as* a will, Heidegger continues to refer to "the proper will of Nietzsche's thought [*den eigentlichen Denkwillen Nietzsches*]" (*Ne*, 1:65; *Ng*, 1:78),[25] or to that "toward which the will of Nietzsche's thought aims [*(darauf) geht Nietzsches Denkwillen*]" (*Ne*, 1:66; *Ng*, 1:79). And finally, taking the matter altogether out of Nietzsche's hands, Heidegger asserts: "Will to power itself, the fundamental character of beings as such, and not 'Herr Nietzsche,' posits the thought of eternal return of the same" (*Ne*, 3:215; *Ng*, 2:290).

The willfulness of these descriptions, their willingness baldly to acknowledge a revision of Nietzsche's explicit statements, differs from the tone of Heidegger's reading of art and truth only by degree. But there is a further, structural radicalization of Heidegger's approach to Nietzsche within this new reading, not unrelated to his increase in vehemence. The radicalization does not occur through an alteration of the form of the reading per se, but rather in its claim for a new type of subject matter, a new content whose status as a paraliptical herald is somewhat counterintuitive. The unification of will to power and eternal recurrence, like the reconfiguration of the relation between art and truth, posits a concordance as the underlying meaning or intention of Nietzsche's text. However, this particular concordance does not occur on the same structural level as that of art and truth. First of all, unlike art and truth, will to power and eternal recurrence never directly or explicitly discord within Nietzsche's writing; he never identifies any misrelation between them. Indeed, although a number of critics before

Heidegger had interpreted these doctrines as contradictory,[26] Heidegger himself, based on his reading of Nietzsche's schematic plans for *Der Wille zur Macht*, considers even the explicit plans, so far as they go, to foretell a unification. Thus for Heidegger's revision-encounter here—and this reading *is* still a revision, since it, too, is viewed as an essential advance on Nietzsche's basic position—a proper reading of Nietzsche must move not against the explicit content of the text, but instead, so to speak, against the text itself *as* text. It is now the very incompleteness of Nietzsche's writing—not simply the fact that Nietzsche didn't declare a concordance, but that he didn't quite get around to declaring it fully—that manifests, or rather simply *is*, the intrinsic paraliptical self-contradiction of Nietzsche's thought to be revised. Not Nietzsche's text, but his very lack of a text, bespeaks his concealed but *gründlich* paraliptical intention.

Thinking as Failure

Heidegger begins this strange rereading perhaps disingenuously, by stating that "nobody knows what would have become of these preliminary sketches had Nietzsche himself been able to transform them into the main work he was planning" (*Ne*, 1:24; *Ng*, 1:32). It is obvious enough that Nietzsche never completed his work on will to power or eternal recurrence. But Heidegger immediately makes clear that any uncertainty about the relation of these doctrines cannot be primarily due to Nietzsche's own stoppage, for between the two doctrines there already exists a more basic and intrinsic connection: they "cohere . . . in the most intimate way" (*Ne*, 1:18; *Ng*, 1:26). Furthermore, the fragmentation of Nietzsche's text is not attributable to the mere fact that Nietzsche didn't finish writing, but to a more intrinsic fragmentariness in Nietzsche's thinking itself, next to which his fragmented text must appear, as it were, a mere symptom: "Everything published in this 'book' is indeed written down by Nietzsche, however he never thought it *like that* [so]" (*Ne*, 4:11; *Ng*, 2:43, Heidegger's emphasis). In general, Heidegger writes, beginning in the same seemingly disingenuous tone as in the passage above about Nietzsche's "preliminary sketches": "We of today do not know the reason [*Grund*] why the innermost core of Nietzsche's metaphysics could not be made public by him, but rather lies concealed in posthumous notes—*still* lies concealed, although these posthumous notes have for the most part become available to us, albeit in a very misleading form" (*Ne*, 4:12; *Ng*, 2:44). Piecing together the fragments will never comprise a proper reading of Nietzsche, because even if they could be made entire, the essentially fragmentary *position* of these texts would keep them "*still* concealed." A proper form of the text, the one that won't "mislead," is the responsibility neither of Nietzsche nor of his editors, but can only belong to a confrontational revision-encounter.[27] In such an encounter, fragmentation itself must be interpreted as an intrinsic facet of the basically limited state— not of Nietzsche's bibliography, which is merely symptomatic—but of his *thought*, an essential "veering-away route" at the ground of the more obviously doctrinal discordances or gaps.

Here the essentializing gesture that regrounds Nietzsche's failure occurs as blatantly as it ever will in Heidegger's reading. Not only does Heidegger attribute Nietzsche's bibliographical incompleteness to the fact that, generally, "a gift for . . . 'systematic philosophizing,' as it is called, Nietzsche utterly lacked" (*Ne*, 3:11; *Ng*, 1:483), but, as he expresses in a tone that clearly shows his awareness of how counterintuitive the conclusion sounds: "The lack of completion [of the 'major work'], if one may dare to assert such a thing, in no way [*keinesfalls*] consists in the fact that a work 'about' the will to power was not finished. Lack of completion could only mean that the inner form of his own unique thought was denied the thinker" (*Ne*, 3:12; *Ng*, 1:485).[28] The "inner form" was denied Nietzsche—and so too, only subsequently, the ability to finish writing. Denied by what or whom? It was denied, of course, by Nietzsche's metaphysical position, which was fundamentally limited. Limited with respect to what? With respect to a further position, a "completed context [*geschlossene(r) Zusammenhang*]" from which one could perceive the ground of Nietzsche's limitation, and therefore complete the text. What is this ground? It is the *Seinsfrage*, to be sure, recollected in its original, unified form; but at the same, it is a perception of the decline of the *Seinsfrage* into the "oblivion [*Vergessenheit*]" that necessarily denies a particular thinker the "inner form of his thought." Here, more than in the reading of art and truth, it is apparent that the thinker, Nietzsche, is not limited through some particular failure of thinking, but rather because thinking itself is essentially failure. Metaphysics, as such, passes down *only* limited, paraliptical versions of the *Seinsfrage*. In this light, the basic historicity of Nietzsche's thinking, its axiomatic relativity within the context of a philosophical history, is a synecdoche for the structural limitation that lies at the ground of metaphysical thinking itself: "The thinker can never himself say what is most of all his own. It must remain unsaid, because what is sayable receives its determination [or 'direction,' or 'voicing'—*Bestimmung*] from what is not sayable" (*EP*, 77–78; *Ng*, 2:484). Nietzsche's "intrinsically" fragmented presentation of will to power and eternal recurrence, his special paralipsis, is thus no more than a special case of the general paralipsis of all Western philosophy, a structural attribute of thinking within metaphysics which, from the proper perspective, grounds the paraliptical limitedness of particular metaphysical systems. Nietzsche's unfinished manuscript is "in no way," for Heidegger, a coincidence of his illness or of his death, but in every way that matters, the effect of thought itself.

The Limit of Metaphysics

Such a description of Nietzsche's limit and its context suggests two possible understandings of the general limitation of thinking. In the first understanding, still within the bracketed or epochal terminology of the "revision-encounter," limitation would be the legacy of Western metaphysics, a particular historical relation of thinking to its origin, "Being": metaphysics is limited, and in turn fragmented, because of its still unrecoverable difference from the originary but concealed unity of Being and becoming. But in the second understanding of limitation, now stepping momentarily out of any *epochē* that would circumscribe the revision-encounter, the limit of a thought can be construed simply as its axiomatic *difference from another thinking*, against which a thought can and indeed must be perceived as relative. From this perspective, thinking is structurally limited simply by virtue of its contrast with the other thinker who comes to confront it.[29] Here the philosopher's "unsayable" would not arise out of the still-concealed inheritance of metaphysics per se, but rather from the mere fact that a philosophy has gotten itself revised, the more or less coincidental event of its being rethought by another *as* against itself. In short, thinking is limited or unfinished because *there is always another thinker*, a different thinker and writer who rereads the thought, and in rereading it, necessarily attempts to revise and complete it.

What is the link between these two possible explanations of the "limitation" of thinking? Between, first, what Heidegger calls the "history of Being," which names the differentiations of a historically discordant metaphysical thinking from its originary and still-concealed concordance, and "revision," the mere quotidian difference of a thought from that of its rereader? These two versions of limitation must provoke two distinct approaches to the problem of revision in the history of philosophy. The first approach, which I have largely followed up to now, and which remains basically loyal to Heidegger's historiography, describes the revision-encounter as the reading's disclosure of the inherent incompletion or self-difference within the text, but relative to the text's own equally inherent metaphysical con-text— and through these identifications, the discovery of its particular "concealed thought-*path* [*verborgenen Gedanken*-Gang]" (*Ne*, 3:14; *Ng*, 1:487, Heidegger's emphasis). But the second approach invokes a more extrinsic kind of difference, a difference created *by* a reader in a rereading *activity*, and retroactively troped as a (paraliptical) self-difference already within the text itself. In what follows I do not intend to choose between these two understandings (as per my *epochē*), but instead to keep both in mind at once, to continue to bracket critical questions about revision while at the same time remaining aware of the artifice of that bracketing, and, as always, to give full shrift to the description of the reading of Nietzsche at hand.

FOUR

Paralipsis, Part 2: Revision as History of Being

Relations do not belong to objects, but to the whole.

— DELEUZE, *Cinema I*

The term "metaphysics" shares a variety of interrelated significations within Heidegger's *Nietzsche* and his other work of this period. At its most conventional, the term identifies a topic originating in Greek philosophy, an inquiry into the underlying character of *physis*, or "nature"—or, in the paraphrase Heidegger prefers, *das Seiende im Ganzen*, "being generally" or "being(s) as a whole." Such an essentialist inquiry is by definition *meta*physical: "To think *das Seiende* as a whole in its truth and to think *the truth in it*—that is metaphysics" (*Ne*, 3:141; *Ng*, 1:637, Heidegger's emphasis). It may be summed up as the search for a single kind of answer: "Metaphysics is the inquiry and the search that always remains guided by the sole question 'What is being' [*was ist das Seiende*]. We therefore call this question the guiding question [*Leitfrage*] of metaphysics" (*Ne*, 2:189–90; *Ng*, 1:454). Systems of metaphysical thought, for instance philosophies, are always seen by Heidegger to complete the proposition *das Seiende ist*. . . . So, for example, "[Nietzsche's] expression 'will to power' provides an answer to the question of what, then, a being is" (*Ne*, 1:4; *Ng*, 1:12).[1] Such a characterization of metaphysics, as an answer to a single question, furnishes a basis for Heidegger's hyperbolic reduction of the history of Western philosophy. By representing all Western thinking as metaphysics, and metaphysics, in turn, as guided by the *Leitfrage*, Heidegger can claim that Western philosophers have thought, explicitly or implicitly, the same thing: "If [philosophy's proper] questions are many, they are nonetheless guided by one single question. In truth, drawn as they are into that question, they are in effect but *one* question" (*Ne*, 2:187; *Ng*, 1:451).

In attempting in every case to answer the leading question or *Leitfrage* of metaphysics, philosophers have always tended to treat the most basic component of metaphysics, ontology, the inquiry about the nature of Being, as though it were fundamentally a question of the underlying character of the particular beings that comprise the world. As Heidegger says, metaphysics treats ontology from the point of view of *das Seiende*. But to ask what a being [*das Seiende*] *is*, metaphysics must already have presumed to comprehend what exactly this "is"—the is-ness [*seiendheit*] of the being—itself is. The very inquiry into what or how a particular being stands in the world requires such a question already to have been answered, and the nature of the "to be [*das Sein*]" to have been supposed. Thus the question of the nature of the "to be" itself, Heidegger asserts, has been entirely taken for granted as obvious or already understood throughout the history of Western thinking. As a result, metaphysical thinkers have remained blind to the premises of their own inquiries and claims about beings.[2] Here we confront not simply a historical or historiographical complaint about the inadequacies of specific thought systems, but rather a structural explanation for the fact that philosophy in the West has appeared *as* metaphysics, a type of inquiry always already on the decline from a potential full self-understanding. Philosophy, in each case posing the *Leitfrage* of the character of *das Seiende*, is always already an assumption about, and a certain concealed preunderstanding of, what Being itself [*das Sein*] *is*.

Therefore, precisely insofar as metaphysics is defined as the asking of the *Leitfrage*, it is likewise defined as the nonasking of the *Grundfrage* or "grounding question," the question of "what Being as such" is, or of what "the *Being* of *beings* [*das Sein des Seiendes*]" is. The difference between this basic "whatness" or "what-being [*Was-sein*]" of *das Seiende* and the "thatness" or "that-being [*Daß-sein*]" of *das Sein des Seiendes* is the "metaphysical distinction [*metaphysische Unterscheidung*]" which "although everywhere claimed [or, taken for granted], is the unknown and ungrounded ground of all metaphysics" (*Ne*, 4:155; *Ng*, 2:210).

A variety of descriptions of the opposition of quiddity and quoddity have been explicitly known throughout the history of philosophy, and indeed philosophers have customarily offered definitions of the "Being of beings" as the ground of their own theories of what the world is, and how it is. For Heidegger, the version of the "*das Sein des Seiendes*" most prevalent in Western thinking, and which leads eventually to the positivism out of which Nietzsche's own critique of philosophy arises, is that "*das Seiende* is [the] actual." In the following passage, note the paraliptical "*as*" that characterizes concealed Being in its explicit metaphysical manifestations:

> For a long time the proper nature of Being has announced itself as "actuality." "Actuality" often means "existence" [*Dasein*] as well. Thus Kant speaks of the "proofs for God's existence." . . . In the language of metaphysics, "actuality" [*Wirklichkeit*], "*Dasein*" and "*Existenz*" say the same thing. Yet what these names say is by no means definite or unequivocal. This is not due to a sloppiness of word usage, but comes rather from Being itself. (*EP*, 1–2; *Ng*, 2:400)[3]

What Heidegger here names as the "unknown and ungrounded" ground is clearly meant to entail some notion of the manner of *das Sein* other than that invoked by such traditional ontologies, since this latter type of thinking is considered a *"flight* in the face of the unknown ground" (*Ne*, 4:155; *Ng*, 2:210, Heidegger's emphasis). The most essential *Seinsfrage*, that which asks about what comes "from Being itself"—*as* a question—is new for philosophy, even if Heidegger claims that in terms of its basicness it is the oldest and most original, the *Grundfrage*. And the difference between what it asks about and what is asked about in the conventional *Leitfrage*—which difference is newly uncovered as the potential questioning of "ontological difference [*ontologische Differenz*]" only in our epoch of thought[4]—is given to constitute the underlying mechanism of the history of metaphysical thinking as a whole, even as the essence of the differentiation remains "outside" of metaphysics:

> The differentiation of beings and Being proves to be that *selfsame* from which all metaphysics arises, and in arising also immediately and inevitably escapes; that selfsame which, as such, metaphysics leaves behind and outside its domain, and which it no longer especially considers and no longer feels a need to consider. The differentiation of beings and Being makes possible every naming, experiencing, and conceiving of *das Seiende* as such. (*Ne*, 4:154; *Ng*, 2:208)

The difference from Being identified here is itself something different from the differentiation from Being that Platonic thought has "always and everywhere" posited as the basic character of *das Seiende*, its mere distance from its basic form or essence. This different difference of Being is, in short, no particular difference, but rather a grounding structural difference that inevitably escapes metaphysical thinking, a difference which underlies the still-implicit presupposition and preunderstanding of metaphysics' own differentiations. This different difference is also, therefore, the difference between the possibility of thinking "*ontologische Differenz*" itself, which Heidegger is here approaching, and the circumscription of the rest of philosophical thinking in the West. For what Heidegger's identification of the "grounding question" inaugurates is the reduction of previous Western philosophy to that single inquiry which did *not* ask the grounding question. Thus the "grounding question" also points, albeit obliquely, paraliptically, to the difference between Heidegger's reading of philosophy and philosophy itself. It names, again, obliquely, paraliptically, the uniqueness of Heidegger's revision of metaphysics, which in its inauguration of the question of ontological difference exposes the "essential" limitedness of "the entire history of previous Western philosophy" (*Ne*, 2:198; *Ng*, 1:463).[5] This reading interprets philosophy's erstwhile failure, both to ask about the *Sein des Seiendes*, and to ask about its own failure to do so—its failure, in short, to read *as* Heidegger reads. But to arrive at a point from which such a connection between Being and reading might be fleshed out, I must define more specifically what Heidegger sees as the difference introduced by an incipient epoch of the questioning of ontological difference itself.

A Genealogy of Metaphysical Differentiation

In the fourth *Nietzsche* lecture course, Heidegger presents an almost Nietzschean genealogy of the origins of metaphysical inquiry.[6] The story runs as follows:

The early Greek thinkers invent a protometaphysics in the form of a question about what is a priori in our perceptions of being (*das Seiende*). It is a question for them of whether, for instance, our ability to perceive likeness or equality or other manners of Being (*das Sein*) among particular beings is itself prior to their existing as such, or whether beings must first *be* as such in order for our respective perceptions of their relations to arise. The conclusion for the Greeks,

Heidegger claims generally, is that the particular being, *das Seiende*, is prior to its way of *"seiend"* in a given perception of it; that is, beings are prior *pros hēmas*, "with reference to us" (*Ne*, 4:161; *Ng*, 2:216).[7] But this, Heidegger asserts, is a conclusion only about the sequence of our knowing and does not yet touch on the character of the *Sein des Seiendes* itself.

For the Greeks, *das Sein* is first *physis*, which Heidegger interprets and translates as—I leave it in the German—"das von-sich-aus-Aufgehen und so wesenhaft sich-in-den-Aufgang-Stellen, das ins-Offene-sich-Offenbaren" (*Ng*, 2:216).[8] With respect to *physis*, "*tēi physei*," and no longer with respect to us, it is *das Sein* that is prior to *das Seiende*. But grasping this priority entails that we consider, with Plato, that Being means presence (*Anwesenheit*), *ousia*, and specifically the presence of the *Seiende* that *is*. *Ousia* is "the presence of what endures in the unconcealed" (*Ne*, 4:161; *Ng*, 2:217),[9] that is, the manner of *Sein*, or *Seiendheit*, of that which self-presents or self-upsurges, a manner such as likeness or equality (*Ne*, 4:162; *Ng*, 2:217).

With respect to, or, as Heidegger writes, "*tēi physei*, from the point of view of Being itself [*vom Sein selbst her gesehen*]," it is the priority of the manner in which a being *is*, the manner of "upsurgence" that Heidegger will also call its presencing (*Anwesen*), that allows *das Seiende* to present itself in a particular way (see *Ne*, 4:161; *Ng*, 2:217). Thus most originally, for the Greeks (although historically this fact begins immediately to be concealed) it is *das Sein*, the "to be," that is prior to *das Seiende*, in contradistinction to the order of our own perception of beings. Heidegger writes, "According to its own essence, *das Sein* is the *proteron*, the *a priori*, the prior, although not in the order in which it gets grasped through us [*des Erfaßtwerdens durch uns*], but with regard to what first shows itself *to us*, what first of all and on its own presences to [or, toward] us into the open" (*Ne*, 4:163; *Ng*, 2:219). As a form of inquiry, metaphysics first arises with the questioning of this apriority (*Apriorität*) of Being itself, that is, a questioning of the being-ness of *das Seiende*, first identified in a limited way, as we shall see, by Plato

(*Ne*, 4:164; *Ne*, 2:220). "Seen from the point of view of *das Seiende*," and therefore not merely from "our" point of view, *das Sein* as the *prior* "reigns over *das Seiende*, and shows itself as something that lies above *das Seiende*, *ta physei onta*" (*Ne*, 4:164; *Ng*, 2:219–20). In turn, the knowledge of *das Seiende*, of *ta physei onta*, becomes a knowledge of *das Sein* itself in the sense of self-emerging physis just elaborated. In short, this knowledge becomes *epistēmē physikē*, knowledge of *ta physika*. And since *das Sein*, in accordance with its apriority, is above or beyond any individual being, a knowledge that inquires into the *Sein* of *das Seiende* is a *meta*physics: "Cognition and knowledge of Being [*Das Erkennen und Wissen des Seins*], of that which is (*proteron tēi physei*) essentially *a priori*—the *Vor-herige*—, must therefore, when seen from the point of view of *das Seiende* [or] of *physika*, surpass [the latter]; that is, the cognition of Being must be *meta ta physika*, must be metaphysics" (*Ne*, 4:164; *Ng*, 2:220). Metaphysics, in the form of a philosophical inquiry, thus emerges because of the general priority of the manner of Being itself over the particular *Seiende* that is. And this priority is due to the essentially *meta*physical structure of (the manner of) *das Sein* itself, even when the priority of the "to be" is concealed within the subsequent history of metaphysics, which always tends, in varying degrees, to view (the manner of) Being as subsequent to the beings that *are*.

Metaphysics, then, is generally the science of the apriority of the being-ness or *Seiendheit* of *das Seiende*, the *ontos on*. But in Heidegger's view, until we consider the specificity of Plato's particular *meta*physical inquiry as the original and essential basis of Western philosophy, the name "metaphysics" still retains its secondary and illusory appearance as a mere branch of philosophy alongside physics, ethics, and politics. Only as Platonic does metaphysics acquire its broader sense—that is, its historical sense—of a general tendency of Western thinkers to explain the world on the basis of a nonmaterial or extraphysical essence. For Plato, the *ousia* of beings, the manner of Being or being-ness that is permanent when beings emerge for us, is *idea*, or as Heidegger translates, "visibleness [*Sichtigkeit*]" (*Ne*, 4:162; *Ng*, 2:217). *Idea*, which for Plato is also *eidos* ("outward appearance [*Aussehen*]") (*Ne*, 4:162; *Ng*, 2:218), is not mere representation of *das Seiende*, but "the name for *das Sein* itself . . . : *proteron tēi physei*, the pre-vious [*Vorherige*] as presencing [*Anwesen*]" (*Ne*, 4:162; *Ng*, 2:218). With this very particular interpretation of the apriority of Being, Western thought launches its epochal valuation of the supersensuous:

> With Plato's interpretation of Being as *idea*, *meta-physics begins*. For all subsequent times, it shapes the essence of Western philosophy, *whose history, from Plato to Nietzsche, is the history of metaphysics*. And because metaphysics begins with the interpretation of Being as "idea", and because that interpretation sets the standard, all philosophy since Plato is "idealism" in the strict sense of the word: Being is sought in the idea, in the idea-like and the ideal. (*Ne*, 4:164; *Ng*, 2:220)

Here "metaphysics" already signifies far more than a topos, but a broad set of presuppositions about what it means for *das Seiende* to *be*, in whatever historical configurations it appears, given the constraints of a particular inquiry's terms and methodology. Because for Heidegger these presuppositions derive first from rereadings and revisions of Plato, despite the decline of Platonic thinking in its Christian-Latin translations, Platonism is said to be the first and last metaphysics:[10] "With respect to the founder of metaphysics, we can therefore say: all Western philosophy is Platonism. Metaphysics, idealism, and Platonism mean in essence the same thing. And they continue to set the standard even when countermovements and reversals come into vogue" (*Ne*, 4:164; *Ng*, 2:220). In short, the metaphysical, especially as the binarism of sensuous and supersensuous, is the core of Western thought: "*Metaphysics* is thus the title for philosophy proper [*die eigentliche Philosophie*] and therefore it always has to do with [*betrifft*] the fundamental thought of a philosophy" (*Ne*, 2:185; *Ng*, 1:449).[11] More precisely, metaphysics is the *structure* of Western philosophical thought, grounded in the self-differentiation of Being itself as it enters into history, as it presences itself.

General Paralipsis: Being is History

Heidegger's description of the original Platonic interpretation of what is *meta ta physika* posits two basic characteristics of philosophy as metaphysics, both grounded in *Dasein*'s original experience of Being as *physis* and the historical descent of philosophy out of that experience. I have alluded to each of them previously, but I want to elaborate them more fully here. First, from Plato onward the history of thinking has a single "simple line" that structures and motivates all thinking about beings *as* beings up to the present moment. Thus Heidegger can speak of "hidden unity" or "the covert unitary essence of metaphysics" and can claim, in the most hyperbolic of synecdoches, that "all great thinkers think the same" (*Ne*, 1:36; *Ng*, 1:46).[12] I have already discussed how this reduction of the essence of philosophical thinking operates on the local level within Heidegger's reading of Nietzsche's special paralipsis: Nietzsche's thought is the "same thought" that grounds the whole history of the West, and it is that synecdochal correspondence that determines Nietzsche's historic importance as a thinker.[13] Second, as declined into Platonism and its various inheritors through Nietzsche, the simple line of Western thinking is "concealed." The fact that the unity of thinking in general is described as "hidden" or "covert" by Heidegger indicates that philosophy's essence appears, from his vantage at the "end" of this concealment, and throughout its history, in the form of paralipsis. More precisely, metaphysics *is* paralipsis, the ironically bespoken nonquestioning of Being; it *is* the *presence* of its own concealment.

These two aspects of metaphysics are both due to Being itself, which from Heidegger's vantage as an interpreter may be now reviewed in the form of its appearance as a paraliptical limitation within all Western philosophy through Nietzsche. Philosophy as a whole is a "history of Being";[14] but precisely insofar as it has entered into history, Being is ironic, different from itself. Even more, Being *is* difference-from-itself—*as* metaphysics. Being "presences" as the history of its own concealment, its own historical lack. But this lack *is* precisely the self-differing and transmuting succession of forms of inquiry into the *Leitfrage*, tantamount to the continual noninquiry into the *Grundfrage*. Therefore Heidegger, in a remarkable essay entitled "Recollection in Metaphysics," can connect Being essentially to history with the following condensed speculative formulation: "The history of Being is Being itself, and only that [*Die Seinsgeschichte ist das Sein selbst und nur dieses*]" (*EP*, 82; *Ng*, 2:489).[15] This statement warns us that it would be a mistake to continue searching for Being within the terms of an ongoing philosophical examination of the particular thing or matter that confronts us, as it were ahistorically—to identify *das Sein des Seiendes* with some *hypokeimenon* of objects that exist autonomously, say, in nature. For each such attempt only brings one back within the metaphysical distinctions already immanent in the history of Being, the ontological difference concealed as metaphysics and the metaphysical, presencing only in the form of differentiations between the object and this or that conception of its most essential quiddity. With Heidegger we are no longer asking what, or even how, a particular thing *is*, but rather, with respect to the statement *that* a thing is, we ask what it could be that constitutes "the that." And the answer is that "the that" is the historicity of *das Seiende*, its becoming in and as a history. Being *is* the history of Being—that is, the becoming-history of Being—and not, as metaphysics continuously assumes, something in itself behind or at the bottom of that history.

For Heidegger's revision-encounter with philosophy, all of the following terms signify the same: Being, difference from Being, history of Being, and metaphysics. But such a sameness can only be a speculative identity, entailing that the terms are all and always connected to one another through a paraliptical *as*: Being *is* (as) history of Being, Being *is* (as) difference from itself and continuous differentiation, Being *is* (as) metaphysics. We could say that a being considered insofar as it is—*das Sein des Seiendes*—has the basic *structure* of "*is as* . . . ," a structural difference-from-self related to its essential historical context. Both the unity and the concealment of the history of metaphysical thoughts about the *is* of *das Seiende* are due to—more properly, they simply *are*—the ever-present "*as* . . ." of Being: Being *as* history.

Despite the extreme speculative complexity entailed by Heidegger's *is* (and its historical *as*), he invokes a number of shorthand terms for signifying it within the *Nietzsche* lectures, a stylistic mannerism that can be both exasperatingly and refreshingly simplistic. Being *as* history is the "abandonment" of, or rather *by*, Being, the *Seinsverlassenheit*. This term signifies a conceptual shift, in which the difference *from* what is named "Being" is given over to the positive *presencing* of Being itself *as* the self-difference of history. Thus Being abandons itself as metaphysics, which therefore is essentially, but paraliptically, a history of Being (*Seinsgeschichte*). The variety, or more precisely the interrelative historicity, of metaphysical positions in Western thought, viewed from the "end," is not a mere loss of the question of Being, but rather *is* the concealed yet abiding presence of Being-as-abandoned.[16] What I would like now to ask is how this speculative identification of Being's historicity as *Seinsverlassenheit* relates to the particular limitation of a given metaphysical thinker—in short, how the general paralipsis of Being *as* a history gives rise, for Heidegger's revision-encounter with philosophy, to the special paralipsis of the thinker's text *as* a specific limited relation to "proper" thought.

The end of metaphysics, which Nietzsche's philosophy paraliptically heralds, is the first potentially proper experience of the essential historicity of thinking, the first experience in which the ever-repeating self-same differentiation of metaphysics, which Hegel called simply the "spectacle [*Anschein*] of so many and so *varied* [*verschiedenen*]

philosophies,"[17] can be properly reviewed as Being's self-abandon-
ment: "The metaphysical differentiation itself—that means always, the
distinction structuring and underlying [*fügend-tragende*] all metaphysics—must first be experienced in its beginning [*Anfang*], so that
metaphysics becomes decisive as *Ereignis* of the history of Being, and
relinquishes the illusory form [*Scheingestalt*] of a doctrine or opinion,
that is, of something produced by man" (*EP*, 82; *Ng*, 2:489).[18] For the
first time, Heidegger claims—although such a move has been continuously anticipated at least since Hegel—the history of thinking may
potentially occur and be appropriated as more than the coincidence of
its development and variety through time, but as a necessary, and
equally necessarily concealed, structure. Because Being is essentially a
history, it may now be reconceived generally as the "saying not-saying
[*sagendes Nichtsagen*]"[19] of itself as metaphysics, the lack-of-itself or difference-from-itself over time which recurs as a "selfsame" structure at
the "end." "Being," as historical, is grasped as general paralipsis, precisely the paralipsis of itself *as* historical. This *Ereignis* of the end of
metaphysics means that one may now begin to unconceal the truth,
the *a-lētheia*, of Being in or *as* its historical absence within the systems
of specific thinkers. But, as Heidegger notes, the uncovering of such a
truth is "granted [*gewährte*]" by Being, and not by the thinker (*EP*, 83;
Ng, 2:490): it is granted by the historicity of the forgottenness of
Being, *Seinsvergessenheit*, and the reduction of this forgottenness,
finally, into its own self-overcoming in Nietzsche's positivistic destruction of Platonism. Nietzsche's philosophy is the "last possible configuration" of metaphysics. But it could not be so—that is, Nietzsche
could not be *read* as (paraliptically) introducing the "new commencement" of the *Ereignis* of the *Seinsfrage*—unless, for Heidegger's own
reading, Being had not granted a finite number of interdeveloping
forms as a single history. Let us suggest another, more provocative way
of putting this point: Nietzsche is named the last because *we* come
after the last. And we come after the last only because now, precisely

due to Nietzsche's destruction of Platonism, Being emerges, dis-covers itself, as the single whole of which Nietzsche's philosophy is the final and concluding part.

The Limit of Being (a Philosophy)

I am describing the structure of a certain historiography of philosophy, but essentially still within the *epochē* of Heidegger's revision-encounter with the whole history of thinking in the West. Being *is* the history of its own nonpresence as metaphysics. What does this mean for any further conceptualization of the particular philosophical text? Thinking, for Heidegger, does not abandon Being, as it appears to do, for instance, in positivism. Rather, Being abandons thinking, or abandons itself *as* thinking. This way of putting the matter is really a way of describing the essential historicity, the essential unity-that-severs-itself, of philosophy (see *Ne*, 1:217; *Ng*, 1:250–51). Thinking is always in the context of a *lack*, a *limit*, and is always a historical decline, at least seen from the perspective of its paraliptical receiver. In short, thinking in philosophy *is* (*as*) limited.

With the possibility of an *Ereignis* of the historicity of thinking generally, we first see that each metaphysics is defined by its particular way of answering the guiding question; this means that each metaphysics has a particular way, as well, of not asking the grounding question, a particular nonrelation to Being as such. But this specific nonrelation *is* the thinking's essential historicity with respect to the origin of thinking itself, the history (of Being) as a whole. A metaphysics *is* (*as*) a particular limitation of Being, and the special character of each metaphysical system with respect to the others is essentially defined as its particular limitation within history as a whole, a history first seen by a reader or revisor such as Heidegger. "Limitation" does not signify such and such a doctrinal absence, but rather the entirely general (non)presence of the whole in a given specific thought system.

In other words, the thinker is limited because, in his own peculiar way, the thinker fails to *end* metaphysics, fails to recuperate the concealed whole of which his thought is only a part, and thus fails to be the postmetaphysical thinker. From the point of view of Heidegger's revision-encounter with philosophy, the thinker fails to be the proper reader—*fails to be Heidegger.* . . .

With this very last assertion I take one small dialectical step, and am now describing, outside of the *epochē* in which my description of the *Seinsgeschichte* has thus far remained, what it means—not for thinking to be generally, structurally, limited—but for the thinker to be, as I said above, limited in his or her "own particular way." Let us pursue this direction, along which "ontological difference" must be reinterpreted as a difference structured by practices of interpretation, by rereading. In turn, rereading must be seen as the motive force of metaphysical systems insofar as they step out on the scene of history, systems structured by the de facto difference between one interpretive act and another, within a set of institutions that has continually demanded such differences-in-sameness. This is the sort of sparing self-differentiation that would establish a *genre*, the difference between *texts* within a single historical whole.

What is it that constitutes the speciality of a thinker's being limited in his or her "own particular way," quite aside from the general sense in which all thinking, retrospectively viewed from the end, may be seen to have been limited? We can begin with Heidegger's own description of the thinker's inner limit, and proceed from there:

> Every thinker oversteps [*überschreitet*] the inner limit of every thinker. But such overstepping is not "knowing it all" [or "knowing it better"—*Besserwissen*] since it only consists in holding the thinker in the direct claim of Being, thus remaining within his limit. This [limit] consists in the fact that the thinker can never

himself say what is most [properly or especially] his own [*sein Eigenstes*]. It must remain unsaid, because what is sayable [*das sagbare Wort*] receives its determination [or "destination" or even "voicing"—*Bestimmung*] from the unsayable. (*EP*, 77–78; *Ng*, 2:484)

The limit with respect to Being is the "unsayable," which bespeaks or determines (*bestimmt*) what is sayable by the thinker. But what is it that remains unsayable in a thinker's thought? It is the unsaid, but troped, with respect to the context of the origin, as un-say-able: it is that particular but crucial thing which, for the rereader, the thinker did not say, essentialized through a synecdochal link to history as such, so that it now means: that which it was not *possible* for the thinker to say: "*Not* to know this inner limit, not to know it thanks to the nearness of the unsaid unsayable [*des ungesagten Unsagbaren*], is the concealed gift [*Geschenk*] of Being" (*EP*, 78; *Ng*, 2:484).

This "unsaid" can be determined or bespoken *only by another thinker*. And only when limitation is named by this other thinker does the unsaid become essentialized as the unsayable, as that which can go to constitute the next thinker's overstepping. The voice that determines or bespeaks what is unsayable—what is therefore the first thinker's proper "ownmost" or "most especial [*sein Eigenstes*]" limitation—occurs only by virtue of a second thinker's activity, through a second thinker's exposing the very ground of the first thinker's context, against which the thought has its limit, and which context, therefore, is axiomatically unavailable to the first thinker. The limit of a thought is essentially the *putative* limit supplied through the rereading that relativizes it, deciding what is proper to (a) philosophy and what is not. Limitation *is* (as) rereading. And therefore what is named "Being," the "to be" of thinking—the positive historicity of metaphysics and the structure of limitation within metaphysics—*is* revision.

Being is Revision?

With this last claim I have decidedly and provocatively overstepped Heidegger's own description of the philosophical canon as a "history of Being." Up to a point I have followed Heidegger's discussion of the *Seinsgeschichte* within an *epochē* of his revision-encounter with the history of philosophy, abstracting from it an argument leading to the conceptualization of the essential limitedness of thought. I then posited a slight revision of that argument, a mere shift in perspective, but one perhaps sufficient to cast the entire question of Being in a new light— although, if such a claim sounds grandiose, we should remind ourselves that it is the sort of claim philosophers continuously make and remake.

I want finally to recall the particular case of Nietzsche's late work, which for Heidegger remains the context within which any essential encounter with Western philosophical history can take place. Nietzsche's limit "oversteps" itself in the paraliptical unification of will to power and eternal recurrence, just as within metaphysics generally "every thinker oversteps the inner limit of every thinker." But where does this ambiguous (self-)overstepping occur? It occurs only within an encounter or confrontation between Nietzsche and Heidegger, a confrontation which Heidegger's reading undertakes to (re)construct—that is, it occurs through Heidegger's revision of Nietzsche. The overstepping is, however, troped by Heidegger's reading as an occurrence within Nietzsche's text, an occurrence due to the structure of thinking, as the general limitation of Being. Yet this structure is essentially indistinguishable—except by a methodological *epochē*— from the simple difference that Heidegger posits between his own reading of philosophy at the end, and the history of philosophy itself. Philosophy *is* the limitation of Being—because, for the moment, Heidegger *is* its reader.

Thus while it is slightly embarrassing to have to recall the simple fact that Heidegger comes historically after Nietzsche, this word "after" must not be taken for granted as characteristic of philosophical chronology, any more than we can continue to take for granted any hypostatic "to be" of philosophical systems in the context of the essential historicity of Being. In the structure of rereading that relates Heidegger's text to Nietzsche's, "after" is not a chronological descriptor, but rather a structural characteristic of the revision-encounter itself, a condition of the Nietzschean paralipsis and its "proper" reception by Heidegger's lectures. If Heidegger *is* posterior to Nietzsche, then this is nonetheless a revisionist posteriority, and therefore a structural priority—here I offer a gloss, and a polemical one, upon Heidegger's notion that a proper philosophical reading looks *ahead* to the *origin*.[20] That is why "Nietzsche's philosophy proper"—which is practically equivalent to "Heidegger's reading of Nietzsche"—can be said in retrospect by Heidegger to have governed the direction of Nietzsche's thinking *from the start*, just as the basic concordance between art and truth governs the eventual discordance of these concepts in Nietzsche's thought, or just as the basic unity of Being and becoming is said to have governed the decline of Western metaphysics into a history of metaphysical distinctions, the nonquestioning of ontological difference. In the revision-encounter, historical posteriority *is* (as) philosophical priority, and philosophies proper are reconstituted ex post facto, *as* origins.

Finally, then, what *is* Being, this "origin" of philosophical thought(s)? What *is* the "to be" of the metaphysical text? Is it just revision, the bespeaking determination (*Bestimmung*) of that which is unsayable in another thinker's thought, and the axiomatic overstepping of the other thinker, given that every thought within a history must have its other, its actual or potential revisor? In any case, the unsayable, depending on the perspective from which it is viewed, *is* either (as) the "transmission [*Zuwurf*]" of Being through the thinker's limited "projects [*Entwürfe*]," or (as) the self-troping of the revision itself, by the revisor, the imputed paraliptical self-differentiation of the reread text.

What Heidegger identifies as the "inheritance of Being" is the historically determined fact that the "thinker can never himself say what is most his own," the retrospectively discovered "inner limit." But the thinker's limit is always already his essential failure *to have been another thinker*, the very thinker who says what the first thinker did not say and could not have said. "Ownmost" and "proper" are first and foremost categories of rereading, for the proper or ownmost limit is that which the thinker paraliptically reveals only through the encounter with another reader. The inheritance of Being is the inheritance of a revision-encounter, probated through the practical medium of textual reinterpretation. A text of metaphysics is (as) its own parapraxis of getting itself reread.

The Reception of Revision

I have been analyzing Heidegger's *Nietzsche* in terms of the shape of its interpretation, the constellation of figural gestures through which Heidegger rereads Nietzsche's texts and repositions his thought. Heidegger's interpretation uncovers in Nietzsche an implicit voice, a paraliptical "bespeaker" of the history of metaphysics, concealed within more explicit assertions—concealed to Nietzsche himself, of course, but also to those who read his work too loyally, since Nietzsche's "fundamental thought" is something other than, even opposed to, what he directly states. Heidegger's interpretation reconstructs this voice in the peculiar form of Nietzsche's "inner limitation," his historically determined inability to ascertain the origin of the discordances and fragmentation that characterize his ambivalent, still-metaphysical thinking. The very being of Nietzsche's self-divided philosophy, grasped "properly," is a paralipsis of concordance and unity, at least for those with ears to hear, that is, for those who hear from a potentially "no-longer-metaphysical" vantage and who therefore reread as strict revisionists.

Throughout the first half of this book, I have followed a phenomenological methodology that has required an *epoché* of critical judgment, bracketing issues of interpretive accuracy or validity until the shape of the reading could be more fully rendered. Such aversion to criticism has a wholly positive significance within the critique of revision. It arises from an understanding that any claim about the degree or quality of a reading's correspondence to, or advance upon, the primary text, or any decision about what is proper or improper to the primary thought, must itself partake of the form of the revision-encounter. By bracketing judgment about the quality or accuracy of Heidegger's reading, and about where and how any critical negotiation between Nietzsche's text and its proper meaning can or ought to take place, one avoids duplicating precisely the revisionist gesture one wants to describe: the philosophical rereader's disarticulation of the text's essential "direction" from its merely "extrinsic" content.

I now want to pose questions of critical value more bluntly and to test the limits of the *epoché* that has so far circumscribed my description of the revision-encounter. Where and how, for instance, does the judgment that I have at times been compelled to make, that Nietzsche is *revised* by Heidegger, occur? I refer here not to the obvious: the sense in which Nietzsche's style or thought patterns, as they reappear within Heidegger's citations and paraphrases, plainly differ from the versions one finds in Nietzsche's texts read on their own. Rather, I am interested in what Heidegger himself identifies as a more basic divergence in respective philosophical positions, a divergence manifest only beyond more obvious differences of statement and style. In the revision-encounter's own terms, this is the divergence not between the thoughts or presentations of "Heidegger" and "Nietzsche" per se, but rather between two facets of Nietzsche's text itself, its "essential" thought and its own future of "self"-revision. Where does such a divergence, a more basic and essential revision-encounter, take place? It would be insufficient to claim merely that the encounter arises *within* Heidegger's reading, in part because Heidegger scrupulously avoids couching his alterations of Nietzsche in revisionist terms, declining to claim for his interpretation a new or revised position. Indeed, he attributes all such alterations not only directly to Nietzsche's text itself, but to the very center of Nietzsche's thinking, its most basic intention and direction. Any decision that Heidegger's text *is* a revision is left as the responsibility of its rereaders, not of Heidegger. For although, to be sure, such a decision occurs "in" the reading of Heidegger's lectures, it can occur only insofar as we ourselves, the audience of those lectures, are willing to engage in a collaborating negotiation between Nietzsche's text, Heidegger's text, and our own "text," whether we construct new interpretations in the future (such as the one I am constructing here), or contrast more ostensibly loyal representations of Nietzsche's texts with Heidegger's "distortions" of the past.

I have counseled suspicion about any chronological schema that would straightforwardly place Nietzsche's text "before" Heidegger's in historical time, opting instead for a more rigorously rhetorical under-standing of the historical interrelations of the two thinkers, such that the issue of whose text is primary and whose is secondary itself becomes open to argument. This otherwise counterintuitive impugn-ing of chronology, which to a conventional historiography must seem like idiot questioning, is required precisely because of the equally counterintuitive restructuring of history effected by Heidegger's rein-terpretation of Western philosophy. The historicity of Nietzsche's text, its essential limitation, is the inheritance of "Being itself," not of the particular thinking. Or, to revise this claim along my own lines, the historical import of Nietzsche's text can be determined only with an eye toward its own future of interpretive revisions: the thinker *is* (as) another thinker. Thus, a decision about what is proper to a philosoph-ical text is always a historical decision, in the nuanced sense of "historical" that Heidegger's own historiography enables. It is a decision both about the future historicity of the text in light of other readings, actual or potential, which position and reposition it, and about the present and future meaning of the whole history for which the text serves as a synecdochal and paraliptical proxy. Thus, to begin to answer my own question as to where the decision that Nietzsche is revised by Heidegger takes place: it does *not* take place in Heidegger's text. There is no revision *of* Nietzsche, only a self-revision and a *proper* rereading, in other words, only a more or less persuasive account of the claims that future readers ought to make about what "was" true of Nietzsche's thought. If the thinker *is* another thinker, this is just as true of revisionist rethinking as it is of "primary" thinking itself. The reception of a revision-encounter is also another revision-encounter.

Thus the description of the revision-encounter remains incomplete until we turn to a new topic, the reception of revision, and reception's contribution to the structuring of the rereading process. Philosophical readings such as Heidegger's are never finished because they appear— quite the contrary, their appearance is a "beginning" which they anticipate within themselves, a mere first step onto the scene of philosophical history. If there is a sense of an ending in such a reading, that sense can only be a rhetorical ploy. But even more, a reading contains no single phenomenological moment that we could call appearing or "stepping out," or at least no such moment that isn't reconstructed ex post facto as a proper (or improper) experience of the text by those to whom it appears. There is no *experience* of the philosophical reading, per se, for the philosophical reading is not an aesthetic object but only a conduit between a "proper" content and a future reader who receives that proper content over and against some other. Practically speaking, every student of philosophy is aware of this theoretical fact as she or he attempts to negotiate the complex set of relations involved in reading philosophical texts in the required ways: as they are supposed to be read, as they were already read, as they should be read against authorities, as they are being reread at this moment, and, most important, as they are read with a mind toward what is to be produced later from the encounter with them.

With the sublime confidence of the "great" thinker—a perfectly commonplace confidence within the conventional styles of philosophical interpretation—Heidegger occludes this process of anticipating the text's future reception. While his text proposes a model of the historicity of philosophy in which the text's proper essence arises out of a historical encounter with other texts, he does not theorize his own anticipated historicity with equal rigor or candor. The *epoché* of critical valuation I have invoked in discussing Heidegger's reading of Nietzsche is, in fact, the very one he himself tacitly invokes, asking readers to avoid questioning the role "we" are expected to play in reconstructing and adjudicating Nietzsche's text and the meaning of its paraliptical "center." It is time to question that role ourselves, to bring it to the foreground, for no understanding of the revision-encounter can be complete without a critique of it as well. The revision-encounter is an intentional, even a social phenomenon. And if we were to conceive of the rhetoric of revision as a kind of conversation, for instance between Nietzsche, Heidegger, and ourselves, then such a conversation would be less like an ideal communicative dialogue than like another, more disturbing sort of social intercourse, the kind in which what I say to you intends—but then elides the intention—to influence what you will convey to *others* about me. The revision-encounter is more like gossip than dialogue.

How, then, does one describe a philosophical text *not* as an object of understanding, but rather as the subject of an anticipated but ultimately unmasterable future history of discourses? Such a task is made more difficult by the fact that hermeneutics remains the crucial foundation for most of the available models of the "aesthetics" of reception or "reader response," while "understanding" itself remains a central category of hermeneutics. With the issue of reception, hermeneutics arrives at a kind of limit case, and finds itself impelled toward the borderlands of rhetoric, which may end up a more adequate model for hermeneutics' own central concerns. In the following brief reading, I wish to suggest this blending or dissolution of hermeneutical understanding into rhetorical persuasion by examining some work of Hans Robert Jauss, whose writing exemplifies both the rigor with which a hermeneutical *Rezeptionästhetik* may be conceived and the problem at which it must therefore arrive.

In his central early essay "Literary History as a Challenge to Literary Theory," Jauss lays the groundwork for understanding the literary text as the interrelation of production, reading, and new production. Jauss considerably complicates any model of the text as a straightforward object for the reader's potential understanding. His strength is a focus on the "dialogical and at once processlike relationship between work, audience, and new work" (*AR*, 19), and "the dynamic and dialectical process of canon formation."[1] Jauss's model is particularly useful for its critique of the text as not simply the occasion, but the encapsulation and incorporation of a past and future of reflective readings: "A literary event can continue to have an effect only if those who come after it still or once again respond to it—if there are readers who again appropriate the past work or authors who want to imitate, outdo, or refute it" (*AR*, 22). Thus, for Jauss, "the history of literature is a process of aesthetic reception and production that takes place in the realization of literary texts on the part of the receptive reader, the reflective critic, and the author in his continuing productivity" (*AR*, 21).[2] It is no leap at all to extend this understanding of "literary history" to "philosophical history," precisely because the attributes that constitute the historicity of the philosophical text are identical to those of the literary text: its appropriation of past texts and genres, its proliferation through interpretive readings, and, even more than for literature, the fact that its persistence into the future is tantamount to its ability to engender new texts.

Jauss's model, like a great many historiographies in the German philosophical tradition, reacts to the quasi-theological historiography of Leopold Ranke, who maintains "that each period is immediate vis-à-vis God, and that its value depends not at all on what followed from it, but rather on its own existence, on its own self."[3] For Jauss, such an essentialist faith in the possibility of uncovering, in Ranke's famous phrase, "how it really was [*wie es eigentlich gewesen*]," effectively "cuts the thread between past and present" (*AR*, 8). Worse than that, it opens the door for the scientistic application of what Jauss calls "positivism's blind empiricism" to literary studies, separating off the analysis of history from that of literature, and (we may expand the point) from philosophy, and allying itself with, among other things, the pernicious irrationalism of fascist aesthetics.[4] Against these antihistoricist trends, ironically derived from a historicist realism,[5] Jauss attempts to reestablish a hermeneutical model of literary poetics that would bridge the gap between the historicist and aesthetic strains of literary study, reinstating a proper post-Rankean, or possibly pre-Rankean, understanding of the reader's relation to past texts. The more deliberate or self-conscious hermeneut is indeed interested in "wie es eigentlich gewesen," like any historian, but is also capable of analyzing the historical immanence of his or her own moment of reading in relation to the past—and indeed, the immanence of both past and present within the historical process: "A literary past can return only when a new reception draws it back into the present, whether an altered aesthetic attitude willfully reaches back to reappropriate the past, or an unexpected light falls back on forgotten literature from the new moment of literary evolution, allowing something to be found that one previously could not have sought in it" (*AR*, 35). The answer to the question of how the past text *was* only becomes available in comprehending how the text now *is* (as) reread. With these insights Jauss moves close to a model of textual history as a rhetoric of revision, and verges, at least, on a model of rereading as rhetorical influence and revisionist imposition, much like the one I have begun to suggest in this Interlude. Jauss cites Karel Kosík:

> The work lives to the extent that it has influence. Included within the influence of a work is that which is accomplished in the consumption of the work as well as in the work itself. That which happens with the work is an expression of what the work is. . . . The work is a work and lives as a work for the reason that it *demands* an interpretation and *works* [or effects, or influences (*wirkt*)] in many meanings. (*AR*, 15)[6]

Kosík offers to Jauss's model a tentative step toward a full-scale rhetorical, but therefore potentially antihermeneutical, understanding of texts as pure "becoming," but it is not a step Jauss is fully willing to take. Kosík's model, as his own pun on "work [*wirkt*]" suggests, dissolves the very distinction between work and interpretation upon which an "aesthetics of reception" could distinguish itself from poetics. As Kosík asserts, "the work *is* a work and lives *as* a work" only in its demand for further interpretation: as a work, "it influences or effects [*wirkt*]. . . ." What is an interpretation of a work, here, other than a new work, which influences and works upon further interpretations? And what was the work in the first place, other than yet another interpretation, which gives rise to new works? When we turn to philosophy, it is even less possible for the distinction between work and interpretation or between primary and secondary texts to have a real or independent meaning, because each of these categories is too clearly an artifact, not a presupposition, of the process of interpretation. Philosophical revision-encounters are, in essence, secondary texts that trope their action upon other texts *as* primary—and in doing so redefine which "text" was primary and which was secondary, or which, in other words, is properly originary work and which is rereading. Even more importantly, a philosophical interpretation can only be precisely a new "work" in Kosík's crucially full sense: a thing demanding interpretation, a thing that *is* only (as) interpreted.

We need go no further than Jauss's own literary-critical practice to verify the theoretical indistinguishability of work and interpretation. I would suggest that the similarity between the terms Jauss uses to describe critical histories and those used by Heidegger to describe his relation to Nietzsche and to Western metaphysics (path, limit, gap, perspective, implicit, lack, genuine) are neither coincidental nor the artifact of a common relation to post-Hegelian critical historiography. They are due rather to the very conventionality of the protocols of critical relations to past texts and future readers that make each of these authors, as well as most others published in the genre of philosophical criticism, acceptable to readers and publishers alike. In the following excerpts on the relation of hermeneutics to Marxist and Formalist aesthetics, I wish to call attention not to the content of the specific interpretations offered, but rather to the formal gestures Jauss himself makes while conducting these critical interpretations: "When Lukács relies on Marx's famous fragment on classical art, and claims that even Homer's influence today is 'inseparably bound to the age and the means of production in which or, respectively, under which Homer's work arose,' he once again implicitly presupposes as answered that which, according to Marx, was still to be explained: why a work 'can still provide [us] aesthetic pleasure'" (*AR*, 13). Again: "From this perspective on the reciprocal dilemma of Formalist and Marxist literary theory, a consequence can be seen that was not drawn by either of them. . . . My attempt to bridge the gap between literature and history, between historical and aesthetic approaches, begins at the point at which [the Marxist and Formalist] schools stop" (*AR*, 18). And again: "Both Methods [Marxism and Formalism] lack the reader in his genuine role" (*AR*, 19). Each of these moments of rereading is a call to interpret other interpretive texts anew—but also to reinterpret the broader history of prior texts according to a different path, even a new essential historiography. Each rereading brings a past text "forward" into the present, but always and only in light of a set of interests with which Jauss wants his own readers to be concerned, in light of a potential answer to the question, "To what end and with what right can one today still—or again—study literary history?" (*AR*, 45). In short, this recovery of literary history out of the comparative revisions of a number of different past critical approaches and intentions is an entirely rhetorical gesture, an attempt to work an influence upon a readership, to create a revised future for these past texts. In that light—and I claim nothing at all unusual about Jauss's intentions here; they are entirely typical—each of these critical excerpts is precisely a "work" according to the criterion Jauss himself offers, via Kosík, "for the reason that it *demands* an interpretation and '*works*' in many meanings" (*AR*, 15). In this light, Jauss's hermeneutics of the literary text seems to call for a new rhetorical understanding of critical understanding itself, one in line with the spirit of Kosík's model of textual history. But this would be a posthermeneutical understanding of our relation to texts, an understanding that there is no critical text that "brings forward" another text without being at once a revision and a demand for further interpretation, both of that text and of itself.

Within a hermeneutical model, the process of textual interpretation, as Jauss paraphrases Gadamer, "is to be conceived as a unity of the three moments of understanding (*intelligere*), interpretation (*interpretare*), and application (*applicare*)" (*AR*, 139). By contrast, within the rhetorical understanding of the model I will propose, pursuing the logic of Kosík's suggestion about works, we must conceive the process as follows: what appears to be an understanding of the text is, in fact, the artifact of the application of an interpretation, or in other words, the rhetorical influence of a specific revision of the text occluded as, or in the form of, "wie es eigentlich gewesen." The rhetorical version not only reverses the ordering of the "steps" of the hermeneutical interpretation (*AR*, 140)—"understanding" results from the application of interpretation, not vice versa—but it calls into question entirely the status of an "understanding" of the text as anything potentially independent of the rhetorical situation in which textual rereading arises and is disseminated. In essence, the more radical historicizing gesture of rhetoric undercuts the basis upon which a hermeneutical critique of textual historicity was to be founded, the primacy of a *present* encounter with the text, and the potential for "understanding" as such.

To be sure, Jauss himself, in his own applications of the hermeneutical model to literary texts, remains on the verge of impugning the hermeneutical exemplar even as he invokes it. Here is Jauss in a later essay on Baudelaire:

> I direct my hermeneutic experiment at this problem by dividing into three steps the interpretation of a poem that already has a history of reception. The steps might be described phenomenologically as three successive readings. In dividing the hermeneutical process into these steps the distinction between the three readings must be fabricated to a certain degree; yet only in this manner is it possible to demonstrate what kind of understanding, interpretation, and application might be proper to a text of aesthetic character. (*AR*, 140)[7]

The division of the "three processes" only makes sense "phenomenologically" if the act of dividing is seen not as a transparent methodological hypothesis for the sake of demonstration, but instead as an active occlusion of the real role played by the supposed phenomenologist in "fabricat[ing]," as Jauss suggests, the proper order of textual interpretation. What the "first reading" *is* has everything to do with what a second and third construct it *to have been*. What passes for understanding is an artifact of future rhetorical persuasion, the result, not the initiation, of a historical process of reinterpretation. Jauss all but acknowledges this when he states:

> The priority of aesthetic perception within the triad of literary hermeneutics has need of the *horizon*, but not the temporal priority, of the first reading; this horizon of aesthetic understanding may also be gained only in the course of rereading or with the help of historicist understanding. Aesthetic perception is no universal

code with timeless validity, but rather—like all aesthetic experience—is intertwined with historical experience. (*AR*, 148)

Indeed, a hermeneutics still has a need for the "horizon" of a first reading, but a rhetorical model of the text does not. For a rhetorical model,
the first reading is no horizon, but rather an explicitly manufactured
residue of those historical processes that hermeneutics posits method-
ologically only *after* the "first reading." The logical conclusion from
Jauss's claim is that hermeneutics reaches beyond itself here, and calls
upon itself, in the name of an even more rigorous historicism, to question its own horizon of textual "understanding," a questioning which
threatens to reduce to naught its own notion of the priority of the
"aesthetic" experience of the text. The first of the three "readings" of
the Baudelaire poem is subtitled by Jauss, "A Hermeneutic Reconstruction of the First Reading," almost confessing that hermeneutics
itself is being fabricated by and within his own account of literary history, since the putative "horizon" of the hermeneutical endeavor itself
is "reconstructed" here *by* hermeneutics. It would be more accurate to
say that the "second reading," or even the third, is a horizon within
which the first reading, the "immediate understanding" of "aesthetic
perception," takes place.

In short, Jauss's tentative gesture toward a critique of the primacy
of textual understanding might well signal the destruction of any theoretical or methodological distinction between "readings" at all. But
Jauss is too concerned with retaining the hermeneutical model to risk
dispensing with the terminology that accompanies and enables it. His
theory of the reception of texts rests with the more usual, but also
more problematic, notion that the text is experienced and understood
by a "first audience," and *then* historically received: "The interpretive
reception of a text always presupposes the context of experience of aesthetic perception" (*AR*, 23). Again, Jauss writes, "The way in which a
literary work, at the historical moment of its appearance, satisfies, sur-
passes, disappoints, or refutes the expectations of its first audiences

obviously provides a criterion for the determination of its aesthetic value" (*AR*, 25); and again, "for even the critic, . . . the writer . . . the literary historian . . . etc. are first simply readers before their reflexive relationship to literature can become productive again" (*AR*, 19).[8] One would like to read these instances of the word "first" in the spirit, at least, of the Baudelaire essay, as mere reconstructed "horizons" against which the rhetorical efficacy of particular readings for particular historical audiences are to be judged. Such a revisionist reappraisal of the hermeneutic activity might then run as follows: the text is received precisely *not* by being understood, but by disappearing, becoming transparent, re-presenting only the *other* text, the one it itself receives and passes on. How would hermeneutics propose we "understand" such a text, which vanishes into the future reception of its past, a text with no present? In fact, there is no hermeneut of the revision-encounter, only another revisionist, a rhetor of rereading. Any "understanding" of what the text *is*, is already a *claim* about what it is or was *as*.

In the following two chapters, before returning to Heidegger's text, I will attempt to expand such a rhetoric of philosophical reading, in order to describe the way in which a philosophical revision *is*—not as an object of experience or understanding, but as a nonobjective mode or conduit of persuasion, a refabrication of texts ex post facto.

FIVE

Revision as Canon Formation:
Misreading in Harold Bloom

He had this great quality, which very few of us can claim, that his presence
was as big as his absence.

— G. K. CHESTERTON, "THE SECRET GARDEN"

Harold Bloom's studies of revision concern poetry, but neither his definition of poems nor his understanding of the nature of literary canon
formation will prevent Bloom's work from pertaining to philosophy.
In particular, Bloom will allow us to see in detail what a hermeneutics
such as Jauss's necessitates but leaves abstract, the ex post facto reconstruction of the "aesthetic" of reception and the mechanisms by which
such a "horizon" comes to occupy the concerns of future readers of
past texts. Bloom's rhetoric of revision analyzes what hermeneutics
tends to leave intact as a methodological postulate, the "first reading"
which supposedly begins the historical process, and by virtue of which
a "primary" interpretation of a text is canonized. What will be a stumbling block, however, and what will require us to leave Bloom for

other, more rhetorically severe grounds, are Bloom's own revisionist reading practices, as I will discuss in the latter part of this interpretation of Bloomian revisionism.

The "theory of poetry," as Bloom identifies the middle period of his work,[1] is more broadly a theory of interpretation, for poetry is construed not as a genre of textual forms, but rather as a type of intertextual relationship. The theory begins where Bloom asserts that a poetic text is always a "misprision" of a precursor's poem, a "creative correction that is actually and necessarily a misinterpretation" (*AI*, 30). Such a description of poems as "corrective" is close to my description of Heidegger's reading of Nietzsche as the completion or reception of a "paralipsis." Similarly, Bloom's notion that texts must engage in a "necessary misinterpretation" is close to what Heidegger identifies as the inherent "limitation" of metaphysical thinking. For Heidegger, limitation entails that the exposure of the "proper direction" or "innermost will" of Nietzsche's text is required to correct Nietzsche's explicit but "inessential" self-understanding, and that the correction is itself essentially guided by the putative metaphysical immanence of Nietzsche's thought, now exposed. I noted that Heidegger considers his own revisionist procedure, which in principle opts for the spirit of Nietzsche's text as against the letter, to be a certain appropriation of Nietzsche's own doctrine of perspectivism. Bloom, too, inherits a Nietzschean perspectivism. To comprehend why, for Bloom, the corrective stance of a poem toward its precursor is always not only an interpretation but a *mis*interpretation requires a further examination of his adoption of Nietzschean doctrine.

Bloom's assertion that poetry *is* essentially misreading, like Heidegger's assertion that the history of Being *is* Being itself, must be interpreted as a rigorously speculative sentence: strictly speaking, for Bloom, poems do not arise "through" or "because of" misreading, but *are* misreadings themselves.[2] Hence the first axiom of a Bloomian poetics, even more basic than "misprision" itself, is that a poem can never be understood as a self-contained formal or imaginative construction, but is primarily a relation to another: "a poem is not writing but rewriting,"[3] inextricably linked to the precursors which comprise the canon out of which it arises: "poems . . . are neither about 'subjects' nor about 'themselves.' They are necessarily about *other poems*; a poem is a response to a poem, as a poet is a response to a poet, or a person to his parent" (*MM*, 18). Even more broadly, "Influence, as I conceive it, means that there are *no* texts, but only relationships *between* texts. These relationships depend on a critical act, a misreading or misprision, that one poet performs upon another, and that does not differ in kind from the necessary critical acts performed by every strong reader upon every text he encounters" (*MM*, 3).[4] This antiformalist strain in Bloom's understanding of poetry readily permits his model of poetic historicity to be adapted to a historiography of prose texts as well. For when poems are defined essentially as relation or response, all the conventional formal markers of poetic genre—meter, types of imagery, and so forth—become secondary to the task of interpretation. Other textual types, precisely to the degree that they relate or respond to traditions of their own (and for Bloom they always do), are potentially also "revisionary" and therefore "poetic." For example, Freud is a poet for Bloom, as is Emerson in his prose (more than in his poems), and Norman Mailer and Descartes in their own prose (*MM*, 90; *AI*, 28, 40). Within Bloom's highly "literalis[tic]" appropriation of Nietzschean value theory (*AI*, 8), the poetry of these authors consists not in their respective media, but instead in their relative interpretive "strength" or "severity," their "triumph" over the prior texts, and textual relations, they confront: "a strong reading *is* the only poetic fact, the only revenge against time that endures, that is successful in canonizing one text as opposed to another."[5] Thus Bloom writes, here oddly defining as "love" the reader's presumably requisite "cathe[xis] upon poems," that "the love of poetry is another variant of the love of power. . . . We read to usurp, just as the poet writes to usurp."[6] Poetry—which is to say, interpretive rereading—is will to power.

To this point, Bloom's model of textual historicity basically concurs with Heidegger's, despite Bloom's characteristic distaste for Heideggerian philosophy.[7] To describe textual production as "usurpation" is akin, at least, to describing it as "confrontation [*Auseinandersetzung*]," by virtue of the respective vocabularies of power and potential transmutation that these terms imply. The specific advantage of "usurpation," albeit only a partial advantage, is its acknowledgment of the de facto historical leverage that the later text is able to assert over the prior, revised text, an advantage taken by Heidegger's writing, but not explicitly confessed except in fairly quick and conventional ways. Bloom's text, too, eventually falls back on a commonplace concealment of its own revisionist activity, hiding its practice of usurpation within its own theory of usurping. But Bloom does so in an ambivalent and self-conscious manner that makes his revisionism more useful than Heidegger's as an explicit theorization of revisionism within critical reading practice.

Poetic usurpation is accomplished, for Bloom's theory, through six "revisionary ratios," mechanisms of interrelation through which one poetic text confronts and revises another.[8] Here I will concentrate on the final of the six ratios, the one that completes any revisionist reversal: the "*apophrades*," which Bloom identifies as "revisionism proper" (*MM*, 54). "*Apophrades*" names a Greek holiday on which the dead return to inhabit their old houses—"dead" poets, analogously, return to inhabit the poetry of their literary progeny, in which they are already, of course, somewhat ambivalently housed. In texts, the return or repetition of the dead occurs as a peculiar effect, an uncanny sense for the reader that the precursor's influence is present within the work. If sufficiently controlled by the later poet—if powerfully reread—this ghostly influence may then be altered and overcome, and a different sense engendered.

In part, the domain of *apophrades* includes what we might consider conventional poetic influence, the effects of which Bloom discovers mainly in bad poets.[9] For instance, in Roethke, Bloom identifies the dead precursors' return as a "devastation," which is to say, a blatant yet unconscious plagiarism: "There is late Roethke that is the Stevens of *Transport to Summer*, and late Roethke that is the Whitman of *Lilacs*, but sorrowfully there is very little late Roethke that is late Roethke" (*AI*, 142).[10] This straightforward failure to transcend a text's precursors Bloom terms the "negative *apophrades*." But the "stronger" writer is "the master at reversing," and furnishes his or her reader instead with the uncannier "positive *apophrades*" (*AI*, 142), in which the effects of the precursor's influence, although still present, are subverted: "The uncanny effect is that the new poem's achievement makes it seem to us, not as though the precursor were writing it, but as though the later poet himself had written the precursor's characteristic work" (*AI*, 16). The stronger writer appropriates the mode of the precursor so successfully that it "has been captured by him, inescapably and perhaps forever" (*AI*, 144). In essence, the late poetic text becomes the *Ereignis*, and the *Erinnerung*, of the poet's "own" poetic history. For the acute historicist reader of that poem—a reader whose identity I will discuss in more detail—it will now seem that the future writer influences the past, not vice versa. A revision of the chronology of tradition has been effected, or rather, a new quasi-traditional chronology instantiated. In terms of the revision-encounter, positive *apophrades* is an accomplished paralipsis, a revision which has effectively compelled the prior text to "speak" in the revisor's own way, and to seem, properly and in itself, just as the revisor's text intends it to seem. In Jauss's terms, it has "fabricated" and installed as given what appears in analysis to be the "horizon" of a "first reading."

With Bloom's vocabulary of "effect," "success," "achievement," "seeming," and so on, we confront an aspect of the historicity of texts that typically gets slighted even by theories that take for granted the perspectival creativity of interpretations: the sense in which a reading's creation of the past, or influence over it, is realized through the proleptic revision of future readings. No revision-encounter is complete—is *concrete*—without this essentially rhetorical intention to form an audience for its particular "proper" version of the past text. As a text itself, a revisionist rereading anticipates and requires readers who will read the past as it does: the revisionist poem requires readers for whom it, then, is a proper past, or who receive its version of history's paraliptical voice. Bloom's theorization of the *apophrades* fully implies, and yet, as I will show, does not yet fully account for, this necessary futural moment within the revisionist rereading, or what might be called the essentially futural structure of all texts as revisions of the past.[11]

For the Bloom of *A Map of Misreading*, the exemplary "positive *apophrades*" occurs in Milton, the poet whose effect on poetry persists throughout the romantic period and "down to the best poetry of our own moment" (*MM*, 101). *Paradise Lost* achieves its *apophrades* through a highly detailed allusive practice. Milton evokes prior poets in an almost continual series of images from the literary canon, but retropes each image as limited or belated with respect to his own more "primal vision" of its content, a vision often bolstered by reference to the Old Testament, as an ultimatum of primacy. For instance, Milton invokes the simile of a shield shining "like the moon," a figure with roots in both the *Iliad* and the *Fairie Queene*. But in *Paradise Lost*, the shield-as-moon is updated:

> He [Beelzebub] scarce had ceas't when the superior Fiend
> Was moving toward the shore; his ponderous shield
> Ethereal temper, massy, large and round,
> Behind him cast; the broad circumference
> Hung on his shoulders like the Moon, whose Orb
> Through the Optic Glass the *Tuscan* Artist views
> At Ev'ning from the top of the *Fesole*,
> Or in *Valdarno*, to descry new Lands,
> Rivers or Mountains in her spotty Globe.

The "Tuscan Artist" is Galileo, whom Milton had met, and whose recently invented telescope ("Optic Glass") lends the description of the moon a concreteness that its classical or Spenserian counterpart could not have possessed. According to Bloom, Milton thereby renders his own use of the image decisively modern:

> Homer and Spenser emphasize the moonlike brightness and shining of the shields of Achilles and Radigund; Milton emphasizes size, shape, weight as the common feature of Satan's shield and the moon, for Milton's post-Galilean moon is more of a world and less of a light. Milton and Galileo are *late*, yet they see more, and more significantly, than Homer and Spenser, who were *early*. Milton gives his readers the light, yet also the true dimensions and features of reality. (*MM*, 133)

The figural relation described here is metalepsis, which in *A Map of Misreading* Bloom offers as the specific mechanism of *apophrades*. Metalepsis tropes upon another, prior trope, substituting a new term for one pole of the already figurative relationship.[12] When Milton relocates the moon (within the figure of the shield-as-moon) under the gaze of Galileo, he effectively reverses the prior simile's priority over his own use of it by situating it within necessarily new, but also more essential, connotations.

Generally speaking, metalepsis is "a scheme, frequently allusive, that refers the reader back to any previous figurative scheme" (*MM*, 74). But in a positive *apophrades*, the repetition of the precursor's trope is "allowed" by the later poet only insofar as the trope is revised to make the new figuration more basic, or in Bloom's language "earlier," than the precursor's. For Bloom, the "scheme of transumption" (*MM*, 100),[13] used strongly by a poet, is designed to incorporate or "introject" the precursor's meaning so as to be able to "project" it into future traditions as a new beginning, and therefore to overcome the late poet/reader's otherwise axiomatic belatedness:

> The expansion of this apparently extrinsic image [the shield-as-moon] crowds the reader's imagination, by giving Milton the true priority of *interpretation*, the powerful reading that insists upon its

own uniqueness and its own accuracy. Troping upon his forerun-
ners' tropes, Milton compels us to read as he reads, and to accept
his stance and vision as our origin, his time as true time. His allu-
siveness introjects the past, and projects the future. (*MM*, 132)

As within our reading of Heidegger's *Nietzsche*, the chronology of
texts, their anthological sequence, is no axiomatic fact, but must be reviewed through a powerful historicist lens, one capable of perceiving
what Bloom calls the "true priority of interpretation." Milton's interpretive strength, within such a schema, is described through a psychoanalytic vocabulary, which marks the putatively psychological agon
behind the revision-encounter between Milton and his precursors.
The concepts of "introjection" and "projection" that Bloom invokes in
the above passage, borrowed from the terminologies of Ferenczi and
Freud, are "defenses," which at this period of his work are "interchangeable" with tropes (*MM*, 88–89).

The reading of Milton conducted here includes, among other
things, the basis for a theory of psychological repression as a mechanism of textual production, a notion which is probably the most significant and controversial addition that Bloom's theories make to our
understanding of how canons are formed by the publication of individual texts. I would like to discuss Bloom's notion of repression in
some detail and offer a reconsideration of his poetic psychology in
structural and formal terms that may be more useful for reading texts
within generic histories. First, however, I wish to comment on a crucial word in the above passage, a word that might normally remain
unnoticed because of its very pervasiveness in interpretative discourses:
the word "us." When Bloom refers to "us," as in the statement, "Milton compels *us* to read as he reads," this is *not* simply a conventional
nod to his readership, nor simply the journalistic (or royal) "we" of
academic prose, but rather an essential structural component of the
revision-encounter itself.[14] Since the outcome of Milton's reading is
solely an effect (the *apophrades*), it has no reality without "our" experi-

ence of it, an experience which alone permits Milton's new version of past texts to persist concretely into the future. At least three intertextual events are entailed in understanding Milton's figure of the moon: the simile as it was "originally" written (or projected) by Homer or Spenser, Milton's revision (or introjection and projection) of it, and finally "our" reading (or introjection) of the updated figure through the strong effect of Milton's interpretation.[15] When understood as a fully historical intertext, the figure is the site of an ongoing rereading *process*, a gesture or movement that creates (or anticipates) its perspective upon the past text only through the manipulation of future reading-perspectives, instantiating its "truer" version of the past text through a strong and artful persuasion of a future "us."

But something curious happens in the construction of this "us": another, concealed revision-encounter is interjected between Milton's reading of the classics and "our" reading of Milton himself. This interjection is Bloom's own rereading, for the sake of which Milton is broadly reconstructed as an agonizer upon influences and a revisor of prior poems, largely against prior traditions of Milton scholarship,[16] and through which "we," in turn, are persuaded to accept Milton's poetry as a specific metalepsis of Spenser or Homer. What the sheer (and false) conventionality of Bloom's "us" occludes is that it is Bloom himself, not Milton—the rereader, not the poet—who creates the effect of the Miltonian *apophrades*, impelling "us" to read (or simply to accept) the simile of the moon in such and such a way, to participate in such and such a new critical procedure, indeed to help to canonize it.

In fact, "we" do not experience the effect of Milton's refiguration at all here; rather, we are *told* by Bloom that we experience it. Any "aesthetic" of reception implied here must be at best a horizon, at worst an illusion. What we should be looking for is not an *aesthetic* experience, but rather an *iconography* of revision, signs of the reinterpretation and preinterpretation of what passes for actual or potential experience. Bloom's "we" tacitly adjoins his reader to his (Bloom's) own reading project or projection: our access to Milton's *apophrades* is mediated through the strong but invisible hand of Bloom's own revision-encounter, which deliberately "introjects" and "projects" a quite particular interpretation as though "we" had read it thus and as though it were the reader's proper and even automatic experience of *Paradise Lost*. Only now is there a paralipsis within Milton's text that speaks to "us" in the form of a given truth about that text. Thus there *is*, in a sense, a repression entailed by the structure of introjection and projection in Bloomian revision, but it is *not* a psychological repression, rather a structural occlusion of the paralipsis of the revision-encounter itself, a concealment which persists not so much within Bloom's theory as within his practice of rereading and writing. Bloom's theory is itself an occluded praxis, as all theories probably are, to greater or lesser degrees.

The Primal Scene of Revision

Keeping in mind the importance of the critic's secretive intervention in the rereading of the canonical text, let us now move directly to the core of Bloom's model of poetic influence, and to the idiosyncratic psychologism usually found most objectionable in Bloom's analysis of reading, even by his admirers.[17] Read for its internal logic, Bloom's narrative of influence is a condensed and elegant rendering of the particular dialectical structure of influence—and now we must mean an influence both of the past and of the future—figured in terms of a "family romance" and as a "primal scene of instruction." It is essential that we read the following passage not psychologically but allegorically, as a quasi-mythical rhetoric of powerfully cathected historical interrelations and as a philosophical critique of historical determinism:

> What is the Primal Scene, for a poet *as poet*? It is his Poetic Father's coitus with the Muse. There he was begotten? No—there they failed to beget him. He must be self-begotten, he must

engender himself upon the Muse his mother. But the muse is as pernicious as Sphinx or Covering Cherub,[18] and may identify herself with either, though more usually with the Sphinx. The strong poet fails to beget himself—he must wait for his Son, who will define him even as he has defined his own Poetic Father. To beget here means to usurp. . . . (*AI*, 36–37)

In several senses the simultaneous prospective and retrospective character of influence will never be as explicit for Bloom as it is here, provided we continue to understand this model not as an aesthetics of experience, but as an allegory or iconography of rereading practice. The poet desires "coitus with the muse"; in other words, the muse remains the pure object of desire for the "poet *as poet*." This "as" is Bloom's constant hint that a structural argument, not just a psychological one, is being conducted, or in Bloom's terms, that the poet is in the position of "reader" as well as "subject."[19] As Bloom says elsewhere, poetry "begins because there is an absence,"[20] and poets-as-poets always find themselves already "fallen" into a condition of belatedness. The "father," as Bloom unfortunately calls the precursor, has already had whatever "coitus with the muse" there was to be had, and thus has already given birth to whatever progeny there were to beget. A poet/reader has no direct way of getting around this fact or facticity. The primal completeness of canonical poetry, once witnessed by an ephebe or "son," cannot be simply reversed, but must first be displaced, refigured, dissimulated, or "mistranslat[ed]" (*AI*, 71): "To originate anything in language we must resort to a trope, and that trope must defend us against a prior trope" (*MM*, 69).

Milton's Satan, who awakes to find himself fallen into a wholly foreign place but still willing to appropriate it for his own, is, for Bloom, during this middle period of his theoretical work, the paradigmatic figure for the strong poetic "son" who confronts tradition through a new tropological stance: "Satan, organizing his chaos, imposing a discipline despite the visible darkness, calling his minions to emulate his refusal to mourn, becomes the hero as poet, finding what must suffice, while knowing that nothing can suffice" (*AI*, 22). In structural terms, such a reader is one who discovers him- or herself fallen into a canon that always already defines which poetry may be written. By definition the essential texts are already completed by precursors and, therefore, exclude the possibility of one's own writing. Bloom asserts that "a poem begins because there is an absence"—but this assertion could be made of all texts: a text "begins" in the condition of its *own* absence within a tradition,[21] and writers (or rereaders) therefore begin with the knowledge that they themselves are absent with respect to opportunities already fulfilled. If the opportunity to create an essential text is already fulfilled—and for Bloom's hyperbolic essentialization of tradition it always is—to proceed at all the poet must dialectically refigure this absence. The poet does so by displacing "absence," attributing it to a lack within the tradition itself, thereby opening the possibility of the presence of his or her own poem. It is this refiguration that Bloom identifies as the "*clinamen*" or "misprision," the starting "swerve" of new poetry which "clear[s] imaginative space," characterized by the reversing trope of irony. "'As I fell,' asserts Bloom's hypothetical Satan/poet, '*I swerved*, consequently I lie here in a Hell improved by my own making'" (*AI*, 45).

In short, because the tradition of the precursors—the "Poetic Father's coitus with the Muse"—has failed to beget him, the poet must beget himself: "*where it, the precursor's poem, is there let my poem be*; this is the rational formula of every strong poet" (*AI*, 80, Bloom's emphasis).[22] Yet the logic of the romance of reading-as-influence does not permit any direct or obvious self-engenderment, a fantastic hyperbole which Bloom bluntly calls "the impossibility of *originating [one]self*"[23] and which could as easily be called the paradox of writing entirely outside of a genre. To remain within the tradition, and therefore in a position to make claims upon it, the poet must proceed by a ruse, an antiliteral troping[24] or "lie against time," which Bloom also calls "rebeget[ting]" (*AI*, 64).[25] The poet, always to some (but only some) degree cognizant that the history of texts is complete, swerves the tradition in his own direction through a misreading, positioning it so that it leads necessarily to him: "poetry is always at work *imagining its own origin*, or telling a persuasive lie about itself, to itself."[26] The poet, as poet, *tropes* his own parent, or "gives birth to his own father,"[27] an indulgence in perspectivism which Bloom dramatically calls "the greatest illusion."[28] If successful, the result is *apophrades*, the uncanny effect that the poet has paradoxically subsumed both precursor and tradition, not vice versa. The poet now is, instead of the tradition, the "begetter" of his own writing, as well as of his own canonical past: "each [poet] wants to be the universe, to be the whole of which all other poets are only parts" (*MM*, 52).[29] Poetry (that is, interpretive reading) is essentially a denial of historical determinism.

The Subject of Revision and the Practical Limits of Theory

To this point, Bloom's account of the romance of poetic influence provides a formula, still abstract, for a writer's use of figural language to overcome the influence of canons, that is, to be original. The formula dictates that the writer begin in irony, in negation and reversal, as a stance against absence or lack, and proceed through a series of tropological shifts to establish this ironic negation as a new positive stance. In the structural terms of the revision-encounter, with which I have proposed we refigure Bloom's psychological allegory, the writer begins in revision and concludes by instantiating within the prior text the appearance of an essential paralipsis of his or her very own reading— the poet reinterprets the prior text so as to make it anticipate precisely his or her textual rereading.

Yet in and of itself, the formula does not work: as Bloom writes in the passage with which I began, "the strong poet fails to beget himself." Why? A figural displacement of the poetic self as "father" or as origin is not sufficient for self-begetting, for it does not correctly anticipate the role of future "sons," other readers of the intended effects of poetry. Troping oneself into bed with the muse is insufficient if no one is there to witness the act (as a primal scene of his or her own)—if one does not manage to get it published, so to speak, that the muse is now one's own. In its retroping of the primal scene, poetry is as much exhibitionism as voyeurism. Like all ironies, it requires the audience to understand the swerve of one's poem *as* something swerved, the muse as one's own muse—one's created and imputed paralipsis as the voice of tradition itself.

A further moment of displacement is required by Bloom's theory in order for a poet/reader's lie about origins to complete its self-fulfilling prophesy: a metaleptical trope of trope which instantiates the reader's *own* past as a future of his or her text. The poet "gives birth" to a new line of readers for whom he is the "father," for whom he represents the original essence of written poetry complete in the form of a canon, an already consummated coitus with the muse. These future readers, if all goes well, now read tradition as he reads it, or indeed read tradition *as him*, a paralipsis of his own poetic rereading. The poet therefore blocks their access to the original muse just as the prior poet blocked it from him, becoming the tyrannical father-figure who in his whole-ness neglected or failed to beget *them*. Only thus, once removed, does the poet/reader beget himself as his own parent: "Poetic strength ensues when such lying [about one's own origins] persuades the reader that his own origin has been reimagined by the poem."[30] Poetic "fathers"—even of themselves—become such only through the antici-pated activity of their sons. Fatherhood is a rhetorical accomplish-ment, an act of persuasion. Therefore strong textual reading is no aes-thetic experience, let us say in the "form" of a single poem, but rather a dissimulated paternalistic influence, a residue of family romance, uneasily but unavoidably received.

Poets, then, are metaleptical refigurations of prior figures of the essence of poetry, of the "primal scene for the poet *as poet*." But "coitus with the Muse," it should now be obvious, has never taken place—it is

always infinitely displaced—and there are no "true" (or, in another terminology, "positive") fathers, but only fathers-as-displaced sons, hypostatic father-figures reconstituted ex post facto by their future readers,
as themselves particular readings of the past to be revised and displaced. No primal scene of poetic coitus with the muse has *being*, but
such scenes only constantly re-become, and get themselves reread.
Therefore no such scene is going to get fully remembered by any
amount of poetic refiguration. A poetic canon *is* only a series of repres-
sions, and then a series of figural substitutions for the primal poetic
origin, which remains always one step more absent to memory than
any one poetic reader is able to oversee: "behind all Primal fantasy is
the even more Primal repression that Freud both hypothesized and
evaded" (*MM*, 56).

Practically speaking, this means that "against Freud, the idea of the
most Primal scene as being a scene of instruction goes back to the
roots of the canonical principle and insists that: 'In the beginning was
Interpretation'" (*MM*, 55). Structurally speaking, it becomes insufficiently precise simply to say that "poems are readings": crucially, they
are readings of readings (of readings of readings . . . ad infinitum).
There is (or was) no ur-text or " muse," but only the successive revisions of relations with that muse—readers' incessant repositings of
what constitutes the true or proper beginnings of their readings. In
short, poems *are* the history of poetry, just as for Heidegger "Being *is*
the history of Being." But the origin of such a history is a reconstituted
hypostasis, only troped as "recollected" in and by the appropriating
event (*Ereignis*) of revision. To recast the point in Jauss's terms, the
"first reading" of hermeneutics is precisely a revision *by* hermeneutics.
Or, to put it more polemically in Heidegger's terms, the *Ereignis*—of
the "end of metaphysics and the new commencement" of the epoch of
the proper *Seinsfrage*—is a rereading, in the strongest historicist sense
of this "is" that Heidegger's or Bloom's theory allows.

The logic of Bloom's model of revision demands a strict deconstruction of the subject or ego of the revision-encounter, whose existence at any particular moment within a history of texts is a hypostasis,

and therefore a misreading, of what is actually a continuous historical development between texts and an inherent intentionality toward futures. Readings *stop* history—that which precisely cannot be stopped. In other terms, readings are rhetorical in the strongest possible sense of the term, even magical; they alter the past; they appear to stop time itself. But the supposed subject who pretends to the position of the originary agent of revision is, in fact, always only an anticipation of its own creation ex post facto, by and within another reading process, fully reliant, for its stance toward past texts, on its dissimulated effects upon an audience of future readers. However hyperbolically final or original the poet/reader tropes him- or herself—and as Bloom states somewhere, "all revisionists, however irreligious, are anagogists"—he or she is necessarily only a moment in a halting historical movement, at best a more or less successful attempt to swerve the progress of a text's history, whatever his or her pretense to stopping or ending it.

Yet in his own interpretive practice—even his early practice— Bloom commits many such hypostatical stoppages, reducing the structural poet-as-poet to a specific and reified psychological agent, whose "cathexis upon poems" and resulting anxiety is then seen as both the source of and the reason for revision. Such freezing of the reading subject is deliberate on Bloom's part and explicitly opposed to what he considers an analogous Nietzschean tendency (which I would share) to reduce psychological subjects to intertextual power relations:

> Even the subtlest of contemporary Nietzschean "deconstructors" of texts must *reduce* those texts in a detour or flight from psychology and history. Nothing prevents a reader with my preferences from resolving all linguistic elements in a literary text into history, and similarly tracing all semantic elements in literary discourse to problems of psychology. (*MM*, 85)

While it is perhaps true that nothing prevents such a reduction of language to psychology, or more specifically to anxiety, Bloom's "preference" for psychological subjects prevents him from fully accounting for the revision-encounter in the structure of *text*. His theory of the reading subject stops precisely at the point where the effect of a subject's revision, the *apophrades* or reversal of historical chronology, is merely posited by the reading itself as a "total, final act of taking up a poetic stance in relation to anteriority."[31] In other words, Bloom's theory, despite its explicit advocacy of revision as a *basis*, practically speaking remains in the guise of a hermeneutics of reading, not yet a rhetoric of rereading.

And yet nothing can be total or final here, except perhaps within the reader's own self-construal as a "proper" interpreter, or within the discourse of the conventional "we" who is politely supposed to share in that construal. Despite his severe critique of poetry as misreading, which effectively deconstructs the poet/reader's own pretension to propriety and priority, Bloom eventually rests with a psychological terminology that follows rather than questions the romantic poet's own ambivalent or anxious appraisal of his position: as an end and a beginning, instead of as a mediation and an outcome, of the process of reading and the history of interpretation. We needn't turn to Bloom's latest polemical efforts to legislate the canon, for instance his recent efforts to restore the supposedly lost centrality of Shakespeare,[32] in order to discover a hypostatized perception either of poetic subjects or of inherent literary qualities. Curiously, and ironically, Bloom's unanalytical loyalty to poetry's own ego-ideal is already blatant in what Bloom himself considers his own most critical attack on the pretensions of the poetic subject, the well-known notion that poetry is "unconscious" misreading. Again, I emphasize that Bloom's theory of the poetic subject must be read allegorically and rhetorically, not psychologically: what Bloom names the "unconscious" is in fact the moment in which the difference between the prior text and the later reader is itself effaced—that is, reread and revised—or in which the prior text's all too powerful sameness is dissimulated. Either way, it is the comparison of prior poet and later reader that is "unconsciously" misread by a poetic subject whose supposed "anxiety" drives the reading process and therefore motivates the misreading. But, in fact, what Bloom's theory itself demonstrates is that this moment of "unconsciousness" is itself always uncovered by yet another reading and yet another analysis. The "unconscious" of revision is not *in* the poet's subjectivity, but rather *is* the difference between the poet and his future reader: it is the prolepsis of a new, supplementary revision-encounter, the historically reconstructed unsaid of the text. Where Bloom's theory retains the Freudian "unconscious" as the term for this essentially inter*textual* difference, it occultly metaphorizes, instead of appropriates and deconstructs, the basic historical revisionism of reading practice—and above all, of Bloom's own reading practice.

Indeed, Bloom has always been the arch literary-critical practitioner even in his most theoretical moments. I noted earlier how a certain invisible rereading intervenes between the putative "effect" of Milton's *apophrades* in *Paradise Lost* and the equally putative "experience" of that effect by "us." Both the effect and the experience are the dissimulated products of a concrete interpretive act, namely, Bloom's own reading, which connects the various strands that relate Milton both to his precursors and to his reading progeny ("us"). When a poem or reading such as Milton's is troped as strong or successful, someone (here it is Bloom himself) must always have *decided* that the "experience" of reading Milton causes such-and-such an effect, even though this sort of critical decision is conventionally elided, troped merely as a direct communication between poet and reader. But such a convention itself has essentially a sideways-speaking or paraliptical structure, within which the critic's antithetical reading is imputed to the text itself, just as Heidegger's revision of Nietzsche is imputed to the erstwhile concealed but most proper "center" of Nietzsche's text. The terminology of power in Bloom's writing, which could have served, as it does in Nietzsche, the critical function of exposing the essential structural "error" of interpretation—and thereby also the possibility of a social critique of reading practice—instead limits itself to the very hypostasis of the self-contained strong poetic "man" that his model in its most rigorous theoretical moments ought logically to destroy. In the end, and in all cases, Bloom himself is that "man"—in the role of "strong critic" (*AI*, 93–96) attempting to have the last word, more or less sneakily, about the achievement of revisionist effects, a revisionist gesture which remains an unacknowledged will to power over his own readers and which has become an increasingly strident voice in his work during the past ten years. Yet even in 1975, as a pragmatics of the revising activity, Bloom's theory, like most or perhaps all theories, is *too* pragmatic, for it stops short of theorizing its own practical role in instantiating its topic's "true" paraliptical intention—the same role as that of the poet/readers it is meant to demystify.

SIX

Healthy, Wealthy, and Wise: Rereading in Emerson

Being is being-more.

— WERNER HAMACHER, *Pleroma*

The historiography of philosophy Heidegger constructs in the later portions of the *Nietzsche* lectures demonstrates that the most essential topos of metaphysics is, albeit only proleptically and paraliptically, metaphysics' own historicity: the history of Being *is* Being itself, and nothing more. But the manner in which Being presents itself within this history takes the form of individual thinkers' limitations and, therefore, the form of the revision-encounter, the "saying not-saying" of an imputed paralipsis, always reread by another reader. In the previous chapter, I examined Harold Bloom's theory of poetic revision, which, in its most clear-sighted moments, analyzes exactly such a structure of limitation and (future) completion explicitly as the rhetorical effect of a rereading act. Bloom offers a model for literary or philosophical historiography in which the construction of new texts is an ongoing process through which reinterpreters exhort, if not guarantee, the reception of their respective historical positions. But Bloom stops short of a full structural account of this reception, which any adequate model of rereading and rewriting requires. Instead, he rests with an essentially descriptive, unanalytical terminology of power—"strength," "achievement," "triumph," and so on—which may ultimately be construed as a hyperbole of his own attempt to influence readers.

Such a vocabulary is at least useful for its acknowledgment of the power relations that subsist among text, interpreter, and audience, prior to the communitarian ethic by which philosophical readers abide in their ostensibly mutual quests for truth, accuracy or insight. Historical revision, via Bloom, is an imposition of greater or lesser efficacy, which means that one version of a text will always end by the wayside as another becomes canonical. Thinkers are axiomatically different from other thinkers, although not too different. Only through continual but subtle divergence and dissimulated usurpation is there something like a history of texts. Indeed, texts must accrue difference to exist as such; the accrual of textual difference *is* textual history. While Bloom's terminology productively foregrounds these processes, he consistently declines to scrutinize the same vocabulary as a set of structural conditions through which texts and authors are actually produced. Instead, he rests with a psychology, a story about desires and cathexes, which in a sense already implies their producibility. It is as if, within Bloom's theory, textual usurpation were not a historical but a personal phenomenon, as if, after all Bloom's complex analysis of the dialectical interrelativity of textual histories, the individual writer were still a subject, not chiefly an object, let alone a mere artifact, of the rereading process.

In its recalcitrance, Bloom's theory creates a structural puzzle, yet forsakes it unsolved: How does one account, in useful structural terms, for the historical reconstruction of the subject of textual revision, the subject who emerges out of the revision-encounter in the occlusionary form of its origin or source? Who reads? Who revises? Whoever this subject is, it is not the congenial "we" whom both Bloom and Heidegger, entirely conventionally, still identify as the putative subject of a "confrontation" with prior thinkers, for instance with Nietzsche. Viewing a philosophical historiography such as Heidegger's through the theoretical window opened by Bloom, the task becomes to recast the revision-encounter so that this model will accommodate both the phenomenon of revision and its suppression through mechanisms of reception. If there is an individual or collective "subject" of the revision-encounter, a subject whose "positioning" bequeaths a persuasively stable version of the past, then the collusion of such a subject with its anticipated future readers ought to be examined in its full character as a historical and rhetorical process.

Ralph Waldo Emerson will serve as the exemplar for this next stage of my discussion of the rhetoric of revision. Emerson, particularly in his early essays, is deeply engaged with the problem of how an active and productive subject will be formed against the weighty legacy of European history. This engagement makes Emerson the harbinger of a specifically American critical iconoclasm, whose resonances will be felt in the work of critics such as Bloom and beyond. More crucially, Emerson construes the history of the "self" as a history of textuality, emerging only through an aggressive revision-encounter with the textual past. However—and this is Emerson's most important contribution to this discussion—this revision-encounter is explicitly cast as a rhetorical phenomenon, a quasi-oratorical performance for a future audience. This understanding of the relation to past histories and texts distinguishes Emerson's theory of reading and revision from both Bloom's psychological-conflictual model and Heidegger's more conventional implication of a community ("we") of actual or potential "thinkers" in the here and now. Out of Emerson's prose we get a rhetorical poetics, an antihermeneutical theorization more fully capable of questioning the stance of the reader as an interpreter of both pasts and futures. Indeed, perhaps because of his own distance from hermeneutical traditions, Emerson reenacts, almost in the form of a narrative about his own reading practices, the development of modern hermeneutics from a methodology of exegesis into a theory of the production and reproduction of texts through interpretive action.

"Correspondency" and Active Reading

Emerson's prose is notorious for hindering the extraction of coherent theoretical arguments, so much so that critics have been persuaded that its very equivocity is a positive philosophical strategy.[1] Without encroaching upon any debates on this matter, but still agreeable to equivocity, I will offer an interpretation of two distinct but conflicted moments within Emerson's theory of reading history: the respective accounts within the first two essays of his *First Series*, "History" and "Self-Reliance." Read alongside one another, these two essays enact Emerson's peculiar self-debate over the role of the past in the development of the self, the first essay leaving the problem unresolved in a way that expressly allows room for the second to complete it.

In "History," Emerson describes reading as a sympathy with the historical past: "We as we read must become Greeks, Romans, Turks, priest and king, martyr and executioner" (*E*, 238). When we "put ourselves in the place" of, say, the builders of gothic cathedrals, then "we have, as it were, been the man that made the minster; we have seen how it could and must be" (*E*, 241). What an individual reader derives from sympathetic reading is not mere historical data, but rather a sense of "correspondency" between his own experiences in the moment and the experiences of creators in the past. In Emerson's particular version of a historico-structural cliché, what happened then is less important than what these events mean for us here and now:

> The world exists for the education of each man. . . . He should see that he can live all history in his own person. . . . [Each man] must

transfer the point of view from which history is commonly read, from Rome and Athens and London to himself, and not deny his conviction that he is the court, and that if England or Egypt have any thing to say to him, he will try the case; if not, let them be for ever silent. (*E*, 239–40)

Despite first appearances, Emerson is not a subjectivist. He attempts to elevate the reader's subjective viewpoint on history into a *general* reading practice, so that the sympathy and correspondency of individual experiences of the past become themselves shareable phenomena. To effect this shift, Emerson must consider the correspondence between the reader and the maker of history not as the imposition of particular perspectives upon past facts, but rather as the consequence of an already present universality of experience that, because it is apropos of "men" in all historical periods, guarantees that every historical text will be comprehensible to each new reader: "Every man is an inlet to the same and to all of the same. . . . What Plato has thought, he may think; what a saint has felt, he may feel; what at any time has befallen any man, he can understand" (*E*, 237). In this denial of historical relativism we have a formal equivalent, albeit in cruder terms, of Heidegger's universalizing reduction of the variety of history, the notion that the particular historicities ("limitations") of thinkers are "granted by the 'to be' [*Sein*]" of history, and therefore that all thinkers think "the same." In the following passage, Emerson explains that a reader understands a bit of history not because he forms and manipulates it for his own interests, but rather because it potentially resonates for him in a way that he always already finds familiar: "Every revolution was first a thought in one man's mind, and when the same thought occurs to another man, it is the key to that era. Every reform was once a private opinion, and when it shall be a private opinion again, it will solve the problem of the age" (*E*, 238). History is "subjective" here, to be sure, but only in a sense that is familiar (if debatable) to most forms of hermeneutics: that reading is fundamentally a kind of communication between similar historical subjects, and that experiences are therefore transmittable over the longest gaps in time.[2] Indeed, Emerson is satisfied with nothing less than the complete intelligibility of history for the individual reader, a position he asserts rather than argues: "Universal history, the poets, the romancers, do not in their stateliest pictures—in the sacerdotal, the imperial palaces, in the triumphs of will or of genius—anywhere lose our ear, anywhere make us feel that we intrude, that this is for better men; but rather is it true, that in their grandest strokes we feel most at home" (*E*, 238).[3] Yet in this passage, as in other moments of "History," Emerson's universalism threatens to come undone precisely because he carries it to such extremes. Would it not be far easier to explain the complete intelligibility of historical texts on the basis of an individual's sheer revisionist imposition, rather than on the basis of some fortuitous "correspondency" between past and present historical moments? Of course a reader "feels at home in history" if that reader forms historical events after his or her own image, if he or she recreates them in the form of a paraliptical voice, a prolepsis of the very reading act that now appropriates them. The more a reader imposes a point of view on the facts, naturally the more sympathetically the facts "speak to him" over and against any pesky facticity. Perspectivism, rather than universalism, would seem to be the primary implication of "History," despite what Emerson intends.

In fact, nearly all of the passages in "History" that call for the dialectical overcoming of subjectivism in "correspondency" also imply perspectivism and subjective imposition upon past texts or facts. This conflict surfaces in the polemical tone with which Emerson calls for an aggressive approach to history reading, a tone which belies any notion that the "correspondent" past will easily or automatically resonate for the individual reader: "The student is to read history actively and not passively; to esteem his own life the text, and books the commentary. . . . I have no expectation that any man will read history aright, who thinks that what was done in a remote age, by men whose names have resounded far, has any deeper sense than what he is doing to-day" (*E*, 239). These demands end by privileging the present moment to such a degree that, paradoxically, historicality itself is negated.[4] At several such points, the essay moves surprisingly against its own notion of "sympathy": "All inquiry into antiquity . . . is the desire to do away this wild, savage, and preposterous There or Then, and introduce in its place the Here and the Now" (*E*, 241). Eventually it appears that for Emerson nothing is actually "past," or that the past cannot persist as a phenomenological category—historical facts and artifacts, "read" by individuals, are solely present; "they live again to the mind, or are *now*" (*E*, 241, Emerson's emphasis). History devolves from something that "has happened" before to something "happen*ing*" still, essentially a bildungsroman about the particular self now reading it: "All history becomes subjective; in other words, there is properly no history; only biography" (*E*, 240).[5] Thus, finally, "Who cares what the fact was, when we have made a constellation of it to hang in heaven an immortal sign? London and Paris and New York must go the same way. 'What is History,' said Napoleon, 'but a fable agreed upon?'" (*E*, 240).

The model of reading that begins to emerge in "History" is sufficiently self-contradictory as to seem deliberately incomplete, soliciting rather than begging a resolution. Its polemical form, a call for active, perspectival reading, directly impugns the humanistic tendency of its content, an affirmation of universal sympathy through the correspondency between texts. For if "active reading" is necessary at all, sympathy and correspondency cannot be taken for granted, except perhaps as a mere "fable" of their own. The resolution to this problem will not appear in "History," which ends on a peculiarly ambivalent and self-recanting note—"I reject all I have written, for what is the use of pretending to know what we know not?"[6]—but in the essay that follows it, "Self-Reliance," which takes the self-recanting ambivalence of "History" and sculpts it into a peculiar paraliptical structure. The latter essay recoups the contradictions of "History" for a model, rather than a mere problem, of "active reading," a recuperation which Bloom's work, a century and a half later and in the same theoretical vein, declines or fails to achieve.

The Singular Self

Even though "Self-Reliance," among all of Emerson's writings, calls the most aggressively for an original, declarative, even presumptive style of thinking—asserting that "imitation is suicide"—the essay opens with an uncharacteristic moment of hesitation or humility. The first three sentences tell this anecdote about reliance on another: "I read the other day some verses written by an eminent painter which were original and not conventional. The soul always hears an admonition in such lines, let the subject be what it may. The sentiment they instill is of more value than any thought they may contain" (*E*, 259). This citation of the "eminent painter" is curious, since the verses to which Emerson alludes never appear in the essay, nor does he mention their author again. Instead, Emerson gives a brief explanation of their absence: that the sentiment of such lines is always more valuable than any "thought" contained within them. This is a rhetorician's little joke, based in the self-effacing irony of paralipsis. Whatever lesson the painter's lines may have contained is expressed in the form of being left out: the real "sentiment" of the citation is precisely that nothing need be cited. Following the painter's implicit admonition, therefore, Emerson does not include the lines. But why bother to mention them at all?

Not mentioning the lines, Emerson's or the painter's, is precisely the strategy of most of Emerson's critics, who head directly for the essay's fourth sentence, a comfortably Emersonian "*a priori* deduction"[7]: "To believe your own thought, to believe that what is true for you in your private heart is true for all men,—that is genius." Logically, this apothegm seems to follow from the truncated quasi citation, as though it were precisely the "sentiment" instilled by the absent verses. But rhetorically, it is hard not to think of the fourth sentence, with its strong manifesto of individualism,[8] as a more proper and less artificial beginning for the essay, both stylistically, because it suits the audacious rhetoric of the rest of the text, and theoretically, because the topic of the essay as a whole is independence and autogenesis. The task of reading the essay's first three sentences in light of the fourth sentence is not to explain the absence of the quasi-cited verses—presumably they are absent because you must "believe your *own* thought"— but to explain why their exclusion is incomplete, why they maintain a nagging quasi presence. If we pursue the direction in which the logic of this beginning leads us, we must ask why *self*-reliance (or the essay "Self-Reliance") should be unable to get started except through this ghostly or vestigial reliance on someone else. Why does Emerson introduce the self-reliant self, of all things, through the essentially reliant trope of paralipsis, as a response to the saying not-saying of another text's "sentiment"?

A preliminary answer would be that the other text, typified here by the painter's verses, remains quasi present only as that which has been superseded in the present moment: the "self" learns, by admonition, to rely on itself through a rejection of reliance on others. Such an exercise in rejection is performed by Emerson's opening, which then retains the residue of the rejection as a small didactic reminder. On such a reading, Emerson would hold a more or less dialectical view of a reader and his or her reliances—a reading self is the negation of reliance, while reliances negate the reading self. I say "more or less" dialectical, however, because Emerson portrays the exercise of relying on another in such a one-sided way. His quasi citation of the verses shows little deference to a truly dialectical—that is, a negative—influence on the part of the cited text. His posture toward this bit of the recent past seems something beyond dialectic, as though the interplay of influence or reliance proceeded in one direction more than the other, enabling Emerson to toy with "admonishing" influences with the pretense of being finally free of them. It is here that Emerson's model of textual reading and reception will productively exceed a hermeneutical description of the reader's understanding, and why he will find that a more powerfully rhetorical stance will be necessary to "receive" the text in anything other than a passively historicist way.[9] To read the whole opening of the essay as an allegory of such a quasi freedom from history: it is as though the "self" tropes itself as a *singularity* with respect to influences, exceeding into the future the "reliances" out of which it springs from the past, a whole greater than the sum of its historical parts. And singularity, excess, being "greater," can be nothing other than a creative act toward texts and readers, a rhetoric of historic persuasion and retroactive self-authorization.

The essay "History" had already hinted at such a singular self in its polemical suggestion of a reader for whom facts were mere fable and for whom the entirety of historical determination could be taken or left at will. "Self-Reliance" elevates such a self to the level of structure, an essential component of the reading activity and, therefore, of the relation to pasts and past texts. "Singularity" is only one possible name for this structure, connoting the unique place of a successful self in a continuum of historical time. The singular self could also be named with a word of Emerson's own, one more appropriate to the characteristic audacity of Emerson's polemic within this essay: "impertinence." Emerson first uses this word to characterize the past's own imposition on selves in the present: "history is an impertinence and an injury, if it be any thing more than a cheerful apologue or parable of my being and becoming" (*E*, 270). In "History" Emerson had already suggested that the past can "bull[y]" or "tyrannize over" individuals (*E*, 239, 250).[10] But in "Self-Reliance," the critical rejoinder to history's impertinence will not be some conveniently sympathetic "Mind," but rather the individual's own counterimpertinence, a self-centered and rather unsympathetic eschewal of correspondencies.

For instance, Emerson declares, "What have I to do with the sacredness of traditions, if I live wholly from within?" (*E*, 262), or even more appropriately in light of the quasi citation at the beginning of "Self-Reliance": "when you have life in yourself, it is not by any known or accustomed way; you shall not discern the foot-prints of any other. . . . It shall exclude example and experience" (*E*, 271). Impertinence is singularity with respect to all reliances, a disdain for social, historical, or textual debts, a will-to-negation that makes one capable of uttering "the rude truth in all ways" (*E*, 262). Emerson writes: "Why should we assume the faults of our friend, or wife, or father, or child, because they sit around our hearth or are said to have the same blood?" (*E*, 273). Far from the respectful deference of dialectic—even dialectic that posits its own positive advance on moments of citation or reliance—Emerson advises that one simply dismiss out of hand whatever is not absolutely one's own, for any such dross is a threat to one's independence.[11] Nonetheless, these various rejections, whether they dispense with society, family, friends, books, traditions, or the past as such, still begrudge a connection to some other or otherness, even when the latter merely "pules and whines" (*E*, 262). Whatever its degree of self-reliance, a self is constantly beset by these impertinent externalities, and must constantly repel them—is compelled, perhaps, constantly to treat them rudely, otherwise to succumb to being treated rudely by them. We can reconsider Emerson's quasi citation at the beginning of "Self-Reliance" as a small allegory of such a proactive impertinence: not exactly a concession to the influence of the past text, but a revisionist-tending compensation[12] in the form of an impertinent anticitational reading practice.[13] The self is first a rereader, but foremost a rejecter of texts—a revision*ist* in the rudest and most polemical sense. Consider how far we are here from Heidegger's polite invitation that we "follow the way" that his lectures on Nietzsche have taken.

The fifth sentence of "Self-Reliance," immediately after the quasi citation and its "*a priori* deductive" follow-up, introduces time and history as the proper domain of what the fourth sentence had defined as self-reliance, namely, "genius," or "believing your own thought": "Speak your latent conviction, and it shall be the universal sense; for the inmost in due time becomes the outmost,—and our first thought is rendered back to us by the trumpets of the Last Judgement" (*E*, 259). This command is followed by a series of epitaphs on Moses, Plato, and Milton, whose "highest merit" is that they "set at naught books and traditions."[14] If, for Emerson's previous essay, history is essentially biography, in "Self-Reliance" we are offered a reciprocal demonstration that an individual biography is itself "historical," or, more precisely, that selves are essentially things that assert themselves against the background of a broader temporal continuum, a story about others. The self is something that "degrades the past, turns all riches to poverty . . . shoves Jesus and Judas equally aside" (*E*, 271); it outgrows its past. But because "Self-Reliance" grudgingly acknowledges, as "History" did not, that the rereading self is formed *by* its own historicality, this essay can in turn propose, as the essay "History" could not, that the self may exceed those same reliances, that it may become a new historical beginning through the mechanism of impertinence. The self-reliant self reverses or oversteps, rather than merely absorbs, the past for the benefit of its own becoming. In Bloom's terms, it both introjects and projects the text of the past—but its projection always exceeds, or gets troped as exceeding, its introjection. It is a revisionist, therefore not a proper hermeneut, but more properly a rhetor.

In short, the revisionist self-reliant self creates futures, reversing the direction of past influences that otherwise would have hampered it: "Every true man is a cause . . . —and posterity seem to follow his steps as a train of clients" (*E*, 267)—he is a cause, *and therefore not an effect*. Emerson sums up this singular temporality of the self, as well as the essential connections among reading, history, and "biography," in a single declaration that makes "Self-Reliance" a virtual manifesto of the futuristic rhetoric of rereading: "Perception is not whimsical, but fatal. If I see a trait, my children will see it after me, and in course of time, all mankind,—although it may chance that no one has seen it before me" (*E*, 269). The self is a "fatal perception"—a "transmission," in Heidegger's terms, or a "projection," in Bloom's—of a particular past into the future, a past "introjected" through reading. But Emerson's analysis is a significant improvement, in terms of the structure of rereading, upon Heidegger's analysis of what is "transmitted" through "confrontation." The Emersonian self, unlike the self-effaced discoverer of what is intrinsic or proper in Nietzsche's text, has a positive stake in—explicitly *intends* toward—its future reader, and positively flouts the easy conventionality that would usually conceal such a blatantly rhetorical deportment within polite philosophical society. This moment of intentionality exposes the revisionist activity that links the "proper" past to the future readers whom it is motivated to influence. In short, what Emerson theorizes as "fatal," and which Bloom names (but largely fails to theorize) as "strength," is precisely an exposed version of the moment of the paraliptical transfer of meaning that Heidegger's reading continually effaces. Emerson does not hesitate to acknowledge the impertinence or "rudeness," even the rapaciousness, of such antihistoricist imposition. Compare, for instance, the terminology of coercion in this statement from Emerson's later *Representative Men* (1850), about the influence of Platonic metaphysics, with Heidegger's flatter notion that "all metaphysics is Platonism": "The writings of Plato have preoccupied every school of learning, every lover of thought, every church, every poet—making it impossible to think, on certain levels, except through him. He stands between the truth and every man's mind, and has almost impressed language, and primary forms of thought, with his name and seal."[15] Emerson's language is not only stronger than Heidegger's; it also suggests more explicitly the activity, the *praxis*, that has gone into canonizing Plato's writings. This suggestion is followed out in the general theory of "fatal" reading that Emerson's model of history supplies.

Emerson's formulation also offers an improvement upon Bloom's by virtue of its fuller description of the link between the reader's metaleptical reconstruction of the past and that reconstruction's subsequent reception by future readers. Whereas for Bloom the end of the process of revisionist reading remains the formation of the poetic subject over and against the precursor, Emerson's fatal gesture toward a future is absolutely and inextricably linked to the continual process of acceptance by future readers ("children") of that particular "subjective" vision of the past. In essence, Emerson more fully addresses the Bloomian *apophrades as* an effect—which, like all ironic tropes, entails its own reception—whereas Bloom himself ironically leaves it bound to hypostatic categories such as strength or success. Moreover, for Emerson, the putative subject of reading remains inherently a movement in the process of historical recreation, *both formed and formative*, in the *midst* rather than at the end of the process of influencing. As Emerson writes, again in *Representative Men*, "We are tendencies, or rather, symptoms, and none of us is complete."[16] Emerson's only demand, then, is that the reader, if never complete, at least be excessive, singular, tendentious.

Three Figures of Fatal Perception

The remainder of this chapter is a gloss on the remarkable speculative manifesto from "Self-Reliance" that "perception is fatal," just as Chapter 4 was a gloss on Heidegger's manifesto that "the history of Being is Being itself, and nothing more." I want to analyze three metaphors of self-reliance in Emerson's essay, treating all of them on the same logical-allegorical register as I did Bloom's "father" and "primal scene" in Chapter 5. The first two metaphors, both versions of what Emerson calls the "integrity" of self-reliance, are "health" and "economy." The interplay of these two figures is analogous to the conflicted logic of correspondent versus subjectivist "sympathy" in the essay "History." In turn, they can be seen as representing the poles of a certain dialectic of "art" and "truth"—of revision and essentialization—at the heart of the revision-encounter. The third basic metaphor of Emersonian self-reliance is "manhood," which within Emerson's metaphorical system is oddly equivalent to "divinity." The latter figuration logically concludes Emerson's meditations both on the conflicted notion of history as "sympathy" and on the self-reliant self as historical singularity: when the self as "manhood" revises history, it resolves the problem of relating past to present by positioning itself as an "uncreated creator," one who *forms* historical "correspondencies" into the future, a "fatal perception" of the past.

When we continue to the fourth sentence of "Self-Reliance," we find the beginning of an exhortation to nonconformity,[17] which will climax in a provocative paragraph a few pages later, in which Emerson declares, "Whoso would be a man must be a non-conformist" (*E*, 261). Nonconformity is a favorite Emersonian topic and receives considerable rhetorical flourish in this essay: "What have I to do with the sacredness of traditions, if I live wholly from within"; ". . . if I am the devil's child, I will live then from the Devil"; "No law can be sacred to me but that of my nature"; ". . . the only right is what is after my constitution, the only wrong what is against it"; "I shun father and mother and wife and brother, when my genius calls me" (*E*, 262). In these assertions, as in the most polemical passages of Nietzsche's *Ecce Homo*, which I discuss in the next chapter, a provoking literalism is the text's characteristic rhetorical figure. The discomfiting ambiguity of Emerson's statements is the source of their polemical force: Are they meant seriously, literally, or are they just hyperboles that connote an ultimately milder, figural nonconformism? The more straightforwardly they are read, the more these literalisms serve to cast out whatever conventionally offers itself within society as an individual self's ideal or universal purpose. Emerson, like Nietzsche, encourages the reader to be boldly revisionist in renouncing ideals and idealizations, a practice of renunciation that Emerson continues to characterize as "integrity": "Whoso would be a man must be a non-conformist. He who would gather immortal palms must not be hindered by the name of goodness, but must explore if it be goodness. Nothing is at last sacred but the integrity of your own mind" (*E*, 261).

In general Emerson plays on two senses of "integrity"—that of bodily integrity, in which the healthy body is whole and free of foreign substance, and that of economic integrity, or wholeness in the sense of solvency, freedom from debt, and therefore freedom either to commit to the exchange of assets or refuse it. To be "healthy" is to be "undivided," somewhat like the previous "natural" reader of "History." But in "Self-Reliance," human nature, rather than simply posited, is contextualized within what might be called a minor theory of nature as a whole: "Nature suffers nothing to remain in her kingdoms which cannot help itself. The genesis and maturation of a planet, its poise and orbit, the bended tree recovering itself from the strong wind, the vital resources of every animal and vegetable, are demonstrations of the self-sufficing, and therefore self-relying soul" (*E*, 272). Ultimately, and paradoxically, if still predictably, this naturalism becomes a kind of nativism, as Emerson draws conclusions about the connections between a natural health and a natural home, the latter of which, as usual in such descriptions, is undergoing troubles. For Emerson, the social malaise at home is manifest by the desire of individuals to leave it, and he curiously expends a large portion of the essay discussing the "problem" of foreign travel, despite his disappointment with domestic civil society. The threat of the foreign, as well as its seductiveness, makes a certain sense in the light of the metaphorics of the self as healthful integrity, for by the logic of this metaphor, the body in a foreign place is the counterpart of a foreign substance in the body: "the rage of travelling is a symptom of a deeper unsoundness affecting the whole intellectual action. The intellect is vagabond . . ." (*E*, 278). "Travelling" thus becomes a general rubric for any dissipation of self, and there are any number of ways figuratively to travel: "What is imitation but the travelling of the mind?" (*E*, 278); "As our Religion, our Education, our Art look abroad, so does our spirit of society" (*E*, 279); "[The mob-mentality] goes abroad to beg a cup of water of the urns of other men" (*E*, 272).[18] Foreignness and unhealthiness, metaphorically speaking, are equivalent symptoms of a general "disease of the will": "It is only as man puts off all foreign support, and stands alone, that I see him to be strong and to prevail" (*E*, 281).[19] The "healthy" domestic self is ostensibly the same self to which Emerson alluded in "History," the self that, by contrast, reads history while "sitting solidly at home" (*E*, 239): the "home-keeping wit . . . which finds all the elements of life in its own soil" (*E*, 247). The self is, for instance, the reader who finds the past universally sympathetic from his own vantage—but then it is precisely *not* that other, more polemical reader whom this essay solicits, the reader who transforms the past to suit his or her own biography, reading "actively and not passively."

However, if this initial metaphor of health renders the reading self only in terms of the sympathy between its own past and present, the darker side of Emerson's ambivalent reader/self emerges in his alternative metaphorization of the "integrity" of self as *economy*. This less sympathetic figuration is evident in Emerson's complaints about charity, when he hopes, for instance, that "by and by I shall have the manhood to withhold" the dollar he is tempted to give to the poor (*E*, 263). Given the connection between the metaphorics of health as integrity and the vilification of the foreign, one begins to see why charity would be problematic for Emerson, and why he would treat the concept so impertinently. Charity entails a logic of "virtue" and "obligation" antithetical to the self's appropriation of reliances according to its own standard. As a typical virtue—that is, both as a virtue and as typical— charity is rather a substitute for genuine selfhood than an attribute of it: "Men do what is called a good action, as some piece of courage or charity, much as they would pay a fine in expiation of daily nonappearance on parade. Their works are done as an apology or extenuation of their living in the world,—as invalids and the insane pay a high board" (*E*, 263). Here, while health or bodily integrity remains Emerson's basic metaphor for self-reliance,[20] it begins to merge with a divergent figure, a metaphor of payment or expiation, or more broadly of economic freedom. To be free of the "obligation" to be charitable is to be free to choose whether or not to pay, since charity, like virtue in general, is here considered a kind of social blackmail. For this metaphor, the problem with the morality of society, the solicitor of charity, is that it operates within a static economy, one in which an equilibrium of influences between a person and his or her responsibilities offers no possible gain for either side: "Society never advances. It recedes as fast on one side as it gains on the other. It undergoes continual changes; it is barbarous, it is civilized, it is christianized, it is rich, it is scientific; but this change is not amelioration. For every thing that is given something is taken" (*E*, 279). Thus "no man improves" when the improvement of everyone is the aim of men. Conformity is always, even in altruism, a detriment to the individual's ability to grow, which is also his or her self-sufficiency: "Society is a joint-stock company, in which the members agree, for the better securing of his bread to each shareholder, to surrender the liberty and culture of the eater. The virtue in most request is conformity. Self-Reliance is its aversion" (*E*, 261). Solvency, by contrast, would be precisely a kind of monetary singularity; loosely speaking, an economic "health." More than that, to be "solvent" one must not simply have enough to pay one's "debts," but enough to pay one's "way"—one must, as it were, make *profit*. The economic metaphor centers on what might be called a high-capitalist formulation of the reading self, according to which the "essential" capital that it retains in self-reliance is also something that gains surplus value: "that which a man is does always by necessity acquire, and what the man acquires is living property, which does not wait the beck of rulers, or mobs, or revolutions, or fire, or storm, or bankruptcies, but perpetually renews itself wherever the man breathes" (*E*, 281).

What could "surplus value" be, with respect to a self and, more importantly, with respect to a reader? In the two metaphors I have so far outlined, the same conflict at the root of all Emerson's theorizations of the reader's relation to history again comes to light. With respect to a self troped as health or "soundness," self-reliance consists precisely in remaining at rest, and therefore in an independence from the "foreign," either as reliance or obligation. As health, the self's integrity is a stasis, a dispassionate perception most conducive, perhaps, to a hermeneutical mode of reading. However, for the metaphorics of economy, the self cannot remain still, but *must* become acquisitive: it has a vital interest in moving forward, in acquiring influence or in becoming "fate." Troped as capital, as a *richesse* of "fatal" expenditure, self-reliance is precisely the "aversion" of stasis, conducive, perhaps, to a rhetorical style of rereading.

To understand fully Emerson's characterization of the self/reader as singularity or impertinence, both of these metaphorical systems must be combined. The self, as "capital," is an inherently futural or intentional structure, accruing influence as the basic form of its relation to others. But it does so only *as*, or in the form of, a health, that is, as static or hypostatic in its (self)-established perspective toward past influences. The self that reads self-reliantly is intentional toward futures, but troped as resting in its present "knowledge" of the past. It is an acquisitive capitalist who has succeeded in appearing in the guise of a benefactor instead of a blight, a kind of Carnegie or Morgan of interpretation. In Bloom's work, such a furtive dialectical ambivalence was described as the poet's unconscious refiguration of his own "perverse" perspectival reading into a "health[y]" objectivity: "The strong poet's imagination *cannot see itself as perverse*; its own inclination must be health, the true priority. Hence the *clinamen* [or, 'swerve' of misprision] is that the precursor went wrong by *failing to swerve*, at just such a bias, just then and there, at one angle of vision, whether acute or obtuse" (*AI*, 85). But what Bloom identifies as an "unconscious" trope need not be considered as such, although it may yet persist as a kind of delusion. Following the logic of Emerson's metaphorics, the putative health of the revisor is not, precisely, his *own* false self-hypostasis, but rather the retrospective hypostatic position he is granted by the readers who trope him as the objective perceiver of an essentially paraliptical past. In other words, "health" is not a subjective stance so much as the metaphor of a consummated fatality of reading, an influence fully purchased. And thus the unconscious "mis-" of "misreading" is a structural attribute of the reading process, like Nietzsche's "error" or Heidegger's "limitation"—a difference not of two voices "in" the self, but between one "healthy" reading and another.

"Self-reliance" has the structure of what Bloom calls, vaguely, a "strong" revision, one with historical effects. But I would call this structure, more concretely, *an accomplished paralipsis*, the construction of a past fated to future readers as the meaning that the revision itself reads, but effectively effaced *as* a revision and therefore troped as "healthy" rather than "perverse." Economic integrity, like capital itself, has an occult quality. Like an accumulation of capital sufficiently great to accrue profit with no apparent effort, the reader "who has more obedience than I masters me, though he should not raise his finger. Round him I must revolve by the gravitation of spirits" (*E*, 272). This occlusion of the reading self, which in Heidegger's *Nietzsche* occurs as the elision of his own activity by the imputation of the "proper" meaning within Nietzsche's text, is a moment of furtive interpretive blackmail, a fateful and manipulative anticipation, extending into the future, of the reading and all its potential new encounters. It is the coercion of another revision-encounter, in the guise of free trade.

"Manhood": Force and Causation

I turn, finally, to Emerson's third and oddest metaphorization of self-reliance in the essay. Emerson writes: "Who can . . . avoid all pledges, and having observed, observe again from the same unaffected, unbiased, unbridled, unaffrighted innocence, must always be formidable" (*E*, 261). Such an "innocence," or immunity from the effects of biases or reliances, Emerson names "manhood."[21] Describing an impertinent "formidable" man, Emerson writes, "He would utter opinions on all passing affairs, which being seen to be not private, but necessary, would sink like darts into the ears of men, and put them in fear" (*E*, 261). The rapacious tone of "sink" and "darts" is just as characteristic of the essay as any of its other impertinent polemics. In general, when impertinence is retroped as "manhood," Emerson's analysis of the integrity of self-reliance becomes bound to a phallic and rather violent sexual metaphorics. Self-reliance is "firmness," and to be "firm" is what is required of the self that would create futures: "Ask nothing of men, and in the endless mutation, thou only firm column must presently appear the upholder of all that surrounds thee" (*E*, 282). To be firm requires "force," as in the phrase "force of character": "Act singly, and what you have already done singly will justify you now. Greatness appeals to the future. If I can be firm enough to-day to do right, and scorn eyes, I must have done so much right before as to defend me now. . . . Always scorn appearances, and you always may. The force of character is cumulative. All the foregone days of virtue work their health into this" (*E*, 266). Emerson repeats the word "force" throughout the essay: the self is "force"; he speaks of "the cumulative force of a whole life's cultivation" with which one can present a truly self-reliant opinion (*E*, 278); and he warns that by failing to abide by our own impressions we "shall be forced to take with shame our own opinion from another" (*E*, 259).

Moreover, the threat of social obligations or debts is directly absorbed into the figure of "force." Social convention, as one would expect, but in a phrasing that perhaps rings surprisingly of the biblical injunction against onanism, is seen, in its own "deadness," as diminishing or deadening the force of the individual:

> The objection to conforming to usages that have become dead to you is, that it *scatters your force*. It loses your time and blurs the impression of your character. If you maintain a dead church, contribute to a dead Bible-society, vote with a great party either for the government or against it, spread your table like base housekeepers,—under all these screens I have difficulty to detect the precise man you are. And, of course, so much *force* is withdrawn from your proper life. But do your work and I shall know you. Do your work, and you shall *reinforce* yourself. (*E*, 263–64, my emphasis)

Death and "scattered force" can be linked by Emerson because the logic of the metaphors, like that of "impertinence," associates a personal or subjective ethics with creation: force is like potency or fertility, and, because fertility is seen as male attribute, "scattered force" is like "spilled seed." These figural connections are already apparent where Emerson wishes to have the "manhood to withhold" the charitable dollar, and perhaps even when he claims that it is preferable to be inconsistent than to follow the precedent of one's own erstwhile opinions. A demand for creation, for the new, is asserted over and against *any* repetition:

> Suppose you should contradict yourself; what then? It seems to be a rule of wisdom never to rely on your memory alone, scarcely even in acts of pure memory, but to bring the past for judgment into the thousand-eyed present, and live ever in a new day. . . . Speak what you think now in hard words, and to-morrow speak what to-morrow thinks in hard words again, though it contradict every thing you said to-day. (*E*, 265)

But above all—and this provides the crux of the entire metaphorical system of "Self-Reliance"—firmness, force, hardness, and manhood are all linked by Emerson's repeated exhortation to *cause*.[22] Here the one-sided quasi dialectic of impertinence, and in fact all of the various moments in which Emerson persuades the rereader to exert influence rather than *be* influenced him- or herself, are grounded in a basic metaphor of sexual creativity.[23] Properly conserved, for Emerson, "manhood" is a potency, and potency essentially fertility.[24] A "man's" progeny, or, as I cited earlier, his fated "children," are the thoughts and actions of other "men," which he creates by engendering himself as their historical precedent:

> The man must be so much, that he must make all circumstances indifferent. Every true man is a cause, a country, and an age; requires infinite spaces and numbers and time fully to accomplish his design;—and posterity seems to follow his steps as a train of clients. A man Caesar is born, and for ages after we have a Roman

Empire. Christ is born, and millions of minds so grow and cleave to his genius, that he is confounded with virtue and the possible of man. An institution is the lengthened shadow of one man . . . , and all history resolves itself very easily into the biography of a few stout and earnest persons. (*E*, 267)

Avoid influences, be original, and you provide yourself the opportunity to create yourself *as an influence on someone else*,[25] to become the paraliptical bespeaker of another's rereading of the past. Self-reliance, standing above the fate of received convention, becomes itself the fate of future readings, even if, ironically, it is reliant on being interpreted *as* such. We may recall what I earlier called Emerson's manifesto of the interpretive self as a historical singularity: "Perception is not whimsical, but fatal. If I see a trait, my children will see it after me, and in course of time, all mankind,—although it may chance that no one has seen it before me" (*E*, 269). The "man" engenders his "children" at the same moment as, and because, he resists being engendered by another—because only he is (indirectly, through them) his own parent. Thus although every "man" is potentially causal, the "man" who fails to be original produces only illusionary progeny, has a false pregnancy, a deliverance which does not itself deliver; he is insufficiently forceful and pays the price by failing to engender those who will engender *him*.

Here is a wholly rhetorical understanding of textual histories, not merely in the sense that "the historical" is a product of persuasion, of the rhetorical process of the reader and writer of history, but in the more crucial sense, that the reader and writer of history becomes its interpreter by *resisting* the fatalism of the past, resisting *understanding* the (historical) determinism of texts whose completedness tends to persist into the future. To revise the past forcefully means to have compelled it to speak a revisionist language, a *new* perception, as its own, not as rhetoric but as a fate, a "truth." In the history of texts, rereading represses itself, and *is* its own oblivion, in the form of persistence into futures *as* a mere past, as something merely understood. In the words of Siegfried Kracauer, who shares with Emerson almost to the letter the terminology of a historical fatalism despite differing theoretical aims: "Once a vision becomes an institution, clouds of dust gather about it, blurring its contours and contents. The history of ideas is a history of misunderstandings."[26]

Divinity

Being a "man," for Emerson, inasmuch as the metaphorics of manhood in this essay are bound up with the thematics of historical influence, means to impose, even to rape, to "sink like darts into the ears of other men." But we should not balk at the possibility that even such violent figures represent quite typical and conventional structures of academic reading—that even the genteel "correction" of the revision-encounter characteristically, and even structurally, takes a rapacious stance toward the future readers it attempts to sway, albeit a stance effaced as the confidence of a healthy, objective integrity (*E*, 260).[27] Such imposition can be viewed as a combination of the figure of integrity with the demand to look to the future. To be a reading "self" would be to engage in the practice of *revising* the future's rereading of the past, but to do so precisely by virtue of a healthily occluded parapractice of rereading paralipses.

I began by noting that Emerson couches his initial analysis of selfhood in terms of a radical anticitational practice; but I ended, just now, by describing that same practice as bound to the veiled exertion of will to power over other readers. The dialectic of influence under which "self-reliance" forms itself entails that a singularity achieved by impertinent reading of historical texts is impossible without the creation of future reading practices that acknowledge one's revision(ism) *as* the "proper" understanding, future readings to which one's perception of the past, qua perception, is fated. Thus any revisionist anticitational reading practice is tantamount to the causing of a future practice that *will* cite; that is, will cite precisely oneself, or rather, one's own reading. For a "self" that rereads is, strictly speaking, no "subject," but rather a coercive anticipation of its own ex post facto reconstruction, a prolepsis in which one's rereading becomes the fateful object, or strong paraliptical intention, for the rereadings of other "subject"-readers.

What I am describing is what Emerson calls the "divinity" or "the divine idea"[28] of self-reliance, its capacity to *be*—which, I would assert, means *to get itself troped as*—an "unmoved mover" or "uncreated creator," a moment of relation to history in which a created change supersedes an inherited determinism.[29] Since the revisor that Emerson tropes as "man" is a "fate," it already supersedes itself in becoming itself. Logically speaking (if no longer quite pragmatically), the revisor is already *übermenschlich*, a superhuman or overhuman agent.[30] More properly, the reader is an agent that no "man" could be, but only a whole history of men and women who reread, and have reread, "him." A successful revision, one that subverts historical chronology sufficiently to get its own *apophrades* troped as a "truth" about the historical text, is a superperformative "lie" against the historical determinism which forms all reading subjects: "Self-existence is the attribute of the Supreme Cause, and it constitutes the measure of good by the degree to which *it enters into all lower forms*" (*E*, 272, my emphasis). As Bloom writes, "The poet steps out from man into god" (*AI*, 116); or Nietzsche: "I am no man, I am dynamite."[31]

The "divinity" I describe is, in the end, neither an attribute of reading selves, nor just a romantic hyperbole (despite the extravagant terminology), but simply the metaphor of a structural condition of even the most mundane revisionist practices, the most conventional revision-encounters. This the case, first, because the authority granted to a particular revision as a "truth" about the text—say, Heidegger's self-effacing confrontation with Nietzsche's text as an implicit anticipation of the question of Being—fully relies on whatever "humane" readership it is able to muster, a readership whose faith in the revision is, as it were, freely given, and may be rescinded at the instigation of a new revision-encounter. Second, it is the case because the most common conventions of revisionist practice—the synecdochal "we" that effaces the will to power of the revisor over a future readership; the claim that a revised text is "experienced" when in fact the "experience" is self-effacingly imputed *by* the revision; the denial of perspectivism, and of the artificiality of the prior text's paraliptical voice, in the conventional pretense to a rigorous or objective "*letting* the text *speak*"—are themselves tools for the manufacture of authority, dissimulated mechanisms of a reading's auto-genesis *as* historical *fact*. All these conventions are quite tenuous. They exist to be exposed, not by "criticism" so much as by a further revision-encounter, the substitution of yet a new authority over the text, and therefore a new campaign for election to interpretive "truth" among readers:

> The divine authority of the man thus should be the surest defense which secures the doctrine and keeps from it at all the majestic distance of the divine all impertinences; instead of which the content and the form of the doctrine must allow itself to be criticized and sniffed at—before one is able in this way to reach the conclusion that it was a revelation or no. And meanwhile the apostle and God must presumably wait at the door or in the porter's lodge until the case has been decided by the wise men in the *belétage*.[32]

SEVEN

Thought for Food (Eating Eternal Return)

They treat the philosopher's hat
Left thoughtlessly behind
As one of the relics of the mind.

— WALLACE STEVENS, "THE PREJUDICE AGAINST THE PAST"

Posthumous Thinking

"Some are born posthumously," Nietzsche writes about himself in *Ecce Homo*, a formula which suggests the structure of the revision-encounter.[1] Heidegger seems to paraphrase such a formula in an early section his lectures in which he gives a brief history of Nietzsche's published oeuvre: "[Nietzsche's] philosophy proper was left behind as posthumous work [*Nachlaß*]" (*Ne*, 1:9; *Ng*, 1:17). Heidegger's aim here is to criticize the editors of Nietzsche's *Nachlaß*, who, although they did make public Nietzsche's writing, specifically the previously uncollated fragments of *Der Wille zur Macht*, nevertheless did not and could not achieve the publication of Nietzsche's "genuine philosophical thought [*Nietzsches eigentliches philosophisches Denken*]" (*Ne*, 1:24; *Ng*,

1:32). Mere publication fails, for Heidegger, to be genuine philosophy because what is genuine or proper among Nietzsche's leavings cannot be equivalent to what merely comes authentically from his pen. Such a legacy is posthumous in far too mundane and merely *historisch* a sense. Indeed, with respect to Nietzsche it is precisely what was *not* put on paper that matters. As the reading of the relation of art and truth demonstrates, Nietzsche's proper thought is that which he didn't and couldn't actually write. Because the too-scholarly editors of the *Nachlaß* do not *read*—which is to say, since they do not *revise*—Nietzsche's fragmentary work, their presentation is too factually correct to be true to Nietzsche's "essential philosophical thought," which instead will have to be drawn out of the "innermost will" of the materials attributed to Nietzsche's pen. As I began to argue in earlier chapters, Nietzsche's fragmentariness is no "extrinsic" coincidence of his biography or bibliography, but rather a structural condition of his essentially limited metaphysical perspective, a limitation to be read in such a way that a proper Nietzsche may be born posthumously through Heidegger's rereading, or through our own if we follow Heidegger's "thought-path."

So while it may appear obvious that *Der Wille zur Macht* lies in pieces for unastonishing reasons, for instance because Nietzsche went insane before he could finish it, precisely the obviousness of such a conclusion is contested by Heidegger's lectures, which consistently scorn the sort of biographical study that could lead to it. In his second lecture course in 1937, entitled "The Eternal Recurrence of the Same," Heidegger attributes Nietzsche's fragmentariness to "something that no longer pertains to him, the thinker, but to which he can only devote himself" (*Ne*, 2:13; *Ng*, 1:264).[2] This "something" is Nietzsche's "metaphysical task [*metaphysische Aufgabe*]," and Heidegger hyperbolically declares that "for [Nietzsche] that task alone is reality proper" (*Ne*, 2:10; *Ng*, 1:261). But the fulfillment of the task is also identified by Heidegger's reading as the proper *Ereignis* of Nietzsche's particular limited insight into the history of Being, an "event" that of course remains only implicit until drawn out by a rereading:[3]

> The range of the thinker's insight is no longer [within] the horizon of his "personal experiences"; something other than he himself passes beneath, above [and beyond] him and is henceforth there, something that no longer belongs to him, the thinker, but to which he can only devote himself. This characteristic of the *Ereignis* is not contradicted by the fact that the thinker at first and for a long time preserves the insight as his own, inasmuch as he must become the site of its development. (*Ne*, 2:13; *Ng*, 1:264)

Heidegger's language, as usual, dislodges Nietzsche's volition as a potential source of his proper philosophy, positioning Nietzsche's writing as only the "site [*Stätte*]" of a reflection and development that is immanent in a far larger historical movement, one which remains essentially beyond Nietzsche, "rooted in the historical context of two millennia" (*Ne*, 2:23–24; *Ng*, 1:275). From such an angle of vision, the circumstances of Nietzsche's writing, for instance his biographical or publishing history—in general the local and personal conditions which contributed to the text's production—*must* be less important than the inherited historical-metaphysical conditions that define what the specific written statements do *not* state; and all the more because Nietzsche is not fully aware of these latter conditions, even though he is quite deliberate in his focus on the former. The reading of Emerson's work I have conducted in the previous chapter ought to lead us to suspect any such conditioning of "Nietzsche's fundamental thought." If what Nietzsche left unsaid was actually unsayable by him—if his limitation is construed, within the *epochē* of the revision-encounter, as a metaphysical limitation, not merely as the axiomatic difference between one writer (who didn't finish) and another (who perhaps has)—then such an "inherent" inability is likely the product, not the starting point, of Heidegger's encounter with Nietzsche's text. Nietzsche, Heidegger suggests, was fatally, not coincidently, incapable of finishing. But the difficulty of persuading his readers of the plausibility of this bit of antihistoricist impertinence emerges in the often strange thought-paths along which Heidegger must proceed in order to establish the metaphysical immanence of Nietzsche's work, and the irrelevance to which Heidegger must attempt to relegate the peculiar historical circumstances of that work.

In fact, despite Heidegger's declaration that he will de-emphasize Nietzsche's "personal experiences" in deference to his more crucial posthumous task, the problem of Nietzsche's autobiographical texts continues with surprising persistence to occupy Heidegger's second lecture course, ultimately taking up most of the space that was supposed to be devoted to more obviously metaphysical matters such as the relation between will to power and eternal return. I will argue that Heidegger's ambivalence over Nietzsche's personal history arises because, particularly with respect to the doctrine of the eternal return, Nietzsche's use of autobiographical data, and more generally of the concept of "life," are intimately bound up with his philosophical thinking, and especially his late thinking. Heidegger is required rather more blatantly than usual to revise instead of merely sidestep Nietzsche's own relation to personal experience, although the difficulty of doing so is indicated even by the sheer space Heidegger devotes to what he calls a "preliminary" matter. Overall, my argument in this final chapter is twofold: on the one hand, I analyze a new instance of Heidegger's revision-encounter with Nietzsche, a divergence over the status of autobiographical texts, the concept of "life," and, finally, the particular figure of food or eating. On the other hand, I engage in specific criticisms of Heidegger's reading, an activity which must be considered as initiating a revision-encounter of my own with Heidegger's text, one which oversteps what I have called the *epochē* of my description of Heidegger's revisionism. Such overstepping may be thought of as an Emersonian rudeness toward the occluded hypostases with which Heidegger's text requires one to concur in order to "follow" him down his putatively more essentially Nietzschean thought-path.

Preliminaries

Throughout his lectures, Heidegger's explicit goal remains to establish Nietzsche's "fundamental metaphysical position [*metaphysische Grund-stellung*],"[4] although what Heidegger construes to be the content of that position shifts over time. In the lectures of the summer of 1937, Heidegger asserts that Nietzsche's position is "captured [*bezeichnet*]" by the "eternal return of the same" (*Ne*, 2:5; *Ng*, 1:255),[5] which he now calls Nietzsche's "fundamental doctrine [*Grundlehre*]" (*Ne*, 2:6; *Ng*, 1:256).[6] An interpretation of eternal return therefore becomes, at this stage, Heidegger's crucial step toward identifying Nietzsche's relation to the history of metaphysics, and in turn for locating that history overall with respect to Heidegger's own thought. Because Nietzsche's fundamental position is the "last [position] that Western thought has achieved" (*Ne*, 2:7; *Ng*, 1:258), the doctrine of eternal return—the "capturing" doctrine of that position—"ends" metaphysics, which now appears and can be understood in its entirety: "Nietzsche's doctrine of eternal return is not merely one doctrine among others about *das Seiende*; it arises from the most stringent confrontation with Platonic-Christian ways of thinking and from their impact on, and deterioration in, modern times. Nietzsche posits these ways of thinking as the fundamental earmark [*Grundzug*] of Western thinking as such and of its history" (*Ne*, 2:7; *Ng*, 1:257–58). Heidegger's strategy, within this characteristic apocalyptic setting, is always to interpret the doctrine of eternal return insofar *as* it is, paraliptically, the last metaphysics. He asks, in other words, why and how Western philosophy anticipates its own ending when Nietzsche thinks this particular thought, and what metaphysics *is*, such that the thought of eternal return concludes it.[7]

Since this one doctrine is the synecdoche of metaphysics overall, it also becomes our access to the original ground of metaphysics after Nietzsche, or more precisely, after the historical moment in which Being, in and as its own history, has "granted" the capturing doctrine. Eternal return is, for this moment, the presencing nonpresence, the saying not-saying, of the "to be" of philosophical history itself, expressed within the limitation of Nietzsche's thought.

Yet for all its hyperbolic reach, the doctrine of eternal return remains tied to very particular texts and contexts, namely, to a certain peculiar nineteenth-century writer's life, a tie which Nietzsche himself foregrounds. For instance in *Ecce Homo* he gives detailed descriptions of the "history" of his life at the moment the thought "came to him," describing date, time, place, the medium on which the thought was written down, the fact that he had "gone walking," and so on:[8]

> I shall now relate the history of *Zarathustra*. The basic conception of the work, *the thought of eternal return*, the highest formula of affirmation that can ever be achieved, belongs to the month of August of the year 1881. It is jotted on a page signed with the phrase "6,000 feet beyond humanity and time." On that day I had gone walking in the woods by the lake of Silvaplana. By a mightily towering pyramidal boulder not far from Surlei I stopped. The thought came to me then.[9]

The hints of supernatural qualities in this setting do not obscure the fact that Nietzsche arrived at his thought, or it arrived at him, on his more or less daily walk. Other matters of local history also intrude upon the originary scene of the thought. As Heidegger is compelled to note, some of the sources of the doctrine of return are quite particular nineteenth-century models of cosmology and the natural sciences to which Nietzsche seems to have ascribed. Indeed, as Heidegger notes with apparent scorn, Nietzsche himself "pursued a 'scientific side' to the doctrine of return" (*Ne*, 2:83; *Ng*, 1:340).[10] And Heidegger comments that "in letters written during these years [he] speaks of plans to study mathematics and the natural sciences," ostensibly to establish eternal return as a scientifically supportable doctrine.[11] All of these contextual details, like the "scholarly" efforts of the *Nachlaß* publishers, must be explained or overstepped if we are to "really penetrate the fundamental thought of Nietzsche's philosophy proper" (*Ne*, 2:15; *Ng*, 1:266).

Therefore, before setting out on the monumental venture of reading eternal return as a synecdoche of metaphysics, Heidegger launches into what appears to be a nonphilosophical or prephilosophical digression, "a preliminary presentation of the doctrine of the eternal return of the same in terms of its genesis, its configurations, and its domain" (*Ne*, 2:8; *Ng*, 1:258). This preliminary work fulfills certain academic obligations, such as citing the places where eternal return appears in Nietzsche's work, defining the historical and philosophical scope of the doctrine's application, and examining autobiographical materials that pertain to Nietzsche's discovery of it. For instance, Heidegger's "preliminary report" includes background material about the nihilism of Platonic metaphysics, as well as a discussion of natural science as the source of the language in Nietzsche's "proofs" of return, because both of these matters bear upon what Nietzsche believed to be the framework and context of return. In addition, Heidegger goes to some lengths to connect some seemingly noncrucial matters to his analysis of Nietzsche's doctrine, for instance the fact that Nietzsche was thinking about "rings" and "encircling" already at the age of nineteen, in this brief reflection on ambition: "Where is the ring that ultimately encircles [the human being]? Is it the world? Is it God?"[12] Heidegger concludes that this bit of text from Nietzsche's school years foreshadows his concern for things that return in his philosophy "two decades later." In any case, the citation seems preliminary enough alongside the far more comprehensive problem of reading eternal return as the end of Western philosophy, especially considering Heidegger's customary disdain for biographical or historical-contextual study.[13]

It is surprising, then, that autobiographical fragments like the one just cited get considerable attention in Heidegger's "preliminary report" and, moreover, as I have noted, that the "report" itself swells until it consumes the bulk of the second lecture course. It is not until about the last fifth of the course that Heidegger actually gets back to the issue of Nietzsche's "fundamental metaphysical position." Or, to describe the shape of this course more exactly, the problem of Nietzsche's fundamental position is eventually woven into what was to have been preliminary, but which persists as the central focus all the way through, namely, the "genesis, configurations, and domain" of return. These matters, then, would seem to have been more than "preliminary" after all, more than just the preparatory chore of documenting the "context and mode of presentation" of Nietzsche's "philosophical communication" (*Ne*, 2:19; *Ng*, 1:269). But why should a "preliminary report" acquire this dominant position? The answer to this question, I will argue, is that certain facets of *Nietzsche's* thinking about return demand precisely such a lengthy consideration of what might otherwise have been, for Heidegger, mere artifacts of the historical timing of the thought's discovery. Nietzsche's own polemical concentration on just this sort of artifact, within discussions of return and topics such as "life" that relate to it, demands both attention and revision from Heidegger's reading, whereas elsewhere Heidegger can afford some degree of contempt for these issues. Particularly here, within the reading of return, Heidegger's usual interpretive technique of "simplifying" Nietzsche's presentation to its essence is compelled to accommodate itself to a number of "inessential" or para-textual matters.

A second, more specific aspect of Heidegger's procedure also requires notice. His emphasis on Nietzsche's autobiographical fragments, that is to say, on the portion of the "preliminary report" about the "genesis" of return, adopts a rather peculiar attitude. There is a persistent and sometimes hyperbolic ethical tone in Heidegger's references to Nietzsche's life, underscored, for instance, by the superlative "never" in this passage: "Nietzsche's reports about himself may therefore never [*niemals*] be read as though they were just someone's diary entries, or solely to satisfy our idle curiosity" (*Ne*, 2:10; *Ng*, 1:261). The same rigorous criteria are applied even to the passage I cited above from Nietzsche's nineteenth year, on "rings" and "encircling," thus bringing it under the purview of a philosophical project that seems far beyond its scope: "If Nietzsche repeatedly meditates on himself, yet it is the very opposite of a vain self-mirroring. It is in fact his ever renewed readiness for the sacrifice that his task demanded of him; it is a necessity that Nietzsche had sensed ever since the days of his wakeful youth" (*Ne*, 2:9; *Ng*, 1:260). Something in these statements seems defensive, as if Heidegger were in fact conceding the plausibility of reading Nietzsche's texts as no more than "vain self-mirroring." Just earlier he admits that Nietzsche can appear to demonstrate "an exaggerated tendency to self-observation and self-exhibition" (*Ne*, 2:9; *Ng*, 1:259). But for Heidegger precisely such an appearance of frivolity and exaggeration must be counteracted for the reader: "*all* of Nietzsche's autobiographical observations" must be read as though "they pertain to the uniqueness of his mission [*Sendung*], a mission that was his and his alone" (*Ne*, 2:10; *Ng*, 1:261). These are exacting restrictions to place upon fragments spanning twenty-five years, and which rarely even try to make themselves cohere. But the restrictions become simply outrageous when Heidegger also demands that the reader obey them "no matter how often appearances might suggest the contrary" (*Ne*, 2:10; *Ng*, 1:261).

Here is interpretation by hermeneutical *fiat*, or, in short, no longer interpretation at all; it is with such statements that Heidegger comes closest to Emerson's impertinent "self-reliant" reader, at least in practice if not in spirit. For to presume that all fragments of a person's life history can point in only one direction rudely forecloses any possible reading of these fragments such as they *are*, namely, as fragments of an idiosyncratic and uncompleted biography. In the mode in which Heidegger demands we read, it can no longer be the "self" telling its story in Nietzsche's autobiography, but someone or something considerably more knowledgeable. And thus a text quite other than autobiography is being interpreted by Heidegger in the "preliminaries" to this course, no matter what he would prefer appearances to suggest: not the relation of Nietzsche's life to his philosophy, nor "life" as a context for thinking, but simply the same implicit paraliptical directedness that makes Nietzsche's work putatively about the concordance of art and truth or the synthesis of will to power and eternal return, a directedness toward "tasks" that are in fact discerned and/or supplied after the fact through an elaborate rhetorical mechanism. What Nietzsche left in a fragmented form, Heidegger will "sacrifice [*opfern*]," to adopt his own word, to his own "task" of unifying Nietzsche's work. Thus—and note the superlatives here—"*Nietzsche's retrospective and circumspective glances at his life are only ever prospective glances into his task. For him that [task] itself is reality proper*" (*Ne*, 2:10; *Ng*, 1:261, Heidegger's emphasis).

Why should the reader accept such a claim? It is one thing to understand Heidegger's aspiration to unify will to power and eternal return, and thereby to overcome what he construes as the essential fragmentariness of the texts in which these doctrines appear. It is more difficult to grasp, first, Heidegger's need to concentrate on the autobiographical texts at all and, second, even given that concentration, his drive to herd Nietzsche's life so doggedly into a single direction. The topic at hand, after all, is not Nietzsche's autobiography per se, but rather the doctrine of eternal return as the "thought of thoughts," and "a matter for this century and the century to come" (*Ne*, 2:83; *Ng*, 1:340). What has Nietzsche's life, such as it was, got to do with these historic matters? To pursue this question, and to pursue Heidegger's peculiar revision or suppression of it, we must look more closely at the doctrine of return itself.

The Return of the Thinker

In a passage in *Thus Spoke Zarathustra* entitled "The Vision and the Riddle," Zarathustra tells how he climbed up a mountain, bearing on his shoulders a dwarf he calls a "spirit of gravity."[14] At a point in the story Zarathustra decides to unburden himself of this dwarf. He does so by piquing the dwarf's curiosity with a riddle, challenging him to respond to what Zarathustra calls "my abysmal thought." The dwarf, intrigued, jumps to the ground. The pair now stands beside a gateway, upon which is inscribed the word "Moment [*Augenblick*]":[15]

> "Behold this gateway, dwarf! . . . It has two faces; two paths meet here; no one has yet followed either to its end. This long lane stretches back for an eternity. And the long lane out there, that is another eternity. They contradict one another, these paths; they butt heads against one another [*sie stoßen sich gerade vor den Kopf*]; and it is here at this gateway that they come together. The name of the gateway is inscribed above: "Moment." But whoever would follow one of them, on and on, farther and farther—do you believe, dwarf, that these paths contradict each other eternally?"[16]

The dwarf answers this question with a piece of "wisdom" that sounds like a paraphrase or parody of what is presumably Zarathustra's or Nietzsche's own conclusion: "'Everything straight deceives,' murmured the dwarf contemptuously. 'All truth is curved; time itself is a circle.'"[17] In fact the dwarf has guessed Zarathustra's riddle: if the two paths continue to eternity, one forward and one backward, they both end up in the same place. This answer to the riddle *is* the doctrine of the eternal return in a nutshell; there is nothing lacking in the dwarf's figuration. Or, as Heidegger writes: "The two of them, the dwarf and Zarathustra, say the same thing" (*Ne*, 2:53; *Ng*, 1:307).

Nevertheless the dwarf's answer displeases Zarathustra, who replies angrily, "You spirit of gravity . . . don't make things too easy for yourself!" (*Ne*, 2:42; *Ng*, 1:200). Zarathustra does not suggest that the dwarf's answer is incorrect; only that he has answered too easily—"dwarfishly."[18] In some sense, still vague, the dwarf has failed to account for the fact that the two paths "offend" or "contradict" or "butt heads with" one another (*sich stoßen vor den Kopf*) despite their ultimate identity. Or, as Heidegger suggests, to guess (*erraten*) the riddle is not the same as really to get hold of (*fassen*) it (*Ne*, 2:42, 43; *Ng*, 1:294, 295). What, then, is the difference between the dwarf's response and the response Zarathustra is looking for? Or in other words, what will constitute Zarathustra's revision of the dwarf's version of eternal return?

Zarathustra rephrases the dwarf's answer in the form of a new question, this time not demanding an answer, but rather the proper *way* of questioning, the proper emphasis:

> "Behold," I went on, "this moment. . . . What do you make of this moment, Dwarf? Must not this gateway, too, already have been there? And are not all things knotted together so firmly that this moment draws after it *all* that is to come? Therefore—itself too? . . .
>
> "And this slow spider, which crawls in the moonlight, and I and you in the gateway, whispering together, whispering of eternal things—must not all of us have been there before? And return [*wiederkommen*] and walk in that other lane, out there, before us, in this long dreadful lane—must we not eternally return [*ewig wiederkommen*]?"[19]

What is properly to be thought here is not the returning itself, but the moment—presumably, the very moment in which the thinker is standing in the gateway—the moment of thinking about return that the gateway itself labels, the same moment in which "you and I . . . [are] whispering of eternal things." Considering return in this light, what we perceive to return are not "events" generally, or the abstraction "time" within the content of the thought, but rather the activity of thinking return itself, which *is* the particular moment at hand, the moment occurring now, beneath the gateway. If we can palpably imagine—and take ourselves seriously in imagining—that the gateway, and ourselves, and this moment of thinking are precisely the things that return, then within the logic of the figure we compel this thinking itself to return: we render thinking eternal. Return troped as a gateway in an unending path is a paradigmatic self-actualizing reflection, a thought of considerable performative or self-performative power. By thinking return at this particular "moment" of the path, *the thinker* "returns."[20]

The proper thinking of this particular thought is sheer action, an effective willing; what we think, now, in the moment, is what *will* then return. This is also the source of the difficulty of answering Zarathustra's question. Heidegger glosses Nietzsche's assertion that the two paths "butt heads against one another" as follows: "Whoever stands in the moment is turned in two ways: for him past and future run up *against one another.* He lets what runs counter to [or in] itself come to collision, though not to a standstill, by cultivating and sustaining the strife between what is assigned him as a task [*Aufgegebenen*] and what has been given him as his endowment [*Mitgegebenen*]" (*Ne*, 2:57; *Ng*, 1:311–12, Heidegger's emphasis). But the dwarf's abstract or objective answer about "circles" and "eternity" does not "sustain the strife" implied by the moment of return; as Heidegger says, the dwarf "keeps to the outside, perches on the periphery" (*Ne*, 2:57; *Ng*, 1:312).[21] He treats the moment merely categorically, like any other passing bit of time, and therefore gains no power from the act of thinking to determine what will return, no power of decision. In short, the dwarf's answer is the sort that Heidegger would call "logically correct but metaphysically untrue" (*Ne*, 1:147; *Ng*, 1:173), an empty shell or mere simulacrum of thought, a mere content but not yet a *proper* thinking activity. Return as a falsifiable statement about the world has no effect on anything. But as a reflection on its own activity, the thought has the uncanny potency to alter the world's history in surprising ways.

Thus eternal return becomes, through Heidegger's reading, the paradigmatic thought about the determinative, creative capacity of the action of thinking in and upon life. With this in mind we can begin to construct an argument as to why Heidegger's interpretation of eternal return, and of Nietzsche's "fundamental metaphysical position," should require the oddly emphatic references to Nietzsche's autobiography. The initial premises of the argument will be familiar: first, Nietzsche's thinking, as Heidegger continues to insist, is the culmination of Western philosophy. Second, especially in the context of this lecture course, Nietzsche's fundamental thought is the doctrine of eternal return. A third, more novel premise can now be suggested: the most crucial aspect of the thought of return, and thus of Nietzsche's "metaphysics" at large, is the thinker in the moment of thinking. We cannot forget, as the hyperbolic idealism of Platonism or the dwarfish pessimism of a nihilistic positivism would tempt us to do, that the thinker is neither an abstraction nor a mere object, but rather a *living* thinker, who therefore always thinks from a particular perspective. Thinking is an activity of a specific life.

Philosophy and Autobiography

Provisionally conceding eternal return, with Heidegger, to be the central thought of metaphysics, we may conclude the following: Western philosophy, which begins as a question about Being, "ends" with a particular moment in the life of a thinker, a particular living perspective of what Nietzsche calls the "organic world."[22] Here my own reading borders on somewhat new territory, a Nietzschean revision-encounter with Heidegger himself, even though Heidegger acknowledges, albeit somewhat in the same "objective" manner in which the dwarf avers the circularity of time, that "philosophy is [always] located in a particular place."[23] For Nietzsche—and then, far more problematically, for Heidegger rereading Nietzsche—metaphysics is reduced to a real life-context, to a physics of a sort, the thinking of a "real" moment. In Nietzsche such a reduction is more or less explicitly a critical gesture toward the idealism of Platonism, and a destruction of metaphysics inasmuch as the latter is organized around abstract categories and abstractionist habits. What was excluded or benighted for Platonic metaphysics, a certain interpretation of the sensuous—but in addition, I will argue, was excluded by Heidegger's attempt to dispense with the "preliminaries" of return—is, through Nietzsche's critical reversal of Platonism, seen to be primary, indeed to have been primary all along.

As I suggested earlier, with respect to Nietzsche's description in *Ecce Homo* of the moment of the first thought of return—and this is apparent throughout *Ecce Homo*—part of Nietzsche's critical practice is to invoke himself as the primary example of the active thinker. For this reason, the critique of philosophical thinking as an activity of life occurs substantially in his autobiographical texts. Heidegger acknowledges the importance of this self-referentiality in the following passage, which interprets eternal return as a "counterthought" through which a theoretical thinking is remerged with the *praxis* from which, in the Platonic tradition, it had sought to distinguish itself:

> Part of [Nietzsche's mission] consisted in making visible through the telling of his own history, that in a time of decline, a time when everything is made counterfeit, a time of mere busy-ness [*Betriebsamkeit*], *thinking in the grand style* is real action [*ein echtes Handeln*], indeed action in its most powerful, albeit *most silent* form. Here the usually easy distinction between "mere theory" and useful "praxis" no longer makes sense. (*Ne*, 2:10–11; *Ng*, 1:261)

For Heidegger, the version of return that Nietzsche presents in *Zarathustra* is not independent of the auto-historical "mission" described here. In an exegetical lecture given in 1953,[24] Heidegger asks the question: "Who is Nietzsche's Zarathustra?"—that is, who is the "thinker of return"—and the answer he gives, with some qualifications, is "Nietzsche himself"[25]—Nietzsche insofar as he is the teacher of return and of the overman, the thinker of the end of thinking. But if Nietzsche himself, in this capacity, perhaps obliquely figuring himself as Zarathustra, is the exemplary living thinker who thinks return, then we would have indeed a strong reason to consider Nietzsche's journals and self-referential fragments with care. For Western metaphysics, insofar as it is, in the end, the activity of thinking eternal return, culminates neither with Nietzsche's thinking per se, nor simply with *some* person's life-perspective (for instance, the dwarf's) but rather with Nietzsche's *own* life. In its particular critical approach to Platonism, Nietzsche's autobiography is the "end of philosophy."

In turn, Heidegger's ambivalence toward autobiography and other putatively contextual matters—identifying them as "preliminary" yet dwelling on them for most of his course—indicates the strange role that such particulars must play in what is after all intended to be an essentializing and systematizing reading of Nietzsche. In invoking Nietzsche's most auto-referential moments, even if only to subordinate them to an essentially posthumous "task," Heidegger necessarily raises the specter of the strong criticisms, both of thinking in general and of the pretensions of Western metaphysics in particular, that run precisely through these texts. For instance, Nietzsche devotes considerable effort in *Ecce Homo* to demonstrating that the thinking person's stance is subordinate to explicitly nonmetaphysical life-activities such as eating, drinking, sleeping, and so forth: "These small things—nutrition, place, climate, recreation, the whole casuistry of selfishness—are inconceivably more important than everything one has taken to be important so far. . . . All the problems of politics, of social organization, and of education have been falsified through and through because . . . one learned to despise 'little' things, which means the basic concerns of life itself."[26] I cited a passage above in which Heidegger, too, notes the essential "locatedness [*Standortcharakter*]" of philosophy, as against the pretension of a pure objective stance for metaphysical inquiry. But to conceive of thinking not simply as "located" (and thus opposed to an equally abstract *Standpunktslosigkeit*, or "standpointlessness") but as perduring alongside, say, eating, drinking, sex, and defecation, would be a polemically destructive antimetaphysical gesture toward the idealizations of Platonism that is difficult to subsume under the (perhaps still idealistic) rubric of a metaphysical task, even a negative one. If Heidegger wishes to see metaphysical tasks—and, crucially, *only* metaphysical tasks—in Nietzsche's life-descriptions, then he is obliged to deal somehow with the particularly virulent antimetaphysical form that those descriptions tend to take within Nietzsche's writing.

Thinking Eating

I want to analyze the figure of food or eating as a critical example of "life-activity" in Heidegger's revision-encounter with eternal return. This is not an arbitrary choice, since eating is more than just one example of life's physical aspect. It also serves a conventional but ambivalent metaphorical function with respect to the status of thinking generally, at once the figure of the consumption and incorporation of thought in the dialectical processes of philosophy, and the corresponding catachresis which potentially ruins the "incorporation" metaphor by polemically reminding thinking of the excessively nonmetaphysical origins of its dialectical and spiritual desires. The figure is a favorite of German speculative philosophers, at least since Hegel's early interpretations of the transubstantiation and symbolization of food in the New Testament, and of their analogy to the logic of dialectic itself. Timothy Bahti notes that "the very example of digestion is also *of* the spirit, that is, of the appropriation, interiorization, and assimilation of the outer into the inner—or, . . . of the body by the spirit."[27] Indeed, via the metaphorics of transformation that Christian doctrine conveniently provides, food can serve philosophy as a primary example of exemplarity itself, examples being the material particulars which, by their very nature, get sublated into the universal: "The example of the body is overcome here in its exemplification of the spirit: digestion is digested, or 'the process of digestion' processes or digests the 'merely bodily object' of its knowledge, namely, the animal-like *function* of digestion."[28]

In a variegation and complication of this speculative usage of eating and digestion, Nietzsche's references to food in *Ecce Homo* employ a wide range of rhetorical forms and functions. There are statements about food that show a specifically metaphorical bent, apparently supporting Heidegger's reading of Nietzsche's autobiography as a proleptic reflection on the task of revaluating Western thought. For example, "Till I reached a very mature age I always ate *badly*; morally speaking, 'impersonally,' 'selflessly,' 'altruistically'—for the benefit of cooks and other fellow Christians." Or again, "I . . . do not know how to advise all *more spiritual* natures earnestly enough to abstain entirely from alcohol."[29] Here food is figured in the service of traditional dialectical argument, abetting a metaphysical problematic such as the critique of Christian values or the need for an ascetic attitude toward the body in order to achieve a "lightness" of "spirit" for thinking.[30] However, nestled among these figurative evocations of eating as spiritual exercise are passages of a far more literalistic tendency, exhibiting a tone I would call "polemically mundane." Nietzsche says, for instance, "The best cuisine is that of *Piedmont*," and, "*Tea* is wholesome only in the morning."[31] And he registers the following complaints about German food: ". . . overcooked meats, vegetables cooked with fat and flour; the degeneration of pastries and puddings into paperweights!"[32] What purpose could these comments serve as conceptual examples within a putative "critique of metaphysics"? Of course, nothing entirely proscribes a reader such as Heidegger from interpreting these passages as references to, or preparations for, a thinking task, even a critique of metaphysics, or even as exemplary figurations of philosophical thinking itself. But would it be possible to interpret them, to use Heidegger's phrasing, as "always only" or "nothing but" (*immer nur*) that? (*Ne*, 2:10; *Ng*, 1:261); to rudely erase the belligerent attitude of these "reports" toward the idealizations conventionally entailed by thinking, or to remove their savage irony toward the conventional "tasks" of philosophy? Nietzsche's attribution of higher thinking to indigestion, and of spiritual quests to the bad influence of beer or pastries, seems more the severe humorist's assault on the very spiritual pretense of speculation itself, a caustic insinuation rather than a dialectical or logical attack, akin to Ebenezer Scrooge's initial pique of skepticism against Jacob Marley's ghost: "You *may* be an undigested bit of beef, a blot of mustard, a crumb of cheese, a fragment of an underdone potato." Once such an insinuation is proffered, and so long as the reader remains sufficiently skeptical, he or she may never be entirely sure that the entire long night of metaphysical reverie and spiritual edification, however miraculously substantial and complete it has appeared, isn't finally traceable to the underdone potato. It is perhaps this possibility, and the need to overlook it, that can make Heidegger's descriptions of Nietzsche's figural styles seem miserly, or makes his disrespect of Nietzsche's particularist autobiography seem too blatantly impertinent.

Nietzsche's polemically mundane statements about food suggest that there are at least two versions of the critical concept of "life" at play in the revision-encounter between Heidegger's and Nietzsche's interpretations of that concept. The first is a critical-metaphysical category, a dialectical negation of thinking, but therefore recuperable as an example of, or figure for, thought; something like what Heidegger describes, glossing the notion of perspectivism, as the essential "*Standortcharakter*" of philosophy. The other version of "life," however, would be a severely ironic or even catachrestic extension of precisely this same dialectical exemplarity, a tendency within the concept of "life" that pushes it in the direction of a more literal and therefore more polemical attack on thinking as such: an attack that would explain why a book of "philosophy," ostensibly devoted to metaphysical tasks, sees fit to pronounce upon tea and bad pastry.[33] These two versions of "life" are not exactly opposed, but one is entailed by or even parasitic upon the other. If there is a real difference between the two, a difference useful in defining the divergence between Nietzsche's thought and its revision in Heidegger's reading, then it will be a difference not on par with the "metaphysical distinction" that, for Heidegger, historically structures the difference between general and particular in philosophical thinking, nor, for instance, with the distinction between "life" and "*Dasein*" in Heidegger's earlier, more subtle work on this topic, but with the ironic paraliptical difference that structures the historical shapes that occur between thoughts, the difference compelled by the mere fact that philosophy continues successively to alter itself through rereadings and revisions. The difference between "food for thought" and "thought *as* (mere) food"—or between a *Geist* and a potato—or even between a "digestible" potato and an "undigestible" one—is just such a difference between two versions of life, a difference made only by *reading* in a practical encounter with texts, and by the degree of irony or *skepsis* conjured by a particular angle of vision and revision.

In general, therefore, when Heidegger's reading takes up the question of eternal return—which, because it is interpreted as a doctrine fundamentally about action and life-praxis, leads fairly directly to Nietzsche's polemical autobiographical writing—it enters a double-bind. The desire to position eternal return as Nietzsche's central critique of Western philosophical thought leads Heidegger to autobiographical texts such as *Ecce Homo*, because, as he says, part of Nietzsche's revaluative task consists in "telling his own story," and eternal return is not strictly separable from those moments in which Nietzsche does so—the doctrine of return is simply *in* those texts. Yet Nietzsche's critique of thinking, exemplified by those same texts, tends strongly toward an absolute reduction of, for instance, thought to a kind of eating or other "mundane" life activity, and Heidegger will consistently resist following this particular reduction to its end. Such reduction would eviscerate any attempt to see Nietzsche's focus on life activities such as eating as fundamentally or "only" thought categories in the service of, say, a critique of the metaphysics of Platonism. Bluntly: for Heidegger it is fine for philosophy to end as a "life" activity, so long as "life" itself remains recuperable as a category of a "thought" or "thought-project," so long as it is not too lively to be thought *through*.

The Burden of Food

Heidegger's discussion of Nietzsche's "first communication" of the doctrine of return is an exemplary moment for his dealing (or not dealing) with an excessively lively instance of Nietzsche's figuration of life. The passage in question occurs near the end of *The Gay Science* Part IV, and is entitled "The Greatest Burden [*Das größte Schwergewicht*]" (*S*, 3:570):

> What if one day or night a demon were to steal upon you in[to] your loneliest loneliness and say to you: "This life, as you are now living it, and have lived it, you will have to live, once more and countless times more. . . . Would you not throw yourself down and gnash your teeth and curse the demon who spoke thus? Or have you ever experienced a tremendous moment when you would reply to him, "You are a god, and never have I heard anything more godly!" (*Ne*, 2:19–20; *Ng*, 1:270; see *The Gay Science*, par. 341; *S*, 3:570)

Return is not yet a "doctrine" here, but only a suggestion. It invites the reader to consider particular events *as though* they will recur infinitely, to consider them as possessing an importance they would not appear to possess as isolated moments in time.[34] The suggestion of return is a "weight" or "burden [*Schwergewicht*]" added to a person's thoughts about his or her life:

> The question with respect to each and every thing: "Do you will this once more and countless times more?" would lie upon your actions as the greatest burden! Or how well [disposed] would you have to become toward yourself and toward life *to demand nothing more* than this ultimate eternal sanction and seal? (*Ne*, 2:20; *Ng*, 1:270; see *The Gay Science*, par. 341; *S*, 3:570)

Heidegger glosses the word "burden" in a relentlessly positive light, as something that "hinders vacillation, brings a calmness and steadfastness, draws all forces together upon itself, gathers them and gives them definition" (*Ne*, 2:21; *Ng*, 1:272). A burden is "determinative [*bestimmend*]" (*Ne*, 2:22; *Ng*, 1:273) because it "lies upon our *acting* [*Handeln*]," and the thought of eternal return is the "greatest burden" by virtue of its domain: the fact that every action, no matter how insignificant, must return. Heidegger writes, "The thought of eternal return is to be a burden, that is to say, determinative, for [our] envelopment within beings as a whole [*für das Mitteninnestehen im Seienden im Ganzen*]" (*Ne*, 2:22; *Ng*, 1:273).

The fact that the thought of return is capable of affecting everything in one's life seems adequate to explain why it can be troped as burdensome. Return becomes, as Heidegger's reading shows, a kind of paradigm for the burdensomeness or determinativeness of thought itself, potentially more influential upon one's actions than ideologies, prejudices, moralities, or religions, all of which are subsumed under the domain of eternal return—all of which will themselves *return*. Yet despite the availability of this paradigmatic instance of a burdensome thought, Heidegger still feels compelled to defend a general notion that thoughts can be burdensome or determinative at all. To his gloss of Nietzsche's passage he adds these remarks, as though through an objecting interlocutor: "Yet now we would really have to ask: How can a thought possess determinative power [*bestimmende Kraft*]? 'Thoughts!' Such fleeting things are to be a center of gravity [*Schwerpunkt*]? On the contrary, is not what is determinative for man precisely what crowds around him [*was um ihn herumsteht*], his circumstances [*Umstände*], his 'foodstuffs' [*Nahrung*] . . ." (*Ne*, 2:22; *Ng*, 1:273). Why does food appear just here, at the moment when the power of thoughts was to be vindicated? Heidegger's phrase "his 'foodstuffs' seems innocent enough: food is simply an example of the environment or circumstances that always "stand around" the human being, of the sorts of things that first impinge upon thinking, but later, when thought gets going, are "digested" to become the fodder for its idealizations and spiritualizations. Yet for Nietzsche, as I've already noted, food is no mere example, but in itself an elaborate problematic, particularly in *Ecce Homo*. And food serves as a critical locus for Nietzsche not simply because it is just one of these things that crowd around us along with climate, locality, and so forth, but also precisely because it is the classic referent for a conventional metaphor of idealization or spiritualization—of transubstantiation—in a Platonic-Christian tradition, one which Nietzsche consistently attempts to ironize and revise. The critical thrust of *Ecce Homo*, when it traces types of thinking back to types of food, is to invert this ritual, to resubstantiate the spiritualized body back into mere bread and wine, or into bratwurst and beer: "The origin of the *German spirit* . . . [is] distressed intestines. The German spirit is an indigestion: it does not finish with anything."[35] Metaphor is the trope of *finishing* impugned by this sarcasm, the figure that would subsume and transubstantiate the material object into meaning across the gap that separates the material and the *geistig*. Nietzsche's figure, on the other hand, which revulgarizes the sacrament of metaphor, is a catachresis, a severe ironic abuse of the transubstantive process of figuration itself.

More particularly, Nietzsche's abuse of the metaphorical use of eating could be called a "literalization," if that itself were the name of a figure. Indeed, precisely the difficulty of reading Nietzsche's statements about food *as* figural, their seeming indigestibility as metaphors, or the excessive specificity that makes them difficult to sublimate as concepts—"overcooked meats, vegetables cooked with fat and flour"— provides their specific critical power. But literalization can appear excessive only in light of a metaphorical logic that would relegate such fodder to complete consumption in idealization—or in other words, to consumption in the cause of the "task" or the philosophical "work." Nietzsche's use or abuse of food in *Ecce Homo* both adopts, at times, a version of the paradigmatic Platonic-Christian metaphor of transubstantiation, and at other times deflates or debunks it by polemically leaning on its most mundane significations. Such doubleness is a thorough-going ambivalence, and thus an immanent-critical sarcasm: Nietzsche's concentration on the literal—beer and beef in lieu of the "blood" and "body"—attacks precisely the particular spiritualization that the metaphor of eating itself intends, the full assimilation or *Aufhebung* of what is material about food; it is a *reductio ad absurdum* of the figure of "food for thought." The human is, far more than the run of philosophical tradition would allow, "what he eats."

Despite Nietzsche's obvious fondness for polemical mundanities, Heidegger's argument takes a subtle but crucial turn away from Nietzsche precisely at this point. He attributes the idea that foodstuffs, or climate or locale, are determinative for man *not* to Nietzsche, but to Feuerbach; I continue the passage I started to cite above:

> . . . Is not rather what is determinative for man precisely what crowds around him, his circumstances, his "foodstuffs," as in that maxim of Feuerbach's: "Man is what he eats"? And, along with nourishment, location, or, after the then contemporary teachings of English and French Sociology, the "*milieu*," meaning both the general atmosphere and the social order? But in no way "thoughts"! (*Ne*, 2:22; *Ng*, 1:272)

Since within *Ecce Homo*, opinions like those of Feuerbach and the classical sociologists are quite explicitly, if ambivalently, expressed, it is odd for Heidegger to turn all the way back to Feuerbach to find a voice for these sentiments, with Nietzsche himself so close at hand. Of course it is possible that Feuerbach is more convenient simply because in his work the argument for the influence of foodstuffs is doctrinal rather than parodic. But I would argue rather that Nietzsche, in his catachrestic literalness, is not being sufficiently paraliptical for Heidegger at this moment, not sufficiently proleptic, precisely where Heidegger wishes to insert his own more "proper" metaphysical point into the discussion of "life" and "foodstuffs." To put it bluntly, Heidegger has a very particular revisionist rationale for *not* citing Nietzsche just at this moment. His next sentence reads: "To this Nietzsche would retort [*würde dem entgegnen*]: it is precisely a matter of 'thoughts' [*Gerade die 'Gedanken'*], since these determine man even more [than those other things]; they determine him foremost [*erst*] with respect to these very foodstuffs, to this locality, to this atmosphere and social order" (*Ne*, 2:22; *Ng*, 1:273). As I have tried to demonstrate, it is quite unlikely that Nietzsche "would retort" in such a fashion, particularly in *Ecce Homo*.[36] Normally Heidegger couches such revisionist claims within a hermeneutical overview of Nietzsche's "philosophy proper," sustainable aside from, and even despite, Nietzsche's "own" opinions. In this particular passage, however, Heidegger appears to confuse Nietzsche "himself" with the paraliptical, "proper" Nietzsche that *is* (proleptically) Heidegger, where otherwise one expects the antithetical sentiment to originate in what Heidegger calls the "innermost will" of the text, not at its surface. Thus here Heidegger exposes his interpretation to a much stronger objection on the grounds of "mere" scholarly accuracy than he is normally wont to do.

Heidegger's statements about foodstuffs bear unusually explicit witness to the moment of essentialization that occurs throughout his reading of Nietzsche, the moment in which a new interpretation of

Nietzsche is imputed to the central intention or tendency of Nietzsche's text itself—to whatever it paraliptically *"would* retort" or *"would* have retorted" if asked the proper questions. In this instance, I have for the first time attempted a critical evaluation of this characteristic revisionist gesture of Heidegger's reading, to show perhaps what distortions or reductions are entailed by its gesture of essentialization. This passage especially lends itself to such an approach, precisely because it uncharacteristically declines carefully to distinguish the paraliptical or "inner" will of Nietzsche's text from the text's explicit statement.

The retort to Feuerbach that Heidegger puts into Nietzsche's mouth accompanies a particular interpretation that Heidegger imposes on food and eating generally in Nietzsche's text, a metaphorical interpretation based on a gloss of the term "incorporation [*Enverleibung*]." To illustrate what he claims to be Nietzsche's usage of "eating," but which is in fact only one valence of it, and probably its least critical valence, Heidegger cites one of Nietzsche's several plans for a future work on eternal return. Here Nietzsche appears to write the word "incorporation" in a more or less conventional (that is, a metaphorical) way, as a version of the same figure that gives us the "digestion" or "assimilation" of thoughts. The plan reads:

The Return of the same:

Plan.

1. *Incorporation of the fundamental errors* [Grundirrtümer].
2. *Incorporation of the passions.*
3. *Incorporation of knowledge.* (Passion of insight [*Erkenntnis*].)
4. *The Innocent. The individual as experiment.* . . .
5. The new *burden: the eternal return of the same.* Infinite importance of our knowing, erring, our habits, ways of life, for everything to come. . . . (*Ne,* 2:74; *Ng,* 1:330; see *S,* 11:141)

The specific components of the plan are not important for Heidegger, but the "plan's key word [*Leitwort*], . . . 'incorporation,' [*Einverleibung*]" *is* important (*Ne*, 2:75; *Ng*, 1:331). Heidegger constructs the following chain of argument: "We know from *Thus spoke Zarathustra* how essential the question of the 'incorporation' of thought is. . . ." Here Heidegger refers to Zarathustra's emphasis on thinking in the moment, for instance in thinking the thought of return, the proper emphasis that "incorporates" the thinker's presence into the thought, and vice versa: "If we follow the word's signification [*Wortbedeutung*] we arrive at the idea of 'eating,' devouring and digesting [*die Vorstellung des 'Essens,' Zusichnehmens und Verdauens*]. . . ." Heidegger is still following out a conventional metaphorical usage of the term; here is the crux: "Whatever is incorporated is that which makes the body [*Leib*]—and embodiment [*Leiben*]—steady, steadfast and certain [*fest und stehend und sicher*]. Just the same it is something we have finished with and which determines us in the future, the juice with which we feed our powers" (*Ne*, 2:76; *Ng*, 1:331–32). For Heidegger, here, something incorporated, "eaten," is "finished with," assimilated and "sacrificed" to future tasks, just like those fragments of Nietzsche's autobiography that are "sacrificed" to the task of unifying Nietzsche's life's thought. In general, metaphor is paradigmatically the figure that "finishes with" its material, which trans-forms or tran-substantiates material into the ideal—the figure of and for a completed substitution or sublimation.[37] But this is a long way from the figurations of *Ecce Homo*, where Nietzsche complains that the "German spirit is an indigestion—it does not finish with anything." Such contradictions are easily accommodated by Nietzsche's ambivalent, or rather multivalent, use of the figure of food. Only within Heidegger's oddly one-sided interpretation is such contradiction a hazard, where we can object that Nietzsche, in fact, would *not* reply that only thoughts determine our choice of food, or that only tasks of thinking determine our life activities—or that eating is *only* a figure for thoughtful incorporation.

Life

The oddness of Heidegger's procedure here, as well as the tenuousness of his revision (and reduction) of Nietzsche's use of "life" to "incorporation" in the *Nietzsche* lectures, can be confirmed by a comparison with the extreme circumspection with which he treats the concept of "life" in other contexts. Heidegger never systematically criticizes either "life" or "life-philosophy," nor does either category occupy a central position for his work, which from the start was concerned with the "existential-ontological" problematic of *Dasein* as distinct from what he identifies as a "biological-ontic" problematic (*BT*, 229 [247]). Nonetheless, the foil of *Lebensphilosophie* remains in the background of his thinking at least through *Being and Time*, and is apparent in the earlier versions of this work, such as the 1925–1926 lecture series now published as *The History of the Concept of Time*.[38] Both in this work and in *Being and Time* itself the main advocate of *Lebensphilosophie* is Dilthey, along with his correspondent Count Yorck, although Husserl is also invoked. These sources usually supply counterpoints for Heidegger's "existential analytic," representing, along with the natural sciences more generally, an essentially derivative or inadequate conceptualization of *Dasein* as a "living being."

"Life" can neither serve as an explanation of *Dasein*, nor is it useful as a critical opposition to something like a *res cogitans*, for *Dasein* is not properly understood as something that exists either as, or in addition to, what is "merely living about" a human being. In short, *Dasein* is essentially *not* a Cartesian *animal rationale* or any component thereof. For one thing, since *Dasein* is constituted as "potentiality" or "Being-ahead-of itself" (*BT*, 179 [192]) (or more basically, as "care [*Sorge*]"), "the existential interpretation of death is prior to [*liegt vor*] any biology and ontology of life" (*BT*, 229 [247]). But neither can *Dasein* then be considered a kind of subgenre of living being that merely contains or is characterized by this "Being-ahead-of-itself," for instance some living thing that historicizes itself, cares, worships, and so on, in addition to eating, sleeping, and so forth (*BT*, 46 [49–50]). Such conceptualizations limit "life" to a biological-anthropological figuration of the human being to which the notion of *Dasein* is related as ontological ground, implicit within the interpretation but as yet "unexpressed."[39] In short, *Dasein* is more fundamental than "life," and therefore never a version or type of it, or even its opposite. *Lebensphilosophie*, in its own quasi-materialist critique of the *animale rationale*, remains on a par, and even bound up with, the ontic sciences of "anthropology, psychology, and biology," all of which fail "to give an unequivocal and ontologically founded answer to the question about the *kind of Being* [which is] this being [*nach der* Seinsart *dieses Seienden*] which we ourselves are" (*BT*, 46 [50]).

Yet Heidegger's discussions of "personal experiences" and autobiography in the *Nietzsche* lectures, while they do not precisely contradict an assertion of the ontological primacy of *Dasein* over "life"— since, for one thing, autobiography is already a historical as well as a biological activity—nonetheless significantly simplify the hermeneutical schema that relates *Dasein* to "life," especially considering Nietzsche's particular emphasis on life *as* "biological" process. Moreover, Heidegger's metaphor of "incorporation" itself certainly entails a "biological-ontic" structuring of the human being that can oppose food to *Geist* as though within a biological/spiritual or a physical/metaphysical dualism. Such a dualism, from the vantage of *Being and Time*, must remain "ontologically indefinite [*ontologisch unbestimmt*]" (*BT*, 46 [50]). Nonetheless it continues to hold sway in what would have to be seen, again from Heidegger's very own prior vantage, as Nietzsche's prephenomenological criticism of metaphysics. As a metaphor, eating (or, for Heidegger, "finishing with" the fodder of thinking) essentially sidesteps the potential for a deeper critique of life and of life's relation to metaphysical thinking, which type of thinking, in Heidegger's earlier work, appeared as the paraliptical call of an implicit, more basic ontological structure (*Dasein*) which could ground the ontic involvement of the human being with *both* "foodstuffs" and "thought." In short, Heidegger never does to Nietzsche or to Feuerbach what he does to Dilthey and Count Yorck: identifying a paraliptically anticipated, more essential "existential interpretation" of *Dasein*'s "life" within the description of the human being provided by a *Lebensphilosophie*.

Especially in light of the critique he *could* have conducted, Heidegger's description of Nietzsche's use of the figure of the life-activity of eating is uncharacteristically a severely limited reading, which forecloses all but one of the figure's many valences, namely, the metaphorical, in its effort to make Nietzsche's autobiography appear properly paraliptical. Indeed, it ironically verges on an interpretation of body function that is a throwback not only to much earlier German speculative philosophy but also to precisely the most traditionally Christian influences upon that philosophy, the interpretation of Christianity as "the absolute predominance of the ideal over the real, of the spiritual over the corporeal."[40] Most importantly, in his rereading of Nietzsche's last texts, Heidegger forecloses precisely the most polemical of Nietzsche's figural implications, the possibility of interpreting the quasi figure of food literally, or as strongly tending toward literalness, an antimetaphorical and also critically antiphilosophical and anti-Christian usage.

But Heidegger's reading requires the metaphorical interpretation. Without it, as I have tried to show, Nietzsche's "reduction" of the figure of food, the catachrestic tendency that parasitizes its metaphorization—and which provides the critical thrust, the excessive irony, the polemical mundanity, of food-for-life—threatens also to reduce the possibility of reading Nietzsche's thought as directed toward a task of metaphysical revision that after all Heidegger, not Nietzsche, has set up. Here again we see the duplicity that was evident in the way "life" first arose within the difficult gray area between Heidegger's and Nietzsche's texts. "Life" gets used as a critical category of thought, a metaphysical signifier subordinate to the task of overturning Platonism—and yet, it is also a more polemical antithought, tending to be so critical that it begins to polemicize against thinking as such, thereby amplifying the shock value of Nietzsche's antiphilosophical gestures. The line between these two usages is obviously extremely fine. Indeed, it is the same "smallest gap [*kleinste Kluft*]" or "rainbow bridge [*Schein-brücke*]" (*Ne*, 2:182; *Ng*, 1:446) that Heidegger uses to characterize the divergence between the dwarf's and Zarathustra's respective interpretations of eternal return. The width of the gap is dependent solely on the perspective from which one decides to invoke the word "life": roughly, a "Heideggerian" versus a "Nietzschean" perspective. More precisely, the perspectival gap is a gap of reading, a gap in how one rereads Nietzsche's figure, but not then of the figure's content per se, for the literalization with which Nietzsche polemically deconstructs the metaphor of food-for-thought hyperbolically emphasizes precisely the same content that the metaphor itself requires for its transubstantive sublimation into concept.[41]

What does the interpretation (and restriction) of eating as the metaphor of incorporation do for Heidegger? It allows him to close this "smallest gap," to make the critically cathected eating, and all those things in (Nietzsche's) life that "crowd around" the thinker, subordinate to a critique that remains fully immanent in a tradition of metaphysical philosophy that provides its own self-overcoming, in its own terms. In this sense, the reading of food as a metaphor serves precisely the same function as the prior interpretation of Nietzsche's autobiography as "only ever" task-driven. However, when we reopen the gap by pointing out the incongruity of Heidegger's putting contradictions of Feuerbach into Nietzsche's mouth—or posthumous metaphysical tasks into his teenage autobiography—we reopen at the same time the possibility that Nietzsche escapes metaphysics, which would be to say that he escapes the synecdochal restriction of his positioning by Heidegger's revision; escapes it in a way that Heidegger, who remains intent on calling Nietzsche the "last [Platonic] metaphysician," can't quite accommodate. Reading the ambivalent rhetoric of Nietzsche's literalistic figures, we have executed, ourselves, a (paraliptical) revision against Heidegger's own more conventional (or at least more traditional) reading—repositing an essential paraliptical but properly *improper* Nietzsche, say, the "polemically mundane" Nietzsche, as against Heidegger's "properly" posthumous metaphysician.

Spitting Out Philosophy

The "smallest gap" between Nietzsche's figuration of eating and Heidegger's revision or regression of the figure as a metaphor may be seen again in one last, strange instance of eating that suddenly intrudes on the scene of eternal return in *Thus Spoke Zarathustra*. This instance also allows us to see the absolutely necessary critical negotiation into which we must enter simply to accept Heidegger's reading of Nietzsche, let alone to reject, revise, or overstep it. Just as Zarathustra has finished angrily re-posing the question of return to his sullen dwarf, especially emphasizing the gateway labeled "Moment," he suddenly finds both gateway and dwarf vanished:

> Among wild cliffs I stood suddenly alone, bleak, in the bleakest moonlight. *But there lay a man!. . . .* A young shepherd I saw, writhing, gagging, in spasms, his face distorted, and a heavy [*schwere*] black snake hung out of his mouth. Had I ever seen so much nausea and pale horror on one face? He seemed to have been asleep when the snake crawled into his throat, and there bit itself fast. My hand tore at the snake and tore in vain!; it did not tear the snake out of his throat. Then it cried out of me: "Bite! Bite! Bite its head off!" Thus it cried out of me—my horror, my hatred, my nausea, my pity, all that is good and wicked in me cried out of me with a single cry.[42]

The shepherd follows this advice, bites the head off the snake "with a good bite!," and spits the head "far away."[43] At this point he jumps up, transformed, and begins to laugh, as Nietzsche writes, "with a laughter no longer human."[44]

Here then is a violent reversal of the "incorporation" of return, not a swallowing and digesting, but rather a spitting out, an impetuous rejection or castration of the figure of food as conceptual digestion.[45] If this is a new figure for thinking return—and the snake, as Heidegger points out, is explicitly associated by Zarathustra with return[46]— then we have thinking not as incorporation, but rather as conceptual bulimia, eating without "proper" ingestion, and therefore without sound dialectical nutrition: an "eating not-eating."

What does Heidegger make of this scene of biting snakes, of snakes that bite and are bitten? First, he asserts that "the young shepherd *is* Zarathustra himself" (*Ne*, 2:180; *Ng*, 1:443), and this also means for Heidegger, as I have discussed, that the shepherd is a more or less oblique figure for Nietzsche himself, the exemplary thinker of return. Second, Heidegger interprets the biting and bitten snake quite narrowly—indeed exactly as narrowly as he had interpreted Nietzsche's autobiography and as narrowly as he had interpreted the figure of eating itself: "the bite is nothing other than [*nichts anderes als*] the overcoming of nihilism" (*Ne*, 2:180; *Ng*, 1:443)—thus the snake is a very particular symbol, and the action performed upon it a particular metaphor for overcoming: the snake is nothing other than "nihilism itself" (*Ne*, 2:179; *Ng*, 1:442). Heidegger's "itself [*selbst*]" is the rhetorical equivalent of his description of Nietzsche's autobiography as "only ever [*immer nur*]" to be read as anticipating a metaphysical "task": a hyperbolic limitation, and fundamentally a revision, of Nietzsche's text.

Since snakes are, in fact, symbols of circularity and return in *Zarathustra*, for Heidegger this particular black nihilistic snake in the shepherd's mouth becomes a nihilistic counterversion of return. Of course, the thought of return always has its potential nihilistic side, an aspect in which it causes precisely the opposite of creative action, a mere disgust with the present whose effect on life is a crippling apathy.

Such nihilistic potential was apparent in Nietzsche's earliest presentation of the doctrine from *The Gay Science*, in which a demon comes to you and suggests that every moment of your life will return infinitely. It is always possible—indeed, this possibility provides the story's all-important personal pathos—that you will "gnash your teeth" and "curse," that the thought of everything coming back again just as it is will seem to make it entirely moot how you act, since whatever you do or don't do will return anyway. Action becomes meaningless and purposeless.[47] Of course, such a nihilistic understanding of return is "*logisch richtig*," but as Heidegger writes, it provides the wrong emphasis with which to think the doctrine, the "dwarfish" emphasis, and therefore fails to account for the return of the "moment" itself, the moment in which what you think or do determines exactly what it is that will return. In short, despite its correctness, such a dwarfish, nihilistic interpretation remains "*metaphysisch unwahr*." Still, the apathetic, stultifying version of return is precisely the flip side, the catachrestic parasite, of the active, moment-ous version; there is the "smallest gap" separating them, a gap solely of interpretive perspective. When we "incorporate" return properly, for Heidegger, by thinking it in terms of the moment, we "bite" off the improper, nihilistic version. Incorporating the true return is tantamount to biting and spitting out the untrue, nihilistic one.

Two types of eating, two ways of thinking eternal return, one eating for each version of return. This makes things convenient for Heidegger's reading, which had tended all along to interpret the proper thinking of return in "the moment" as a grand metaphor for the overcoming of Western metaphysics and of the nihilism of Platonic thought. Such an overcoming was to be Nietzsche's fundamental (if proleptic) task, and to comprise his fundamental metaphysical position, to which his personal experiences were, as it were metaphorically, devoted. The correspondence of two types of eating for the two types of return fits the scheme nicely, for by incorporating return properly we are able to spit out the unhealthy nihilistic portions, the metaphysical gristle. But to what lengths must a reader go in order to accept such a distinction?

By contrast, what if—in deference to the real disgust evoked by a literal reading of the shepherd with a black snake biting his throat—we simply elect not to make such a distinction between types of eating? The snake, after all, is a symbol of return. Can we not more easily interpret the logic of the figure as implying that the shepherd (Zarathustra—the living thinker—Nietzsche) must bite off and spit out *the doctrine of return itself*? Is it not easier to permit the possibility that thinking or "swallowing" (incorporating) a thought like that of return would be, in and of itself, an enterprise that contains an essential moment of nihilism? I earlier suggested that return has the structure of self-recantation, a thought about thought that refutes itself as thought, and the more rigorously it is thought "in the moment," the more severe becomes its tendency against thinking as such and toward the reduction of thought to a life-activity. In this light, the proper "incorporation" of the thought, if we may still speak this way, could ironically be tantamount to spitting the thought out, to precisely *not* incorporating it. We may still agree with Heidegger that "the thought only *is* as that bite" (*Ne*, 2:181; *Ng*, 1:445), without limiting whatever is bitten off only to nihilism, the "bad" side of return.

There is that same "smallest gap, the rainbow bridge," between the reading I have just offered and Heidegger's—here the gap consists solely in how the audience of either the primary text or the revisionist secondary text elects to interpret the figure of the shepherd's black snake: as a metaphor just for bad, nihilistic return, or as a catachresis for thought itself, a parasitic literalistic excess coming on the tail of the allegorical thought-experiment that Zarathustra has just concluded at the expense of the dwarf. In such a catachresis the snake represents (if, strictly speaking, it can still "represent" at all) the repulsiveness of thought itself—which we would find, precisely through thinking return as literally as possible, that we must bite off and spit out if we are not to choke on it. If eating eternal return is at the same time tantamount to spitting it out—if for Nietzsche thinking must disgorge itself so as not to shortchange its very *life*—then it becomes increasingly difficult to imagine eating, and all life activities that tag along with it in its tropological usage, as moments subordinate to a critical-metaphysical task of overcoming Platonism. For if the thought of return teaches us to spit out thinking to go on living, then it might not be so easy thoughtfully to distinguish which thinking—or which aspect of autobiography, or which interpretation of food—to spit out and which to swallow.

A Suggestion About Canon Formation in Philosophy

The epilogue is not a conclusion, properly speaking. What I offer instead are some suggestions about how a critique of philosophical revision might continue. In the last chapter, I contrived a partial return to the more open-ended tropology and discordant tone of Nietzsche's last texts. I objected to Heidegger's overly placid reading of the metaphor of eating, ultimately a restrictive and regressively metaphysical figuration, and described Heidegger's interpretation as incapable of accounting for the crucial literalism of Nietzsche's thoughts on philosophical thinking. Despite my differences with Heidegger, all my interpretive gestures are formally identical to those of Heidegger's own revision-encounter with Nietzsche, and of such encounters generally in the field of philosophy. Moreover, my presumptive challenge to Heidegger's dramatic essentialization of the "direction" of Nietzsche's philosophy, or of philosophical history at large, is presumptuous only in a conventional sense, calling for the sort of grand shift in "our" collective vision of the philosophical canon for which any number of texts call. Nothing is more commonplace in philosophy than hyperbolic overviews that reverse whole histories or metaphysical trends with only the most abstract anticipation of an audience or actual effect. This is only to say that philosophical critique, my own included, accedes to conventional demands for large-scale canon formation, and assents to a rhetoric of historic interventionism almost always out of proportion to its real power.

The equivocity of the rereader's commonplace hyperbole or mundane "divinity" brings the critique of philosophical reading practice back to the pair of Hegelian premises with which I began this book, that philosophies are "complete" in themselves and nevertheless must "step out" into history. But the fullest elaboration of these antithetical premises could only follow upon a wider critique of the institutional practices and settings within which philosophy emerges onto the scene of textual canon formation—a phenomenology, perhaps, of publishing houses and university seminars. Such socioeconomic analysis would address itself to the basic conditions of textual fabrication and distribution, the domain of what Gérard Genette calls the "paratext":

> [The paratext] constitutes a zone between text and off-text, a zone not only of transition but also of *transaction*: a privileged place of a pragmatics and a strategy, of an influence on the public, an influence that—whether well or poorly understood or achieved—is at the service of a better reception for the text and a more pertinent reading of it (more pertinent, of course, in the eyes of the author and his allies).[1]

To study philosophy as revision, as textual historicity, is ultimately to orient one's view toward this horizon of paratextual commerce, beyond which one begins to uncover the historical and institutional conditions that make possible the presentation of philosophy for a professional public, much as we have become used to considering these conditions as a productive horizon for literary studies.

We are by now sufficiently accustomed to such notions that it can no longer raise eyebrows to reread Philippe Lacoue-Labarthe's polemical question of 1979: "What if, after all, philosophy were nothing but literature?"[2] Clearly philosophy is no longer able to define itself "*against* what we call literature," as Lacoue-Labarthe could suggest it still did two decades ago. That the literariness of philosophy no longer surprises can be traced to what is sometimes called the "linguistic turn" of late philosophical inquiry, but even more to the fact that suspicions such as those of Lacoue-Labarthe have become thoroughly conventional; this is not to deny their erstwhile radicality—quite the contrary. With the times, then, let us assume, rather than insinuate or forebode, that philosophy is nothing but a kind of literature. Or let us assume what may amount to the same thing, that philosophy's *paratext* must be considered as essential to it as it is to the object of literary studies: What does this mean? First and foremost, it means that philosophy is a book—to be more mundane but more precise, philosophizing is an activity of producing books, or, if one prefers, books and articles. Even more precisely and mundanely: philosophizing is a professional practice of writing, reading, publishing, rereading, and republishing books and articles and of engaging in all of these activities with respect to books and articles already written and published, all of this within a highly organized disciplinary context. The field of philosophy, for most of us who practice within or alongside it, is an institutional history of interconnected manufactured artifacts, designed to make other artifacts "speak" in certain ways for those who rediscover them. Such a para-ontology of philosophy would have to begin where I only end, with my revised answer to philosophy's "basic question": the history of philosophy is revision itself, and only revision.

In what remains of the Epilogue, I want to indicate briefly one direction in which the critique of philosophy might proceed, toward the question of philosophical canon formation, a question whose long-time prevalence within literary studies has yet to impress the neighboring discipline of philosophy. In particular, I wish to develop further the notion that philosophical readings are essentially rhetorical, in the fullest sense, and that philosophy's relation to its own past is therefore inherently an anticipation, a para-practical prolepsis, of that tradition's own future, mediated through interpretive rereadings.

In my discussions of the reception of the philosophical revision-encounter, I have generally eschewed the most readily available traditions of *Rezeptionästhetik* and related hermeneutical models of interpretation in favor of an Emersonian terminology which would perceive philosophical history as the ongoing production of occluded rhetorical appeals to audiences. To the degree that there is a post-Emersonian tradition of interpretation available for the continuation of this rhetorical critique, it persists intermittently, offering mere glimpses of an alternative to well-established hermeneutical paradigms of interpretation within the discipline. Here I will look briefly at two critics whom I see as belonging to a post-Emersonian rhetorical tradition of historiography: Stanley Fish, in his work on "interpretive communities" within literary studies, and Richard Rorty, in his speculations on the pragmatics of philosophical canon formation. We can consider the rather notorious glibness, or even simplicity, of these two critics with respect to the epistemological dilemma of the "subject" of reading encounters, as a positive trait, a methodological perpetuation of Emersonian "rudeness," or extradialectical singularity with respect to historicity. In particular, this rudeness or crudeness permits to emerge, precisely because of its simultaneous obviousness and profundity, a crucial aspect of philosophical canon formation which *Rezeptionästhetik* leaves relatively occluded: the ambivalent role of the author as a "primary" interpreter of his or her own text, and the counterintuitive antichronology into which such a role recasts the history of a text's reception.

Much of what remains provocative for the study of canon formation within Fish's central book *Is There a Text in this Class?* is contained in the essay "What Makes an Interpretation Acceptable." The essay makes strong claims for the relativism of textual interpretations within the histories in which texts are received by readers. For instance, in his reading of Blake's "The Tyger," Fish asserts that although certain potential readings of the poem will certainly fall outside the protocols agreed upon by the "interpretive community" that negotiates the publication of such readings, the interpreted text itself "cannot be the location of the core of agreement by means of which we reject interpretations."[3] Fish's "cannot" suggests a polemical position, and indeed his examples are all designed to provoke interpretive extremes. Both for Blake's poem and for Jane Austen's *Pride and Prejudice*, he proposes alternative readings sufficiently radical to offend the interpretive norms of possibly all extant literary-critical communities—a "Tyger" read as a treatise on the indigestibility of tiger meat ("'Did he who made the lamb make thee?'"),[4] and Austen's novel read as a celebration, not a satire, of the "narrow and circumscribed life of a country gentry," or of "marriage, the preservation of great houses, and so on."[5] These otherwise ridiculous counterreadings serve as a heuristic lesson that "we are never without canons of acceptability: we are always right to rule out certain readings."[6] Most importantly, Fish claims, the very possibility of such readings can show that the "canon of acceptability" by which we reject them must be a literary-critical conception, not strictly a literary one, since (ostensibly) nothing strictly within these texts proscribes them. "Acceptability" belongs to the history of the text's reception, not to anything like the text "itself."

Such an observation is valuable both because it removes the text as the locus of interpretive value and because it calls attention to the institutional protocols that constitute the text as such a locus in the first place. Fish effectively demonstrates that only by virtue of a set of rules that comes to seem like hermeneutical "common sense" can one delimit a horizon of textual liberty, within which a professional or institutional community can agree to disagree. In the context of such a project, the simplicity or the audacity of Fish's examples is to their advantage. But this simplicity betrays Fish's cause in other ways, and brings us to the limit of his proposals about the protocols of rereading. While Fish is persuasive that the community, not the text itself, grounds interpretation, this does not mean that the two positions represented here—text versus community as the "core of agreement"— really oppose one another, except with respect to the most drastic interpretive travesties. For the author is already part of that same interpretive community that would revise her or him, and for that reason it is difficult to imagine another *real* community within which truly radical rereadings would be accepted. Fish is right that the "text itself" never starts out as some "core" of interpreted meaning, but it *can* still ground the history of its rereadings, precisely because its author was its earliest "communal" receiver: the poem or novel (or philosophy) was always already an interpretation of itself, and a rhetorically privileged one. Thus the text *is* a basis for ruling out, say, the outrageous readings Fish offers, not because the author has written anything "in itself," but because the author was, from the start, already an occluded participant in the same community of textual receivers that constructs new interpretations. Interpretative history begins in medias res; texts are already readings of themselves in advance, and are already parts—and rhetorically powerful parts—of their own reception.

Thus we confidently disallow an interpretation of Blake's poetry as a diet, or of Austen's novel as adulation, because such revisionism seems unpersuasive next to Blake's and Austen's own previsions, which seem more than potent enough to establish the text as a "core" of meaning or critical agreement, at least with respect to these particular counterreadings. Less radical alternatives would also have to establish their plausibility alongside and against the author's own perceived interpretive prevision. The real lesson of Fish's extreme examples is not the relative liberty of reading, but rather precisely the power we concede to the "first" reading, that of the author, to circumscribe our rereading practices. In this light, to reread Fish's question, "Is there a text in this class?" is simply to wonder how literary critics, who reread for a living, continue to be persuaded that a text *could* have been thought to exist outside the history of its own interpretation, how a *writing* and a *reading* could ever have seemed so qualitatively distinguishable—and how Fish's thesis that "there is no text" could have come to appear radical. In fact, what interpretations continually show—and philosophy is the paradigmatic instance for such a demonstration, because its very mode is interpretive from the start—is that texts *are* their own revisions, that writers prerevise themselves, albeit in rhetorically sneaky ways.

It is not that agreement or disagreement cannot be "located" in the text—indeed, as Fish himself asserts, it is continually relocated there as a "rhetorical ploy"[7]—but that the meaning of that "core" itself is always renegotiated, and whatever has gotten itself construed as the primary "text itself" has a considerable head start, a kind of ace in the hole, in this negotiation. It is this successfully hypostatic self-revision that Fish's improbable readings expose: the "first" reader's foreclosure, through an interpretive proscription, of future interpretive breadth. It is precisely to such a foreclosure, for instance, that I was compelled to appeal in the final chapter, in order to claim that Heidegger fails to see the essentially ambiguous literalism of Nietzsche's autobiographical texts. There I allied myself with "Nietzsche" as a reader of his own text *against* Heidegger as its improper rereader. A revision-encounter cannot do otherwise.

The philosophical counterpart to Fish's rude reinterpretations of Blake and Austen is Richard Rorty's speculation on the rapaciousness of canon formation in philosophy, which suggests a language that might describe what remains implicit within Fish's model: the retrospective reconstruction of the text as a "core of agreement" for interpretive history. Rorty's philosophical historiography parallels both Emerson's conception of history and Bloom's of poetry, especially in its understanding of interpretation as an imposing reconfiguration of prior historical figures for the benefit of a disciplinary readership. This set of historical relationships Rorty represents with sublime insouciance:

> An ideal Gulag guard can eventually be brought to regard himself as having betrayed his loyalty to his fellow Russians. An ideal Aristotle can be brought to describe himself as having mistaken the preparatory taxonomic stages of biological research for the essence of all inquiry. Each of these imaginary people, by the time he has been brought to accept such a new description of what he meant or did, has become "one of us." He is our contemporary, or our fellow-citizen, or a fellow-member of the same disciplinary matrix.[8]

In a brilliant metonymy, which is already a twist on both a Bloomian *apophrades* and an Emersonian notion of "fateful perception," Rorty describes these characters who get reread by new interpretive interlocutors as "the re-educated dead," a figure which should, like revision itself, be allowed to reside with all the sinister resonances it can evoke.[9] The "dead" are "re-educated" by virtue of a revision-encounter, a structure which Rorty understands, as he makes immediately clear, as a process of rhetorical interaction or "conversation." For instance, he describes P. F. Strawson's reading of Kant simultaneously in terms of communal conversation and rhetorical competition: "Strawson's conversation with Kant is the sort one has with somebody who is brilliantly and originally right about something dear to one's heart, but who exasperatingly mixes up this topic with a lot of outdated foolishness."[10] Here both the essentialist and revisionist strains of the revision-encounter are explicit, if simplified: Strawson's simultaneous loyalty to Kant, and his disappointment in the latter's inherent limitation, along with the imperative to link these two strains in order to correct and complete Kant's thought.

In general, Rorty is interested in describing the characteristics of the process by which a reader such as Strawson produces philosophical readings in light of such an oddly ambivalent relationship to his subject matter. Rorty describes reading in terms of "autonomy" and "freedom," characteristics of what he calls "ironist theory," a kind of play with metaphysics that ultimately intends to dispense with it: "Ironist Theory is thus a ladder which is to be thrown away as soon as one has figured out what it was that drove one's predecessors to theorize."[11] It is with this useful glance toward philosophy's possible futures that Rorty makes the most of his Emersonian inheritance, describing the essence of a philosopher's work as the mere prolepsis of its future revisions, and the reading subject as a retrospective reconstruction. Here he couches the revisionist paralipticism of philosophical writing in his characteristic liberalistic mode, as a conversation between reasonable individuals:

> People often say, quite reasonably, that they only found out what they meant by listening to what they said later on—when they heard themselves reacting to the consequences of their original utterance. It is perfectly reasonable to describe Locke as finding out what he really means, what he was really getting at in the *Second Treatise*, only after conversations in heaven with, successively, Jefferson, Marx, and Rawls.[12]

What Rorty calls "perfectly reasonable" here, that Locke finds out what he was about after his death, in a kind of liberals' heaven, hanging out with Jefferson, Marx, and Rawls, I want to render a bit less reasonable but a bit more pragmatic. This "heaven" is nothing if not the conventional afterlife of texts, their reception in the form of the production of new texts (Rorty's "conversations") that follow and revise them. Jefferson, Marx, and Rawls *are* the heaven (or hell) of Locke's text, or rather their audiences *are*, and these thinkers, in turn, serve as guardian angels or as Bloom's "covering cherub," alternately preserving and "blocking" for those audiences "what [Locke] really means."

Like Fish's model, Rorty's is most useful where it most strongly avers its points, and where its antihermeneutical rudeness allows it presumptively to advocate one sort of philosophical historiography over another. Such advocations serve to expose clearly and distinctly the possible modes of philosophical interrelation, and are the closest thing we have in the philosophical discipline to Bloom's aggressive demystification of poetic self-containment. As Rorty says, again with his characteristic glibness, his work is an attempt "to get rid of the idea that philosophy is a natural kind."[13] This is a worthy goal, although the notion of philosophy's naturalness is not so easily gotten rid of, precisely because philosophical revision-encounters entail the obfuscation of revisionism *as such*, and operate on the rhetorical principle that what a textual reading reveals to its audiences is *the text itself*, its proper or natural utterance, previously concealed. As even a brief glance at Fish's interpretations of Blake and Austen shows, it is impossible to remain content with Rorty's characteristic recommendation that we become "ironists," or people "who realize that anything can be made to look good or bad by being redescribed."[14] For this view (ironically) abstracts out the very audience whose reception of that ironic redescription *is* its very existence, and who must be persuaded in order for the irony to come off as a revised reality. If "making things look good or bad" were as easy as Rorty and Fish seem to believe, texts would hardly find the opportunity to form *histories*, let alone canons, for nothing could be critically excluded in order to delimit them as such. It is not ironic redescription, but precisely its occlusion, its paraliptical self-suppression, that permits a reading to enter into a history of textual positions. Irony is not, as Rorty states, "the opposite . . . of common sense,"[15] but rather its very mechanism, tenuously connected to the institutional and conventional procedures required to make "common" some particular sense of a text.

The critique of philosophy needs to be less unironic about the oxymoron of an individual "sensory" experience held "in common." What is interpretive common sense but an occluded demand that we experience the text in this or that way, an insidious attempt to make us believe we "sense" in the text what another has *told* us is there, before we summon the impertinence to say otherwise?

Reference Matter

Notes

INTRODUCTION

1. In my approach to Heidegger's *Nietzsche* I diverge from the emphases of most critics of these texts. To pick two typical but strong examples: Christopher Fynsk tends to follow Heidegger's own description of his "confrontation [*Auseinandersetzung*]" with Nietzsche as a "liberating engagement," and as the "demarcation of a new historical position" (*Heidegger*, 55–56). With slightly different aims, Reiner Schürmann asserts that "[Heidegger's texts on Nietzsche] speak *formally* about Nietzsche, but *materially* about technology; they describe technology as the closing field in the history of presence, as the 'release of Being into machination,' but they do so with the help of a vocabulary taken from Nietzsche" (*Heidegger on Being and Acting*, 182). In contrast to both Fynsk and Schürmann, I suspend questions of the lectures' overall philosophical gist, or of how they serve Heidegger's general projects. To appropriate Schürmann's vocabulary, I speak *materially* about the *form* of the reading. This ostensibly narrower emphasis on the reading's form must be justified through an examination of the formal nature of philosophical reading itself, and so I leave it for my exposition, especially beginning in Chapter 3.

2. The edited text of the lectures appeared in German in 1961 as *Nietzsche*, vols. 1 and 2, published by Gunther Neske. The two Neske volumes are translated into English in four volumes (with exceptions noted below), edited by David Farrell Krell. In English, the four volumes appear as follows: (1) *The Will to Power as Art* (1979); (2) *The Eternal Recurrence of the Same* (1984); (3) *The Will to Power as Knowledge and as Metaphysics* (1987); and (4) *Nihilism* (1982). These texts are also issued in a two-volume paperback (1991), with form and pagination identical to that of the original four volumes, and with an

added editor's introduction. Heidegger's original lecture notes are gradually being published in his *Gesamtausgabe*, as follows: *Nietzsche: der Wille zur Macht als Kunst* (winter 1936–1937; vol. 43, 1985); *Nietzsches metaphysische Grundstellung in abendländischen Denken: die ewige Wiederkehr des Gleichen* (summer 1937; vol. 44, 1986); *Nietzsches 2d. Unzeitgemäße Betrachtung* (winter 1938/39; vol. 46, in preparation); *Nietzsches Lehre vom Willen zur Macht als Erkenntnis* (summer 1939; vol. 47, 1989); *Nietzsche: der europäische Nihilismus* (2d trimester, 1940; vol. 48, 1986); *Nietzsches Metaphysik* and *Einleitung in die Philosophie— Denken und Dichten* (winter 1944–1945; vol. 50, 1990). Three crucial texts from the 1961 edition of *Nietzsche* are not included in the English translation, but they are available in *The End of Philosophy*, edited by Joan Stambaugh. These are "Metaphysics as History of Being [Metaphysik als Geschichte des Seins]," "Sketches for a History of Being as Metaphysics [Entwürfe zur Geschichte des Seins als Metaphysik]," and "Recollection in Metaphysics [Erinnerung in die Metaphysik]." Stambaugh's book also includes, at Heidegger's request, a text entitled "Overcoming Metaphysics [Überwindung der Metaphysik]," which is a compilation of notes from 1936–1946, published in German in *VA*, 71–99.

3. This is aside from a peculiarly American tradition engaging Nietzsche from concerns arising from traditions of philosophy highly suspicious of metaphysics—most notably, in Arthur Danto's *Nietzsche as Philosopher* (1965), and Alexander Nehamas's *Nietzsche: Life as Literature* (1985). Gilles Deleuze in *Nietzsche and Philosophy* (1962) remains the most important contemporary alternative to the systematic-metaphysical understanding of Nietzsche that Heidegger's texts inaugurate (See also, Deleuze, *Nietzsche* [1965]). An important alternative that precedes Heidegger's reading is Karl Jaspers's *Nietzsche: An Introduction* (1936), largely forgotten perhaps, ironically, because of both its closeness to Heidegger's interpretation of Nietzsche, and Heidegger's own assertions about its distance.

4. Karl Löwith writes: "Wilhelm Szilasi has pointed out that, apart from Schelling and Hegel, no significant philosopher has devoted as large a proportion of his life's work to the interpretation of philosophical texts as Heidegger. He is a lover of the intended word [*des gedachten Wortes*], and precisely for this reason he is against philologists, who simply seize upon the text without also perceiving what is unsaid in it" (Löwith, 99; see Szilasi, 73).

5. Kant, *Critique of Pure Reason*, 17–37 (Preface to the second edition). Also see the Preface to Kant's *Prolegomena*, 1–9. The latter book is a prefatory work composed between the first and second editions of the first *Critique*. By com-

parison to Kant, it may be interesting to compare the Preface of a work almost as bound to the notion of "first principles" as Kant's, namely, Edmund Husserl's *Ideas* (see especially p. xvii). Despite Husserl's ambition to construct a "pure phenomenology," he begins with, and then attempts to overstep, a summary of the concept of "phenomena" in other sciences.

6. Wittgenstein, *Philosophical Investigations*, v–vi. My description requires a qualification, since by at least one account, Wittgenstein could have considered the sole purpose of the *Investigations* to revise the *Tractatus*. Saul Kripke reports, "Wittgenstein himself once found the *Tractatus* theory natural and inevitable—Malcomb says that even in his later period he regarded it as the *only* alternative to his later work—and sometimes he writes as if the reader will naturally be inclined to the *Tractatus* theory unless he personally intervenes to prevent it" (78).

7. Sartre, 35–42.

8. As an example, I offer Rodolphe Gasché's *The Tain of the Mirror*, 1–9. Gasché distinguishes his "philosophical" exegesis of Jacques Derrida's work from what he identifies as "literary" critiques, especially in the United States: "Many deconstructionist critics have chosen simply to ignore the profoundly philosophical thrust of Derridean thought, and have consequently misconstrued what deconstruction consists of and what it seeks to achieve. . . . Yet since this book is concerned neither with the history of deconstructionist criticism and its miscomprehension of deconstruction in a strict sense, . . . I have avoided all detailed debate with deconstructive criticism" (3). Here Gasché, with a powerful but entirely conventional interpretive gesture, "avoids" a debate with "deconstructive critics" precisely by couching his entire project in a revisionist mode, thereby appearing to overstep mere "detailed" polemics by identifying his particular revision of the debate as too essential for argument.

9. For this reason I will generally refer to the "revision-encounter" and not to the "revision" of Nietzsche, a distinction I clarify in Chapter 3.

10. Hegel, *Phenomenology*, 28 [35].

11. Ibid., 2 [4].

12. Ibid., 50 [61].

13. Hegel, *Difference*, 85 [15–16], and 89 [19].

14. Hegel, *Logic*, par. 13 (19 [59]), Hegel's emphasis.

15. Ibid., par. 13 (18–19 [58]), Hegel's emphasis.

16. Ibid., par. 14 (20 [60]).

17. A compact demonstration of this misrelation of philosophy to its particular appearance is available in Paul de Man's reading of Hegel's chapter on

"Sense-Certainty" in the essay "Hypogram and Inscription" (*Resistance*, 41–43). De Man notes that Hegel asks readers to test an "immediate" truth of sense-certainty by preserving it, hence by writing it down; eventually one discovers that it becomes false as a piece of particular knowledge, and true only as an abstract "universal." But here the unsublatable "here and now of inscription"—ironically entailed by the *textual* form in which linguistic statements about exemplary sensual particulars are lent persistence through time (the words "here" and "now" written on a piece of paper, and then reread *later*)— is figured by synecdoche as the unsublatable textual condition of the philosophical system itself: "Because he wrote it down, the existence of a here and a now of Hegel's text is undeniable as well as totally blank. It reduces, for example, the entire text of the *Phenomenology* to the endlessly repeated stutter: *this* piece of paper, *this* piece of paper, and so on" (*Resistance*, 42). Of course the more relentlessly such a reading reduces thought-systems to their particulars—for instance, the *Phenomenologie des Geistes* to "this darned piece of paper"—the more abstract the reduction itself becomes, and therefore the less it can still account, as de Man well knows, for particular attributes of *this* text, *here* and *now*. The analysis of revision, as a subgenre of textualist critique of philosophy, constantly confronts this tension between a loyalty to the particularity of the given interpretation and a temptation to reduce active reading practices to a static model of intertextual relation.

18. Such a distinction takes into account what Jacques Derrida identifies as the "*différance*" or "radical alterity" of the philosophical text *as* text (Derrida, "Différance," in *Speech and Phenomena*, 129–60; see also Andrzej Warminski, *Readings*, 183–91). I use the term "literary" here in the same sense as Philippe Lacoue-Labarthe, as against philosophy's own "insisten[ce] . . . in defining itself against what we call literature," and as a name for "[philosophy's] more or less obscure and silent obsession with the *text*," an obsession which is perhaps no longer either as silent or as obscure as it may have once been (Lacoue-Labarthe, *Subject*, 1). It need hardly be stated—any more than for Lacoue-Labarthe (*Subject*, 1–3)—that a study such as mine owes much to the work of Jacques Derrida, and in my case especially to the essay "Plato's Pharmacy" (Derrida, *Dissemination*, 61–171) However, I am more generally indebted to Luce Irigaray's deep analysis of the peculiar suppressed or "frozen" *time* entailed by philosophical representation and interpretation, in her essay "Plato's Hystera" (Irigaray, *Speculum*, 241–365).

19. Roman Ingarden, *Literary Work*, 4; *Cognition*, 11. See also, in general, Wolfgang Iser's *The Act of Reading* and *The Implied Reader*. My study of revi-

sion quickly diverges from Iser's (or Ingarden's) "aesthetics" of reception, which focuses on "what *happens* to us through . . . texts." Because in philosophical revision a "response" never occurs primarily in the form of an aesthetic experience, but rather always as a new text, such "response" is more properly the subject of a poetics, and eventually, a rhetoric. Iser writes: "It is called aesthetic response because, although it is brought about by the text, it brings into play the imaginative and perceptive faculties of the reader, in order to make him adjust and even differentiate his focus" (*Act*, x). This concentration on "imagination," or on the play of "faculties"—in essence, on "psychological effects" (see Stanley Fish, "Literature in the Reader," in *Is There a Text*, 70)—is inherent in nearly all "reader-response" theories, since they begin by supposing the necessity of a reading *subject*. However, a revisionist *text* cannot in principle achieve its "realization [*Konkretisation*]" (Ingarden) through the single "act" of an individual reader or psyche, however socially immanent or trained, but entails the further real-ization (that is, re*text*ualization) of the reading as well. Indeed it entails a continual process of retextualizing "responses" (See Suleiman, "Introduction," 22). Strictly speaking, a revision is not a "response" per se, but the writing down of a response, always already for the benefit of other responders, and hence not an immediate or "aesthetic" category. See my discussion of "Reception aesthetics [*Rezeptionästhetik*]" in the work of Hans Robert Jauss in the Interlude.

20. This is Kuhn's term for the practice of science conceived within an already established paradigm. See Kuhn, 10.

21. I use "Revolution" also in Kuhn's sense of a critical alteration in a paradigm and, therefore, of an alteration in the practice of "normal" science. See Kuhn, 92–110.

22. The major theory of reception that explicitly addresses a more concrete, textual "response" to texts is Harold Bloom's "theory of poetry," which I discuss separately in Chapter 5.

23. See Victor Farias, *Heidegger and Nazism*, 84. The two other crucial historical works on Heidegger's politics from the approximate time of Farias's are Hugo Ott's *Martin Heidegger: Unterwegs zu seiner Biographie* (1989) and the excellent biography by Rüdiger Safranski, *Martin Heidegger: Between Good and Evil* (1994).

24. See Heidegger, "Nur noch ein Gott kann uns retten," 193–219. This interview was conducted on September 23, 1966, but published only after Heidegger died in 1976. A translation, along with relevant documents, can be found in Neske and Kettering, 41–66.

25. These documents can be found in English in Neske and Kettering, and in Wolin, *Heidegger Controversy*. See especially Heidegger's retrospective text, "The Rectorate 1933/34: Facts and Thoughts," in Neske and Kettering, 15–32. The supposed availability of the facts of the Heidegger case for academic or public readers before the appearance of Farias's book in 1987 has been drastically overdrawn by both critics of Farias and professional readers of Heidegger's texts. Mere availability, or knowledge of existence, particularly among a group of academic professionals, in no way constitutes a public dissemination of facts, let alone debate about their political implications.

26. Derrida writes: "Perhaps Heidegger thought: I can only voice a condemnation of National Socialism if it is possible for me to do so in a language not only at the peak of what I have already said, but also at the peak of what has happened here. He was incapable of doing this. And perhaps his silence is an honest form of admitting he was incapable of it" ("Heidegger's Silence," 148). Gadamer writes: "Here was a man whose thinking held a half-century in its spell, a man who radiated an incomparable power of suggestion, who as a thinker discovered the 'care-structure' of existence in all the behavior of humans toward one another and the world, and (inextricably bound to it) man's tendency toward self-destruction. Yet this man could also, in his own behavior, lose himself in delusions. Heidegger himself recognized this and admitted it through his later silence" ("Political Incompetence," 368).

27. See Farias, *Heidegger and Nazism*, 118; Wolin, *Heidegger Controversy*, 46; Schneeberger, 135–36.

28. Lacoue-Labarthe, *Typography*, 286.

29. Ibid., 288

30. Ibid., 296.

31. Heidegger, "Letter to the Rector," 66.

32. These two comments are from, respectively, Jean-François Lyotard's *Heidegger and "the jews,"* 67, and Richard Wolin's *The Politics of Being*, 56.

33. Fynsk, 233. This comment is from Fynsk's "Postface: The Legibility of the Political," added to the expanded edition of his *Heidegger*.

34. Löwith, 75.

CHAPTER I

1. The German reads: *Über das Verhältnis der* Kunst *zur* Wahrheit *bin ich am frühesten ernst geworden: und noch jetzt stehe ich mit einem heiligen Entsetzen*

vor diesem Zwiespalt. Heidegger cites Nietzsche's *Nachlaß* from the *Großoktavausgabe,* 14:368. Both Neske's German and Krell's English editions of
Nietzsche retain these outdated citations, which are not correlated with the
newer *Kritische Studienausgabe* of Nietzsche's works, edited by Colli and Montinari. The passage of Nietzsche cited by Heidegger continues: "My first book
was devoted to it. *The Birth of Tragedy* believes in art on the background of
another belief—that it *is not possible to live with truth,* that the 'will to truth' is
already a symptom of degeneration [*Entartung*]" (*Ne,* 1:74; *Ng,* 1:88).

2. Krell translates Heidegger's phrase as "a discordance that arouses
dread" and comments, "In the title of this section, *Der erregende Zwiespalt zwis-
chen Wahrheit und Kunst,* the phrase *erregende Zwiespalt* is actually a condensa-
tion of the statement made here. That is to say, discordance between art and
truth 'rages' insofar as it *arouses* dread" (*Ne,* 1:142 n).

3. "Overcome" translates *überwinden,* as distinct from *umkehren* or
umdrehen. See Heidegger's section entitled "Nietzsche's Overturning
[*Umdrehung*] of Platonism" (*Ne,* 1:200–10; *Ng,* 1:231–42).

4. The conclusion of this passage proposes an economy of relatedness or
unity at the root of all discordance and offers an example of sameness-in-dif-
ference that seems to suggest a conservative tendency within Heidegger's
broader philosophical essentialism—or possibly a rationalization for conservative political advocacy: "Only [things] which relate to one another [*was sich
aufeinander bezieht*] can be opposed to one another [*gegeneinander sein*]. But
such opposition is not yet discordance. For surely their being opposed to one
another presupposes a being drawn toward and related to one another
[*Aufeinanderbezogensein*], which is to say, their converging upon and agreeing
with one another [*Übereinkommen*] in one respect. A real political opposition—
not mere dispute—is only present where the selfsame political order is willed;
only here can ways and goals and basic principles diverge [*auseinandergehen*]. In
an opposition, agreement prevails in one respect, whereas in other respects
there is variance [*Verschiedenheit*]. But whatever diverges in the same respect in
which it agrees, slips into discordance. Here the opposition springs from the
divergence of what converged, indeed in such a way that precisely being apart
they enter into the supreme way of belonging together [*die höchste Zusam-
mengehörigkeit*]" (*Ne,* 1:189; *Ng,* 1:219).

5. This passage is particularly resistant to translation. I have bracketed two
of Krell's helpful interpolations.

6. Otto Pöggeler offers an interesting if dated gloss on Heidegger's confrontation with Nietzsche in the context of Heidegger's withdrawal from pub-

lic support of National Socialism, in *Martin Heidegger's Path of Thinking*, 84. Also see Fynsk, 61–64.

7. Invoking this dialectical logic, Heidegger uncharacteristically defers to Hegel, perhaps as much to indicate the preliminary nature of his point as to draw support from precedent: "Since Hegel we have known that a contradiction is not necessarily proof against the truth of a metaphysical statement, but [may be] a proof for it" (*Ne*, 1:22; *Ng*, 1:30–31).

8. Heidegger links the "as-structure" of interpretation to a "fore-having [*Vorhabe*]" and "foresight [*Vorsicht*]," and through these concepts offers a general account of the interpreter's relation to the thing interpreted, an account which is also potentially a model of the inherently revisionist perspectivism of *Dasein*'s "manner of interpreting": "The appropriation [*Zueignung*] of that which is understood but still veiled [*des Verstandenen, aber noch Eingehüllten*] accomplishes the unveiling always under the guidance of a perspective which fixes what is to be understood with regard to [the way] in which it is to be interpreted. The interpretation is grounded for the moment [*jeweils*] in a *foresight* which 'takes a cut at' [*anschneidet*] what has been taken [up] in fore-having, with a definite manner of interpretation [*Auslegbarkeit*]" (*BT*, 140–41 [150]). Also see *BT*, 328 [359].

9. See Heidegger, "Recollection in Metaphysics" (*EP*, 81–82; *Ng*, 2:488–89), and *Ne*, 4:150f; *Ng*, 2:203f.

10. Elsewhere Heidegger states that for Nietzsche "art is affirmation [*Bejahung*] of the sensuous" (*Ne*, 1:162; *Ng*, 1:189), whereas "truth," just as for Plato, describes "knowledge of true Being as philosophy" (*Ne*, 1:163; *Ng*, 1:191).

11. As I will discuss in more detail below and in subsequent chapters, to compel art and truth to concord is a version of an attempt to unify the concept of Being with that of becoming, and more specifically, for Heidegger's reading of Nietzsche, to reconcile "eternal return" with "will to power." In the first lecture course, Heidegger only hints at this underlying context for the interpretation of art and truth, but it remains crucially in the background. Here is a condensed version: "Nietzsche interprets the Being of beings as will to power. Art he considers [as] the highest form of will to power. The proper essence of art is exemplified in the grand style. But the latter, because of its own essential unity [*Wesenseinheit*], points to an original [inter]developing unity [*sich gestaltende Einheit*] of the active and reactive, of Being and becoming. At the same time we must keep in mind what the precedence of the distinction active-reactive, which is expressly [*eigens*] emphasized over the dis-

tinction of Being and becoming, suggests for Nietzsche's metaphysics. For formally one could subsume the distinction active-reactive under one pole of the subordinate distinction of Being and becoming, namely, under becoming. The disposition [*Fügung*] of the active, and of Being and becoming, into an original unity proper to the grand style must therefore be carried out in will to power. But will to power *is* as eternal recurrence. In the latter Nietzsche wants to think together [or, to combine in thought—*zusammendenken*], in an original unity, Being and becoming, action and reaction. Thereby is granted a view [*Ausblick*] onto the metaphysical horizon within which we are to think what Nietzsche names the grand style and art in general" (*Ne*, 1:135–36; *Ng*, 1:160).

12. I may as well note that what I assert here is in contrast, if not necessarily in full opposition, to Theodor Adorno's famous but somewhat routine criticism of Heidegger's vagueness as the attribute of a sacrosanct and anticritical "jargon": "When it dresses empirical words with aura, [the jargon] exaggerates general concepts and ideas of philosophy—as for instance the concept of being—so grossly that that conceptual essence, the mediation through the thinking subject, disappears completely under the varnish" (Adorno, 12). Even more bluntly: "Whoever is versed in the jargon does not have to say what he thinks, does not even have to think it properly. The jargon takes over this task and devaluates thought" (9). Even so, a vagueness that has retained its power to influence critical readings may not be so readily dismissed, not only theoretically, but in practice, whether its influence is due to mere convention or to shared but as yet unstated propositions. It concretizes itself precisely as a historical legacy for other readers; it becomes thought because it is history and has no ulterior thought-in-itself.

13. Heidegger quite deliberately positions his reading within a hyperbolically expansive milieu, the tone of which he clearly inherits in part from Nietzsche's own typical hyperbole, particularly in his late writing, but which he reconstitutes in his own more laconic manner: "If in Nietzsche's thinking the prior tradition of Western thought is gathered and completed in a decisive respect, then the confrontation with Nietzsche becomes one with all Western thought hitherto" (*Ne*, 1:4; *Ng*, 1:13). Nietzsche's "meditation" on art and truth is "a question about the essence of Being" itself, and so with this question the inquiry proceeds such that "nothing further remains outside the question, not even the nothing [*das Nichts*]" (*Ne*, 1:68; *Ng*, 1:81).

14. See the section entitled "Five Statements on Art" (*Ne*, 1:69–76; *Ng*, 1:82–91). The five statements, and their correlations in *The Will to Power*, are: (1) "Art is the most perspicuous [*durchsichtigste*] and familiar form of will to

power" [see *WP*, par. 797]; (2) "Art must be conceived [*begriffen*] in terms of the artist" [see *WP*, par. 797]; (3) "According to the expanded concept of the artist, art is the basic occurrence [*Grundgeschehen*] of every being; a being is, insofar as it is, a self-creating, created [entity]" [see *WP*, par. 797]; (4) "Art is the distinctive countermovement against nihilism" [see *WP*, par. 853, part ii]; and (5) "Art is more valuable than 'truth'" [see *WP*, par. 853, part iv] (*Ne*, 1:75; *Ng*, 1:90).

15. Heidegger writes that "it was just this question of the center [of his own work] that genuinely 'maltreated' [*eigentlich 'malträtierte'*] Nietzsche" (*Ne*, 1:16; *Ng*, 1:24). That Heidegger is coolly describing a facet of *his own* reading in the guise of a portrayal of Nietzsche's own bibliographical difficulties, we can perhaps glean from the rhetoric of obviousness used in the passage immediately following: "Certainly it was not the extrinsic question of finding a suitable connection among the handwritten materials available; it was, without Nietzsche's properly coming to know of it or stumbling across it, the question of the self-grounding of philosophy." Elsewhere Heidegger asserts that "we can see clearly [from certain passages] how unconcerned Nietzsche is with regard to a unified, solidly grounded [*begründeten*] presentation of his teaching. We know that he is only just on the way [*er macht sich erst auf den Weg dahin*], that he is resolutely open [*entschlossen*] [about it]" (*Ne*, 1:50; *Ng*, 1:61).

16. The more "basic" notion of truth is as the emergence or "presencing [*Anwesen*]" of Being (*physis*). See, for instance, Heidegger, *Einführung in die Metaphysik*, 16–18. A translation of the revised edition of these lectures (1953) is available in *Introduction to Metaphysics*, see 14–17.

17. Heidegger offers a detailed analysis of the Platonic term *idea* as "visibleness," and of the conception of *mimēsis* that it entails (see *Ne*, 1:162–99; *Ng*, 1:189–217). He notes that Greek interpretations of *eidos*, or "presencing as outward appearance [*Anwesen in Aussehen*]," presuppose "the interpretation of truth as *alētheia*, non-distortion [*Unverstelltheit*]" (*Ne*, 1:182; *Ng*, 1:212). Thus *mimēsis*, the secondary or tertiary production of the *eidos* in particular materials such as wood or paint, is not mere "copying and reproducing," but "subordinate pro-duction [*nachgeordnetes Her-stellen*]," in which the *eidos* appears or "presences," but only as a *phantasma* from a single particular manner or *tropos* (*Ne*, 1:185–86; *Ng*, 1:215–16). The transcendence of the *eidos* is thus not tantamount to the sovereignty of a pure philosophical access to the "*on as idea*" over and above some nonideal reproduction, but rather to the fact that the thinker of a "visible" thing, unlike, say, the painter of it, can exhibit more than

one *phantasma* at the same time, and therefore does not automatically limit the degree to which the *eidos* may be presented. The difference between the thinker and the artist, and therefore between the pure production of *eidos* (Being) and the limited, phantasmatic production, is, to speak rather loosely, quantitative: "What is decisive for the Greek-Platonic concept of *mimēsis*, of imitation [*Nachahmung*], is *not* reproduction or portraiture, [not the fact] that the painter brings out the same thing once again; rather, [what is decisive is] that this is precisely what he cannot do, that he is even less capable than the craftsman of duplicating the same thing. . . . The *mimētēs* is in its [or his] essence defined by the position of distance, [a distance] which results from the hierarchy established with regard to ways of production and in the light of pure 'outward appearance' [*Aussehen*], Being" (*Ne*, 1:185; *Ng*, 1:215).

18. Heidegger's word is "*herausdrehen*," as in the "twisting free [of Platonism]" (see *Ne*, 1:201; *Ng*, 1:233).

19. See Plato, *Republic*, Book X, approximately lines 595a–609.

20. Heidegger uses the perhaps diminutive term "differs from" or "is something other than" [*Anders . . . ist*] to describe positivism's critique despite the fact that positivism is clearly a deliberate and direct *reversal* of the metaphysical core of Platonism, an *anti*metaphysics (*Ne*, 1:152; *Ng*, 1:178). As I will discuss, Heidegger reserves the term "reversal [*Umkehrung*]" precisely for Nietzsche's own step beyond positivism, in his particular version of the "overturning [*Umdrehung*]" of Platonism.

21. Such a definition is, of course, insufficiently subtle to account for the variety of particular positivistic philosophies, just as the characterization of Platonism was too cursory and general to apply to Plato himself. Positivistic philosophy, like Heidegger's or Nietzsche's own philosophies, tends itself to be a confrontation with the ambivalent dialectics of the *positum* and what is "universal" or "formal" within its presence. What Heidegger represents here as positivism is rather a historical trend, a large-scale moment or "event" (*Ereignis*—a term I discuss in subsequent chapters), one in which Nietzsche, too, participates: "Nietzsche's conception of the essence of truth keeps within the realm of the great tradition of Western thought, no matter how much Nietzsche's particular interpretations of that conception deviate from earlier interpretations" (*Ne*, 1:153; *Ng*, 1:179).

22. For Plato's philosophy—as distinguished from that which, for Heidegger, Nietzsche construes as Platonism—art and truth do not "rage" against each other, but are simply "distant." Indeed, because art is construed broadly

as *poein*, or pro-duction [*Her-stellen*], art and truth are "in a felicitous concordance [*beglückenden Zwiespalt*]" within Plato's thought. See Heidegger's discussion of Plato's *Phaedrus* (*Ne*, 1:188–99; *Ng*, 1:218–31).

23. See Heidegger's discussion of art and *mimēsis* in the *Republic* (*Ne*, 1:171–87; *Ng*, 1:198–217).

24. Briefly to augment the discussion of Platonic "art" and its "distance from the form" begun in the notes above, I need to distinguish more carefully between the "once-removed" craftsman of, say, the bed, and the "twice-removed" artist or painter. What the craftsman, also named a *dēmiourgos*, makes is an "implement" for the use of the people, the *dēmos*, but he does so by producing a copy of the form, which alone possesses permanence and "Being." Thus the craftsman "keeps an eye" on the unchanging form, or *eidos*, while he makes the particular transitory item. Yet the manner in which the form is copied, the *tropos*, or "way" of production, is decisive for the quality of the copy, for as Heidegger writes, "something produced 'is' because the idea lets it be seen as such, lets it come to presence in its outward appearance; which means, lets it 'be.' Only to that extent can that which is produced itself be called 'being' [*seiend*]" (*Ne*, 1:176; *Ng*, 1:204). Even a mere mirror is capable, within a certain *tropos*, of "re-producing" things in the world. But the artist who wields a mirror—like the painter who "mirrors" in paint the production of the craftsman—is not himself a *dēmiourgos*, producing a useful item for *dēmos*, but only a "*mimētēs hou ekeinoi dēmiourgoi*, 'a copier [*Nachmacher*] of the things of which those others are the pro-ducers [*Her-steller*] for the public'" (*Ne*, 1:184–85; *Ng*, 1:214). In all, there are three types of related productions, all organized around "the distance from Being and its pure visibility" (*Ne*, 1:185; *Ng*, 1:215): that of the god, who lets the *idea* itself be fully present, that of the craftsman, who reproduces the idea, making visible a material version of the *eidos* usable by the *dēmos*, and that of the artist, who uselessly copies the production of the *dēmiourgos*. Crucially, the original difference between the three producers is not whether or not they make the *eidos* visible, but rather the degree to which they do so; the artist is capable of "presencing" only the *eidōlon*, the "little" *eidos*. He or she is a poor thinker or discoverer of truth (*alētheia*—which Heidegger translates as *Unverborgenheit*, or "unconcealment").

25. Heidegger provides a brief reading of this figure: Nietzsche distinguishes the organic world from the inorganic by the fact that in the organic each point of force, each occurrence of movement, has a particular perspective in relation to all others. But in this sense *all* being is "organic," and properly

speaking "'there is no inorganic world'" (cited in *Ne*, 1:213; *Ng*, 1:245). Everything that exists is related to everything else through a particular viewpoint or perspective, hence it is "alive" according to the above definition. Nietzsche thus also suggests that "'all Being is essentially [*essentiell*] something perceiving'" (cited in *Ne*, 1:213; *Ng*, 1:245), an idea attributable foremost to Leibniz. Compare *Gay Science*, par. 109, in which Nietzsche offers a formulation that only appears opposed to the above: "Let us beware of saying that death is opposed to life. The living is merely a type of what is dead, and a very rare type" (*Gay Science*, 168; *S*, 3:468).

26. Compare Heidegger: "Reality, Being, is appearance [*Schein*] in the sense of perspectival letting-shine [*perspektivischen Scheinenlassens*]. But to this reality belongs at the same time the majority [*Mehrheit*] of perspectives and so the possibility of illusion [*Anscheins*] and its being made fast [*dessen Fest-machung*], that is, [the possibility of] Truth as a type of appearance in the sense of 'mere' appearance" (*Ne*, 1:215; *Ng*, 1:248).

27. The final subquotation is from Nietzsche's *Nachlaß* (*Großoktavausgabe*, 7:4). Compare: "fixed [*feste*] things, 'objects,' emerge for a living being [*Lebe-wesen*] in what it encounters; constant things with enduring qualities, by which [the living being] gets its bearings. The whole range of what is fixed and constant is, according to the old Platonic conception, the region [*Bezirk*] of 'Being,' of the 'true.' This Being [*Sein*], viewed perspectivally, is but the one-sided, fixed [*festgemachte*] [illusory] appearance [*Anschein*], [taken to be] solely definitive [*maßgebend*], and thus it becomes precisely a mere semblance; Being, the true, is mere semblance, error" (*Ne*, 1:214; *Ng*, 1:246).

CHAPTER 2

1. Nietzsche, *Twilight*, 485–86; *S*, 6:80–81.

2. The word "easily [*leicht*]" is somewhat diverting, since Heidegger has just finished remarking that heretofore no one at all has perceived the impact or clarity of Nietzsche's "final step."

3. Heidegger is increasingly forceful about this point as the lecture courses progress. Compare: "Nietzsche himself quite early characterizes his philosophy as inverted [*umgekehrten*] Platonism. Yet the inversion does not eliminate the fundamental Platonic position [*die Platonische Grundstellung*], but rather, precisely through the appearance [*Anschein*] of eliminating it, [in fact] entrenches [*verfestigt*] it" (*Ne*, 2:205; *Ng*, 1:469).

4. I follow Krell's translation in lieu of several other possibilities such as "frenzy" or "intoxication." See Krell's discussion of the term in *Ne*, 1:92 n.

5. The second of Nietzsche's "five statements on art" asserts that "art must be grasped in terms of the artist." Heidegger expands upon this point: "Nietzsche understands the aesthetic state of the observer and recipient on the basis of the state of the creator. Thus the effect of the artwork is nothing other than a reawakening of the creator's state in the one who enjoys the artwork. Observation of art follows in the wake [*ist ein Nachvollzug*] of creation. Nietzsche says: '—the effect of artworks is *arousal of the art-creating state, rapture*'" (*Ne*, 1:117; *Ng*, 1:137–38; the subquotation is from *WP*, par. 821).

6. The content of this ellipsis is as follows: "It is that attempt to grasp the beautiful which Rilke's "First Elegy" describes wholly in Nietzsche's sense: "'[. . .]For the beautiful is nothing / but the beginning of the terrible, a beginning we but barely endure; / and it amazes us so, since calmly it disdains / to destroy us' ['*Denn das Schöne ist nichts / als des Schrecklichen Anfang, den wir noch grade ertragen, / und wir bewundern es so, weil es gelassen verschmäht, / uns zu zerstören*']."

7. Compare these passages from *Will to Power*: "Before there is 'thought' ['*gedacht*'] there must have been 'inventing' ['*gedichtet*']; the *construction* of identical cases, of the *appearance* of sameness, is more original [*ursprünglicher*] than the *knowledge* of sameness" (par. 544); "We have *created* the world that possesses values! Knowing this, we also know that reverence for truth is already the consequence of an illusion—and that one should value more than truth the force that forms, simplifies, shapes, invents" (par. 602).

8. The speculative copula I invoke here requires at least a brief explanation, which will come more easily in the third and fourth chapters, when I discuss the manner in which revision "*is*" in metaphysics, or what Heidegger calls a "History of Being [*Seinsgeschichte*]." Basically the copula does not indicate a simple predication, but rather a thought-movement that implies a dialectical process relating the subject and predicate, such that their relationship is negotiated over time, not simply named and reified, in the sentence. Such a movement need not be as obscure as it sounds; it occurs wherever a speculative proposition is offered through the medium of an apparent identificational or definitional copula, as in the statements above: "Being *is* truth," or "Becoming *is* art." Put simply, each term's exegesis in the understanding of the proposition requires a mediation or "movement" through the other term, and thus through the proposition as a whole. Compare Hegel's far more elaborate discussion of the speculative copula in *Phenomenology*, 36–41 [44–49].

9. *Being and Time* leaves this issue basically unaddressed, at least with respect to the "history of truth": "A history of the concept of truth, which could only be presented on the basis [*Boden*] of a history of ontology, is not intended here" (*BT*, 198 [214]). However, the following illustration is provided, to distinguish, on an ontological basis, between the historically created true assertion and the truth, or uncovering, of the entities themselves described by those assertions: "[To say that] before Newton his laws were neither true nor false, cannot signify that before him the [kind of] being [*Seiende*] as has been uncovered and pointed out by those laws didn't exist. The laws became true through Newton, and with them, being [*Seiende*] became accessible in itself to *Dasein*. Once a being has been uncovered, it shows itself precisely as the being which beforehand already was. Such uncovering is the kind of Being [*Seinsart*] of 'truth.' That there are 'eternal truths' will not be adequately proved until it has been successfully demonstrated that *Dasein* has been and will be for all eternity" (*BT*, 208 [227]).

10. Both Nietzsche's inadequate view and Heidegger's critique (or "clarification") are troped by Heidegger as thoroughly historically determined: "That a clarification becomes necessary here has its grounds in the concealment [*Verborgenheit*] of the essence of what is named in such words" (*Ne*, 1:143; *Ng*, 1:168). Furthermore, the necessity of this clarification arises first with an essentially phenomenological (hence post-Nietzschean) insight: "Such a clarification is indispensable from the moment the fact is experienced, that human *Dasein*, insofar as it [is]—[and] is itself—is pointed expressly toward the relations [*Bezüge*] named in such basic words and is bound in relation with them [*in diesen Bezug gebunden ist*]" (ibid.).

11. Heidegger writes, in relation to Nietzsche's meditation on the *Grundwort* "art," which for Nietzsche at one point means "a vision of what is perfect [*Der Anblick des Vollkommenen*]": "But Nietzsche knew also of the great difficulty of this task; for who is to determine [*festsetzen*] what the perfect is? It could only be those who are themselves [perfect] and who therefore know [what it means]. Here opens the abyss of that circle within which the whole of human *Dasein* moves. What health is, only the healthy can say. Yet healthfulness is measured [*bemißt sich*] according to the essential starting point [*Wesensansatz*] of health. What truth is, only the truthful one can make out; but who a truthful one is, is determined [*bestimmt sich*] according to the essential starting point of truth" (*Ne*, 1:127; *Ng*, 1:149–50).

12. Krell's translation is "becomes manifest."

13. Compare this passage (which is difficult to translate adequately): "To

be cognizant, to know—that is not mere familiarity with concepts, but rather it is the grasping of what the concept itself grasps hold of: to grasp Being—that is, to remain knowingly exposed to the advance of Being, which is to say, to its presencing [*Erkennen und Wissen—das ist nicht bloße Kenntnis der Begriffe, sondern ist Begreifen des im Begriff Ergriffenen; das Sein begreifen, d.h. dem Angriff des Seins, d.h. dem An-wesen wissentlich ausgesetzt bleiben*]" (*Ne*, 1:59; *Ng*, 1:71).

CHAPTER 3

1. The whole sentence out of which the latter phrase is lifted reads: "As long as we fail to inquire back into this grounding domain we cling to [mere] words and remain stuck in extrinsic calculations of Nietzsche's thinking."

2. The whole sentence reads: "But of course we will never comprehend the innermost historicity of Nietzschean thought, by virtue of which it spans the breadth of centuries, if we only hunt for reminiscences, borrowings, divergences in an extrinsic manner [*äußerlich*]. We must grasp what Nietzsche properly wanted to think [*den eigentlichen Denkwillen Nietzsches*]" (*Ne*, 1:65; *Ng*, 1:78).

3. The paragraph as a whole is instructive. Note that precisely what is "unambiguously" expressed by Nietzsche is actually quite ambiguous, even "incomprehensible," within the "clarified realm" from which Heidegger *now* interprets it: "With the last paragraph of par. 515 [of *The Will to Power*] Nietzsche risks a step into the innermost essence of reason and thinking, unambiguously expressing their biological nature. 'The subjective compulsion by which we are unable to contradict here is a biological compulsion [. . .].' This sentence provides, again, such a compressed formulation that it would almost have to remain incomprehensible if we did not come at it from a more clarified realm. 'The subjective compulsion by which we are unable to contradict here': Where is 'here'? And 'unable to contradict' what? And why 'contradict'? Nietzsche says nothing about these [matters] because he means something other than would appear [*er etwas anderes meint, als es den Anschein hat*]" (*Ne*, 3:102; *Ng*, 1:592).

4. The whole sentence reads: "Nietzsche's saying [*Spruch*]: truth is an illusion [*Illusion*], truth is a kind of error, has as its innermost, and therefore never foremost uttered [*gar nicht erst ausgesprochenen*] presupposition, the traditional and never challenged characterization of truth as the correctness of representing [*Richtigkeit des Vorstellens*]. Yet for Nietzsche this concept of truth changes

[*abwandelt*] peculiarly and inevitably [*eigentümlich und unvermeidlich*]—therefore not at all arbitrarily [*willkürlich*]."

5. Kierkegaard, *Concept of Irony*, 264.

6. This generic definition of irony dates, in its concrete formulation, to the French *Encyclopédie* of 1765, where irony is defined as "a figure of speech by which one indicates the opposite of what one says" (Preminger and Brogan, 634).

7. Cicero, 320–21. The Greek "*para-lipsis*" means a "passing by" or an "omitting" and is rendered in Latin as "*praeteritio*" as well as "*occultatio*": "*Occultatio est cum dicimus nos praeterire aut non scire aut nolle dicere id quod nunc maxime dicimus.*"

8. Cicero, 320–21.

9. I use "trope" in a broader sense than occurs in either Cicero or Quintilian, but a sense more familiar to modern theoreticians of rhetoric. The term "trope" isn't in Cicero, but both he and Quintilian collect and characterize more or less the same "figures of diction" as a subset of figures generally, and Quintilian identifies this subset as the "tropes." For Quintilian, a trope is "an artistic alteration of a word or phrase from its proper meaning to another" (Quintilian, 301), but he notes that "the *genera* and *species* into which tropes may be divided" are controversial and perhaps undeterminable. In the modern usage upon which I rely, "trope" bears much of the more general meaning that "figure" did for the two classical authors. While neither irony or paralipsis is a "trope" (or a "figure of diction") in either of them, the very generality of Quintilian's definition of "trope" allows either irony or paralipsis to be identified as such.

10. I discuss the "reception" of a paraliptical revision in depth in the second half of the book. Let me note briefly that Paul de Man usefully describes the "disjunction" of the ironic writer's "empirical" and "authentic" (or rather, "non-inauthentic") selves. The irony referred to in the following passage need only be attributed to the confrontation *between* two thinkers, instead of to that within the single thinker "him-" or "herself," in order perfectly to describe the effect of the revision-encounter: "The ironic, twofold self that the writer or philosopher constitutes by his language seems able to come into being only at the expense of his empirical self, falling (or rising) from a stage of mystified adjustment into the knowledge of his mystification. The ironic language splits the subject into an empirical self that exists in a state of inauthenticity and a self that exists only in the form of a language that asserts the knowledge of this inauthenticity" (de Man, *Blindness and Insight*, 214).

11. Kierkegaard, *Concept of Irony*, 265.

12. Quintilian, 401.

13. Examples of *antiphrasis* clearly show that with this term Quintilian denotes the same figure Cicero calls *occultatio*: "'I will not plead against you according to the rigour of the law, I will not press the point which I should perhaps be able to make good'; or again, 'Why should I mention his decrees, his acts of plunder, his acquisition, whether by cession or by force, of certain inheritances?', etc." (Quintilian, 401–3).

14. Quintilian, 401. This passage continues: ". . . nay, a man's whole life may be coloured with *irony*, as was the case with Socrates, who was called an *ironist* because he assumed the role of an ignorant man lost in wonder at the wisdom of others. Thus, as continued *metaphor* develops into allegory, so a sustained series of *tropes* develops into this *figure*." Following several examples of *antiphrasis* (see note 13, above), Quintilian further comments: "Such kinds of irony may even be sustained at times through whole sections of our argument" (403).

15. For instance, for Harold Bloom's theory of influence the "misprision" or "misreading" that initiates the encounter between two thinkers or poets is characterized as an irony, a duplicitous intention (*AI*, 19f). Bloom attributes the duplicity of the ironic stance (albeit with a number of complications) to the poet/reader's unconscious. However, the term "unconscious" is here a temptation, too vague and peremptory to explain fully the structure of an ironic revision of something like an entire text. This appears eventually to be true for Bloom as well, since in *A Map of Misreading*, he more or less brackets the psychologistic explanation used to account for the structure of revision in earlier work, providing a complex tropological model in its stead. I discuss Bloom's theory and his "map" in Chapter 5, where I also take up the issue of reception more fully.

16. Heidegger considers these two *Lehren* to be the core of Nietzsche's last and most fully worked out philosophical thinking, his final "*metaphysische Grundstellung*" (*Ne*, 1:25; *Ng*, 1:33). Heidegger furthermore states that the two positions require a third or mediating position, "Revaluation [*Umwertung*]." Although Heidegger identifies these three "guiding phrases [*Leitworte*]" as on a par within Nietzsche's schematic plans for his "major work," *The Will to Power*, he makes it clear that "revaluation" is a more general aspect of each of the other two "doctrines," and therefore not, strictly speaking, doctrinal itself. Thus *Umwertung* signifies an "intrinsic coherence [*innersten Zusammenhang*]" (*Ne*, 1:17; *Ng*, 1:25). Or more precisely: "The unitariness [*Einheitliche*] of this teaching [that is, the coherence of will to power and eternal recurrence] may be seen historically as the revaluation of values hitherto" (*Ne*, 1:18; *Ng*, 1:26).

17. This posthumously collated aphorism dates from 1883–1885. Although Heidegger, in the quotation immediately following this one, writes that "Nietzsche says ... *Recapitulation* ... ," Walter Kaufmann notes that Peter Gast, not Nietzsche, supplied this title (*WP*, 330 n). Colli and Montinari omit the title in their edition of Nietzsche (*S*, 8:320). Krell mentions the title in *Ne*, 1:19 n, and also discusses generally the problem of the relation of will to power and eternal recurrence, and particularly Heidegger's ambivalent debts to Baeumler in the reading of this aphorism (*Ne*, 3:255–76). See also Krell's brief discussion in *Ne*, 2:201 n, in which he cites the text of the aphorism in full. Krell there comments, without further elaboration, that the "sentences from this long note which Heidegger neglects to cite by no means corroborate the use he makes of it."

18. The entire sentence reads: "Nietzsche thinks the thought [of eternal return] in such a way that with his metaphysics he reverts to the beginning [*Anfang*] of Western philosophy; more precisely, to that beginning which Western philosophy became habituated to seeing in the course of its history, a habituation in which Nietzsche joined despite his otherwise original grasp of pre-Socratic philosophy" (*Ne*, 1:19–20; *Ng*, 1:27–28).

19. Heidegger's attribution of these doctrines respectively to Parmenides and Heraclitus is, of course, far more complex than I can indicate here. The passage I cite from Heidegger's text itself confesses a reduction by declaring that the doctrines "being *is*" and "being *becomes*" belong to Parmenides and Heraclitus only "roughly [*im groben*]": "Which are the decisive fundamental positions of the beginning [*Anfang*]? That is, which answers are given to the as yet undeveloped guiding question [*noch nicht entfaltete Leitfrage*], the question as to what *das Seiende* is? The *one* answer says [*lautet*]—it is roughly that of Parmenides—*das Seiende ist*; an odd answer, yet nevertheless a very deep one, for with it is determined [*festgelegt*] for the first time and for all thinkers to come, including Nietzsche, what 'is' and 'being' mean: permanence and presence [*Beständigkeit und Anwesenheit*], the eternal present [*Gegenwart*]. The *other* answer says—it is roughly that of Heraclitus—*das Seiende wird*; the being is [in] being [*seiend ist das Seiende*] in its permanent becoming, its self-unfolding and eventual dissolution [*Zerfallen*]" (*Ne*, 2:200, *Ng*, 1:465).

20. This phrase occurs in Heidegger's discussion of Nietzsche's "physiological aesthetics," which, he declares, "looks like" sheer nihilism. However, the full sentence reads: "And yet as it stands with the innermost will of Nietzsche's thought, things are altogether different" (*Ne*, 1:93; *Ng*, 1:111).

21. Compare what Heidegger writes in a manuscript entitled "Nietzsche's Metaphysics," which was published with the Neske *Nietzsche* volumes: "'Will

to power' says *what* a being [*das Seiende*] as such is, namely, what it is in its constitution [*Verfassung*]. 'Eternal Return of the same' says *how* [a] being [*das Seiende*] is as a whole when it is so constituted. The 'how' of the Being of all beings is determined together [*mitbestimmt*] with the 'what.' . . . The same that recurs has only relative stability [*verhältnismäßigen Bestand*] and is therefore essentially unstable. Its recurrence, however, signifies a continual bringing back into stability [*Bestand*], that is, a permanentizing [*Beständigung*]" (*Ne*, 3:212; *Ng*, 2:287).

22. This quotation and the next one are from Heidegger's 1940 typescript entitled "Nietzsche's Metaphysics," which was included in the Neske edition of *Nietzsche*.

23. Heidegger compares this interpretation with those of Baeumler (*Nietzsche der Philosoph und Politiker*), and Jaspers (*Nietzsche: An Introduction*), each of whom considers "Nietzsche's two basic doctrines" in contradiction, and therefore favor one of the doctrines over the other. The characterization is perhaps unfair at least to Jaspers, whose interpretation of eternal return is in many ways similar to Heidegger's, especially in its emphasis on the "moment [*Augenblick*]" (see Jaspers, 352–67). I discuss eternal return and the "moment" in more detail in the final chapter.

24. For instance, when he declares that "with his doctrine of eternal return Nietzsche thinks in his way nothing other than the thought which, disguised, but still as its proper driving force, pervades the whole of Western philosophy" (*Ne*, 1:19; *Ng*, 1:27).

25. Krell plausibly translates this phrase: "What it was that Nietzsche properly wanted to think."

26. See note 23, above, on Baeumler and Jaspers. Also compare Arthur Danto's logical analysis and partial "refutation" of the doctrine of return by invocation of the second law of thermodynamics (Danto, 205–9). Danto, somewhat like Alexander Nehamas later, considers eternal return invalid or vacuous either as a physical or a metaphysical doctrine, and sees its value only as an "existential" or "ethical" prescription (see Nehamas, 142–54). By contrast, Gilles Deleuze, in partial agreement with Heidegger, whose lectures appeared a year before Deleuze's own *Nietzsche and Philosophy*, asserts: "We can only understand the eternal return as the expression of a principle which serves as an explanation of diversity and its reproduction, of difference and its repetition. Nietzsche presents this principle as one of his most important philosophical discoveries. He calls it *will to power*" (Deleuze, *Nietzsche*, 49).

27. Compare: "Nietzsche did not present his knowledge of European

nihilism in that exhaustively completed coherence [*geschlossenen Zusammenhang*] he surely glimpsed by means of his inner vision [*inneren Blick*], a coherence the pure form of which we neither know nor can ever 'open up' from the fragments of his work that have been preserved" (*Ne*, 4:11; *Ng*, 2:42).

28. The strangeness of this passage, which ascribes to metaphysics itself an incompleteness ostensibly due to the quite glaring biographical facts, should not be overlooked. It may be set against passages from Nietzsche's last year of writing, in which he seems clearly to intend to complete *Der Wille zur Macht*, an intention at least apparently foiled by his mental illness, beginning in 1890.

29. I intend the word "confront" specifically in Heidegger's sense of "confrontation [*Auseinandersetzung*]," a productive "setting-apart" of one thinker from another, or of the reader from the thinker (see *Ne*, 1:4–5; *Ng*, 1:13–14).

CHAPTER 4

1. Heidegger continues, "Since antiquity that question has been *the* question of philosophy."

2. Compare: "Being is for us the emptiest, most universal, most intelligible, most used, most reliable, most forgotten, most said. We scarcely even heed it, and therefore do not know it *as* something opposed to something else. Being remains something neutral for us" (*Ne*, 4:194; *Ng*, 2:253–54).

3. Also compare Aristotle's *Metaphysics*, Book IV (1003a–1012b).

4. Compare: "The reference to the ontological difference names the ground and the 'foundation' [*Fundament*] of all onto-logy, and thus of all metaphysics. The naming of the ontological difference ought to imply [*soll andeuten*] that a historical moment has come [or is coming, *kommt*] in which there is a need, and in which it becomes necessary, to ask about the ground and the foundation of 'onto-logy.' Thus in *Being and Time* there is talk of 'fundamental ontology'" (*Ne*, 4:155; *Ng*, 2:209).

5. What is rendered here is, of course, a particularly powerful "epochal" historicization. Vincent Descombes comments that "epochal thinking . . . seeks to establish a relationship between a particular configuration of human existence and a metaphysical proposition pronounced by a philosopher" (Descombes, 95). He further notes that given such a "hermeneutical" approach, "if something (with regard to metaphysics) is represented at first as being possible, it soon comes to be presented as inevitable. It is as if the mere mention of a possibility by a philosopher were taken as a dare by his succes-

sors" (100). What Descombes identifies here as the inherent revisionism of an epochal metaphysical tendency—"it is evident that . . . there is a movement by which [German Idealists] constantly outdo one another" (101)—I would characterize instead as tendency to hyperbolize the synecdochal "essence" of a philosophical text, reducing it for the benefit of a certain rereading. This is not far from Descombes's description of philosophy, for he, too, notices the *paralipsis* constructed by a philosophical reading, here described as the essentialization of a "possible" interpretation into the text's proper or "inevitable" meaning. This move is characteristic not only of certain hyperbolic "epochal" readings of philosophy, but also probably of all philosophical rereadings inasmuch as they reduce the history of philosophy to certain key figures, and these figures to doctrines, each a synecdoche for the historical whole. To acknowledge that such reductions are positive *actions* by a reader (not just "inevitabilities" of a "proper" interpretation) would mean stepping out of the polite conventions of philosophical criticisms and admitting that possibly all philosophical reading is, in Descombes's definition, "epochal"—precisely insofar as it is perspectival.

6. The section referred to is entitled "Being as *A priori* [*das Sein als* Apriori]" (*Ne*, 4:159f; *Ng*, 2:213f).

7. Or later, "with regard to how *we* specifically [*eigens*] approach Being and beings" (*Ne*, 4:161; *Ng*, 2:216).

8. Translating this phrase is difficult. Krell offers this version: "rising forth from itself and thus essentially self-presenting in upsurgence, self-revealing in the open region" (*Ne*, 4:161). An alternative, or perhaps a complement, might be: "a rising-forth from itself, and thus essentially a self-presenting in forthrising, a self-revealing [or, self-opening] in [an] openness." For a more detailed discussion of nature as *physis*, also see Heidegger, *Introduction to Metaphysics*, 100–15.

9. Compare: "In the beginning [*Im Anfang*] of its history, Being reveals itself [*lichtet sich*] as emerging [*Aufgang*] (*physis*) and discovering [*Entbergung*] (*alētheia*). From there it arrives at the impression of presence and permanence in the sense of enduring [*Verweilens*] (*ousia*). Metaphysics proper begins with this" (*EP*, 4; *Ng*, 2:403). Note that I translate "*Entbergen*" (Heidegger's gloss of *alētheia*) as "dis-covery" here, in lieu of Stambaugh's "unconcealment," since the latter is conventionally reserved for "*Unverborgenheit*."

10. See the section entitled "The Limitation [*Beschränkung*] of Being" in Heidegger, *Introduction to Metaphysics*, 93–206.

11. Compare: "'Metaphysics' is the title for the full range [*Umkreis*] of phi-

losophy's proper questions" (*Ne*, 2:187; *Ng*, 1:451); and "All of western thinking from the Greeks through Nietzsche is metaphysical thinking" (*Ne*, 3:7; *Ng*, 1:478–79). Schürmann gives a brief but useful history of critical responses to the notion that "all" of western thinking is metaphysics (Schürmann, 316 n 10).

12. In a roughly contemporary discussion (1932–1933) Arthur Lovejoy identifies a version of this hyperbolic synecdoche as an attribute of intellectual histories generally, and moreover a "postulate" of their characteristic essentialistic procedure: "The postulate of such a study is that the working of a given conception, of an explicit or tacit presupposition, of a type of mental habit, or of a specific thesis or argument, needs, if its nature and its historic role are to be fully understood, to be traced connectedly through all the phases of men's reflective life in which those workings manifest themselves. . . . It is inspired by the belief that there *is* a great deal more that is common to more than one of these provinces than is usually recognized, that the same idea often appears, sometimes considerably disguised, in the most diverse regions of the intellectual world" (Lovejoy, 15, his emphasis). Lovejoy interestingly refers to this kind of supreme reduction as "the monistic pathos," a subspecies of the "metaphysical pathos" (12–13). On the reduction of historical variation specifically as "synecdochic," also see Hayden White's *Metahistory*, 92, 113–14.

13. Compare this piece of hyperbole on Heidegger's part: "If we do not now thoughtfully formulate our inquiry [*Fragestellung*] so that it is able to conceive [*begreifen*] in a unified way [*einheitlich*] the doctrines of the eternal return of the same and will to power, and these two doctrines in their most intrinsic coherence [*innersten Zusammenhang*] as revaluation, and if we do not at the same time go on to grasp [*fassen*] this fundamental formulation [*Grundfragestellung*] as one which is necessary in the course of Western metaphysics, then we will never grasp Nietzsche's philosophy; and we will understand [*begreifen*] nothing of the twentieth century and of the centuries to come, we will understand nothing of that which is our metaphysical task" (*Ne*, 1:17; *Ng*, 1:25–26).

14. *Geschichte des Seins* or *Seinsgeschichte*. See generally "Metaphysics as History of Being," *EP*, 1–83; *Ng*, 2:399–457.

15. Heidegger also phrases this as "the history of Being, which is solely Being itself [(*d*)*ie Geschichte des Seins, die einzig das Sein selbst ist*]" (*EP*, 79; *Ng*, 2:486).

16. Thus a "proper" inquiry into metaphysics, which Heidegger in this portion of the *Nietzsche* lectures calls "recollection" (or possibly, "interioriza-

tion [*Erinnerung*]"), "does not report [*berichtet*] on past opinions and ideas [*Vorstellungen*] of Being. Nor does it trace the relations of their influence, nor tell about standpoints within a history of ideas [*Begriffsgeschichte*]. It is not concerned with the progression and regression of a series of problems in themselves, which supposedly constitute a history of problems [*Problemgeschichte*]" (*EP*, 77; *Ng*, 2:483).

17. Hegel, *Logic*, par. 13 (19 [58]), Hegel's emphasis.

18. Compare two other passages: "Thus delimited [*eingegrenzt*] to what is metaphysical, humans remain caught within the unexperienced difference of *das Seiende* and *Sein*. The metaphysically marked manner of human representation [*Vorstellens*] finds everywhere only the metaphysically constructed world. Metaphysics belongs to the nature of the human" (*EP*, 87; *VA*, 74); and "The history of Being is neither the history of humans and humanity, nor the history of human relations to *das Seiende* and to Being. . . . However, since Being takes [for] human-being [*Menschenwesen*] [to] the grounding of its truth in *das Seiende*, the human gets drawn into the history of Being" (*EP*, 82; *Ng*, 2:489).

19. "Saying not-saying" is Robert Bernasconi's translation of Heidegger's phrase, more literal but less evocative than Joan Stambaugh's "telling silence." See Heidegger, *Identity and Difference*, 73, 142. In *Identity and Difference* the term is used to denote the possibility of a nonmetaphysical way of speaking, and is offered suggestively at the very end of the book. Bernasconi, by interpolating an essential difference *between* the "saying" and the "not-saying," interprets the phrase specifically as a trope of reading and revision within metaphysics: "The 'saying not-saying' cannot be reduced to the assertion and negation of one and the same proposition in quick succession. It is an invitation to a certain kind of reading where we hear first the metaphysical at work throughout language and then in a second reading the silence, the concealment, that resounds in it" (Bernasconi, 93).

20. In a sense it is irrelevant that one thinker comes "before" or "after" the other, and indeed it may be a hindrance to the understanding of the revision-encounter to heed such a "real" chronology. For instance, Heidegger's reading of Western philosophy posits Descartes as the originator of the specific notion of subjectivity that comes to conclusion in Nietzsche's own work, although Nietzsche is said, as usual, not to understand properly his own relation to Descartes. The "proper" Descartes posited by Heidegger, in the revision-encounter with both thinkers, in fact, comes *after* Nietzsche, despite being his "proper" precursor. It would be an error, in all the Heideggerian-

Nietzschean nuances of this word, to assume that simply because Descartes came first "in time," that he precedes Nietzsche's thought. Such factual chronology hinders the essential ordering of this history within Heidegger's revision-encounter, and occludes its crucial implicit suggestion that a "Descartes proper" (the ostensible precursor to Nietzsche) "*is*" Heidegger himself. In a "proper" reading, according to the logic of the revision-encounter, "we" have, first, Heidegger, then Descartes, then Nietzsche. And this proper "we" who "has" this ordering, to interpolate into Hegel, is analogous to the "we" who finally arrives at a standpoint from which to view the "immediacy of the in-itself [*Unmittelbarkeit des Ansich*]" [of the revision-encounter], and thus "sublates its time form [*hebt . . . seine Zeit-form auf*]" (See Hegel, *Phenomenology*, 487 [524–25]).

INTERLUDE

1. De Man, Introduction to *AR*, xi.

2. Compare: "Literature and art only obtain a history that has the character of a process when the succession of works is mediated not only through the producing subject but also through the consuming subject—through the interaction of author and public" (*AR*, 15).

3. Ranke, quoted in *AR*, 7.

4. Jauss remarks: "*Geistesgeschichte* armed itself with literature, set an aesthetics of irrational creation in opposition to the causal explanation of history, and sought the coherence of literature [*Dichtung*] in the recurrence of atemporal ideas and motifs. In Germany *Geistesgeschichte* allowed itself to be drawn into the preparation and foundation of the 'people's' [*völkischen*] literary studies of National Socialism" (*AR*, 8). In general, see *AR*, 5–9.

5. See Peter Szondi's useful discussion of the history of "the twofold intention that stands at the origin of hermeneutics, along with its motivation: to sublate or, alternatively, to eliminate the historical distance between text and reader" (Szondi, 8). In general, see Szondi, 8–13.

6. See Kosík, 138–39.

7. The essay is entitled "The Poetic Text Within the Change of Horizons of Reading: The Example of Baudelaire's 'Spleen II'" (*AR*, 139–85).

8. Jauss's later work on the aesthetics of reception complicates these notions, especially in their relations to hermeneutics. See, for instance, *Aesthetic Experience*, 22–36, 61–92.

CHAPTER 5

1. From roughly 1973 to 1982. Bloom's crucial books from this period are: *The Anxiety of Influence* (*AI*), *A Map of Misreading* (*MM*), *Kabbalah and Criticism*, *Poetry and Repression*, and *Agon*. In this period, he also published *Figures of Capable Imagination*, *Wallace Stevens: The Poems of Our Climate*, *The Breaking of the Vessels*, a novel, *The Flight to Lucifer*, and, along with de Man, Derrida, Hartman, and Miller, the manifesto *Deconstruction and Criticism*. Finally, although they predate *Anxiety of Influence*, his *Yeats* and the essay collection *The Ringers in the Tower* anticipate much of the theoretical work of the "middle" period.

2. Bloom still sees fit, with more than two decades of hindsight, to reiterate this insight in the Preface to the second edition of *The Anxiety of Influence* (*AI*, xix).

3. Bloom, *Poetry*, 3.

4. This is an antiessentialist form of argument of which Bloom is fond. Compare two formally similar statements, albeit couched in psychological terms: "A poem is not an overcoming of anxiety, but is that anxiety" (*AI*, 94); "Poetry, despite its publicists, is not a struggle against repression but is itself a kind of repression" (*AI*, 99).

5. Bloom, *Poetry*, 6. In an interview with Imre Salusinszky, Bloom states: "What *we* call a poem is mostly what is not there on the page. The strength of any poem is the poems that it has managed to exclude" (Salusinszky, 51).

6. Bloom, *Agon*, 17. I say "presumably" because although, presumably, any reading entails a cathexis or, more generally, a question of desire, there is no necessary reason why this cathexis should be "onto poems," and not, for instance, onto other readers, onto one's academic colleagues, onto the letters section of *The Times Literary Supplement*, or onto any number of other less idealized "sources" of the desire to read. Indeed the very analysis of poetry as will or as will to power should de-center the cathexis of reading and make it an open question whether the object-*text* is what is cathected at all.

7. In the introduction to the second edition of *The Anxiety of Influence*, Bloom comments that he "cheerfully abhor[s]" Heidegger (*AI*, xi). Cheerful abhorrence is itself, I would argue, a Bloomian critical category, and "cheerful," at least, is borrowed from Emerson; I discuss it briefly in the following chapter.

8. I cite the "ratios" as they appear first in *A Map of Misreading*, since there they include both their psychological and tropological significations: *Clinamen*

(reaction-formation; irony); *Tessera* (turning against the self, reversal; synecdoche); *Kenosis* (undoing, isolation, regression; metonymy); *Daemonization* (repression; hyperbole, litotes); *Askesis* (sublimation; metaphor); *Apophrades* (introjection, projection; metalepsis). Between *The Anxiety of Influence* and *A Map of Misreading*, Bloom's "map" shifts in several subtle ways, chiefly, from a formalization of a poet's "life cycle as poet" (*AI*, 152) to a more severely formal tropological pattern within particular poems (see the reading of Browning's "Childe Roland to the Dark Tower Came" in *MM*, 106–22). This divergence between the first and second theoretical works, though drastic, is not irrecoverable within Bloom's Viconian/Freudian dialectics, wherein tropes and psychological defenses are "interchangeable when they appear *in poems*, where after all both appear only as images. What I have called 'revisionary ratios' are tropes and psychic defenses, both and either, and are manifested in poetic imagery. A rhetorical critic can regard a defense as a concealed trope. A psychoanalytic interpreter can regard a trope as a concealed defense" (*MM*, 88–89). More specifically, or more "practically": "Combining Vico and Freud teaches us that the origin of any defense is its stance towards death, just as the origin of any defense is its stance towards proper meaning. . . . Pragmatically, a trope's revenge is against an earlier trope, just as defenses tend to become operations against one another" (*Poetry*, 10). See also *Kabbalah*, 95–126.

9. I assume I need not remark that judgments about the relative quality of poets here are Bloom's, not my own. I will shortly discuss the implications, upon his own theory, of Bloom's proclivity to judge particular writers or texts in such absolute aesthetic terms.

10. In the earlier *Anxiety of Influence*, where Bloom analyzes the ratios as phases in the "life cycle of the poet as poet," the *apophrades* is a trope arising, or dominating the poet's work, in later life. Despite the element of psychobiography apparent in this claim, Bloom describes the domain of *apophrades* in terms that do not appear necessarily to require old age, but rather only a certain rhetorically forceful or ecumenical tendency in the poetry itself: "The wholly mature strong poet is peculiarly vulnerable to this last phase of his revisionary relationship to the dead. This vulnerability is most evident in poems that quest for a final clarity, that seek to be definitive statements, testaments to what is uniquely the strong poet's gift (or what he wishes us to remember as his unique gift)" (*AI*, 139–40).

11. For a lengthy discussion of Bloom's unusual interpretation of the "diachronic rhetoric" of poetic allusion, see Allen, 105–33.

12. Quintilian defines metalepsis as a trope that "provides a transition from

one trope to another" or "form[s] an intermediate step between the term transferred and the thing to which it is transferred" (Quintilian, 322–23).

13. "Transumption [*transumptio*]" is Quintilian's Latin synonym for metalepsis (Quintilian, 322). See Bloom's discussion of the trope in *MM*, 102–3.

14. Hegel, in the *Phenomenology*, explicitly critiques the conventional "us" or "we" as a peculiar effaced "contribution" to the construction of the dialectic of consciousness (see *Phenomenology*, 52–55 [64–68]). For Hegel, the "we" signifies a moment of knowledge of the "absolute" or "in-itself" unavailable to any immanent consciousness involved within the dialectical progression being examined by the philosophical reader. Jean Hyppolite, laying the ground for many similar interpretations, construes the "we" as "the philosopher," to whom a larger picture of the given movement of the movement of Spirit is available than to "consciousness." Hyppolite thereby reduces the critical force of the category of the "we," repositing it within its most conventional signification, the prosaic "we" of academic or philosophical discourse (see Hyppolite, 24–26). Heidegger, in his lectures on Hegel's *Phenomenology*, offers a more complex interpretation of the "we" as a generally "absolvent [*absolvent*]" moment of knowing "*in terms of* absolute knowledge," or in other words a moment in the phenomenological examination of the dialectic in which, although not yet "absolute," the reader is "absolved" of the purely finite or immediate viewpoint of consciousness (see Heidegger, *Hegel's Phenomenology*, 70–74).

15. Of course, this also simplifies the process of reading Milton's figure, on the one hand, because it is Milton's own reception of the simile which itself constitutes it as "first" (or not), and on the other hand, because "our" reading of Bloom's reception of the revised simile must also decide which version of the simile to consider proper, whether with or against Bloom's assessment. In any case, reading *goes on*, and "first," "final," "proper," and so forth are all themselves the effects of further, more or less revisionist, interpretations.

16. Bloom's declared enemy in this context is usually C. S. Lewis and the "angelic school" of Milton criticism, although a more plausible immediate enemy is Stanley Fish in *Surprised by Sin*, to whom Bloom alludes briefly in *Anxiety of Influence*.

17. See, for instance, de Bolla, 15–35. A well-known criticism of Bloom's "intensely (even exclusively) male" model of literary (psycho-)history is that of Gilbert and Gubar in *The Madwoman in the Attic* (46–53). In the discussion following I reproduce precisely the ostensibly patriarchal psycho-historical vocabulary for which Gilbert and Gubar find Bloom both objectionable and

useful as a description of male dominance in the Western literary canon, but I do so with the contention that such a vocabulary must be carefully interpreted as a critical tropology, that is, as an allegory, not a description or even straight-forwardly an "analysis," of literary relationships. Reading Bloom's psycho-logism *psychologically*, Gilbert and Gubar receive his quasi-Freudian terminology with a literalism that itself borders on essentialism or even sexism: "Certainly if we acquiesce in the patriarchal Bloomian model, we can be sure that the female poet does not experience the 'anxiety of influence' in the same way that her male counterpart would, for the simple reason that she must confront pre-cursors who are almost exclusively male, and therefore significantly different from her" (48). For one of Bloom's own responses to this criticism, perhaps no more satisfactory, see Moynihan, 29f.

18. The "cherub" (alluding to the angel placed at the gates of Eden to block the return of Adam and Eve) represents for Bloom a "creative anxiety," the blocking power of the precursor, which cannot merely be pushed aside. The "sphinx" represents "sexual anxiety," more traditionally construed as "sublimated" by poetic figuration, and thereby incorporated in the form of a topos within poetry. Bloom suggests that "it is the high irony of poetic voca-tion that the strong poets can accomplish the greater yet fail the lesser task" (*AI*, 36), that is, that they can "push aside" or sublimate sexual anxiety, but can only repress or misread *creative* anxiety.

19. Compare Bloom's clichéd way of expressing this distinction, which is more complex than he makes it sound: "the poet-in-a-poet *cannot marry*, what-ever the person-in-a-poet chooses to have done" (*MM*, 19); "Perhaps we can say that a man, even as a man, is capable of wishing to die, but by definition no poet, *as poet*, can wish to die for that negates poethood. . . . Death is therefore a kind of literal meaning, or from the standpoint of poetry, *literal meaning is a kind of death* . . ." (*MM*, 91). Paul de Man chooses, fruitfully, to revise this kind of psychologistic hyperbole, looking "underneath" for problems about "the encounter between latecomer and precursor as a displaced version of the par-adigmatic encounter between reader and text" ("Review of Harold Bloom," 273). Bloom's more sophisticated "tropological" version of the dialectic of belatedness in *Map of Misreading* may owe something to this review by de Man; the latter book is dedicated to him.

20. Bloom, *Wallace Stevens*, 375.

21. Compare Maurice Blanchot's essay "From Dread to Language" (Blan-chot, 3–20).

22. Compare: "All quest-romances of the post-Enlightenment, meaning

all Romanticisms whatsoever, are quests to re-beget one's own self, to become one's own Great Original" (*AI*, 64). Also see Bloom's essay "The Internalization of Quest-Romance."

23. Bloom, *Poetry*, 7.

24. Bloom equates literal meaning with the "death" of the poet "as poet": "Death is a kind of literal meaning, or from the standpoint of poetry, *literal meaning is a kind of death. Defenses can be said to trope against death, rather in the same sense that tropes can be said to defend against literal meaning*" (*MM*, 91, Bloom's emphasis).

25. Bloom cites Geoffrey Hartman's comment that "in a poem the identity quest always is something of a deception, because the quest always works as a formal device" (*AI*, 65).

26. Bloom, *Poetry*, 7.

27. Kierkegaard, *Fear and Trembling*, 27; cited by Bloom in *AI*, 72–73.

28. Bloom, *Poetry*, 20.

29. Bloom also writes, "A poem would like to be whole, high and early, and to abound in presence, fullness, innerness" (*MM*, 104). One of Bloom's exemplars for such an ambition, perhaps surprisingly, because so ostensibly post-high-romantic, is Wallace Stevens. Compare excerpts from two Stevens poems: "I myself was the compass of that sea / and what I saw or heard or felt came naught / but from myself and there I found myself more truly and more strange" ("Tea at the Palaz of Hoon," Stevens, 54–55); and "when she sang, the sea, / Whatever self it had, became the self / That was her song, for she was the maker. Then we, / As we beheld her striding there alone, / Knew that there never was a world for her / Except the one she sang and, singing, made" ("The Idea of Order at Key West," Stevens, 98).

30. Bloom, *Poetry*, 7.

31. Ibid., 20.

32. See, for instance, the Preface to the second edition of *AI*, but especially *The Western Canon*, 43f. And see Bloom's recent book *Shakespeare: The Invention of the Human* (1998).

CHAPTER 6

1. See, for instance, Stanley Cavell's "Finding as Founding," in *This New*, 77–121. Compare Eduardo Cadava: "Like the weather, whose variable and unpredictable nature makes it difficult to circumscribe, the gestures of his

writing . . . resist, from the very beginning, all our efforts to bring together or stabilize whatever we might call his thought" (Cadava, 1).

2. See, for instance, Gadamer, *Truth and Method*, 197–221, and Szondi, 4–13, 100–8.

3. Compare: "Everything the individual sees without him corresponds to his states of mind, and every thing is in turn intelligible to him, as his onward thinking leads him into the truth to which that fact or series belongs" (*E*, 247).

4. Compare: "Each new law and political movement has meaning for you. Stand before each of its tablets and say, 'Under this mask did my Proteus nature hide itself.' This remedies the defect of our too great nearness to ourselves. This throws our actions into perspective: and as crabs, goats, scorpions, the balance, and the waterpot lose their meanness when hung as signs in the zodiac, so I can see my own vices without heat in the distant persons of Solomon, Alcibiades, and Catiline" (*E*, 238).

5. Compare: "The advancing man discovers how deep a property he has in literature,—in all fable as well as in all history. He finds that the poet was no odd fellow who described strange and impossible situations, but that universal man wrote by his pen a confession true for one and true for all. His own secret biography he finds in lines wonderfully intelligible to him, dotted down before he was born" (*E*, 250–51).

6. The ending of "History" enacts an odd recantation strangely out of keeping with the rhetoric of the rest of the essay, but which permits the category of the natural to reemerge, a tendency characteristic of other of Emerson's essays from this period. Emerson's final two paragraphs continue from where just cited: "I hold our actual knowledge very cheap. Hear the rats in the wall, see the lizard on the fence, the fungus under foot, the lichen on the log. What do I know, sympathetically, morally, of either of these worlds of life? . . . Nay, what does history yet record of the metaphysical annals of man? What light does it shed on these mysteries which we hide under the names Death and Immortality? . . . I am ashamed to see what a shallow village tale our so-called History is" (*E*, 255–56). By the final line of the essay, the reemphasis on nature is such that where it seems the word "history" should be, the word "nature" is substituted, and the topic of history itself seems to vanish, as if it were the natural, not the historical, world that was to have been "read" here: "The idiot, the Indian, the child, and unschooled farmer's boy, stand nearer to the light by which nature is to be read, than the dissector or the antiquary" (*E*, 256).

7. I borrow this phrase from Matthiessen, who writes of Emerson that "in

spite of his profession of being a seeker, all his mature work proceeded from *a priori* deductive assertion" (Matthiessen, 65).

8. Or antinomianism. Emerson himself addresses the question of whether his statements in this essay are antinomian; he attributes the potential accusation to a conflation of the rejection of "popular standards" with a rejection of standards as such. But since he immediately afterward, as an explanation of the error in this conflation, states that "the law of consciousness abides," it is clear that Emerson *does* mean to hold an apparently antinomian thesis about the origin of moral strictures. This "defense" against the charge of antinomianism appears to be an example of what I argue later might be called an *impertinent* declaration, but hardly an effective "defense."

9. Cadava usefully summarizes two competing trends in Emerson scholarship, especially with respect to Emerson and post-Emersonian models of historicism: "[The] reevaluation—led by critics such as Len Gougeon, Sacvan Bercovitch, Michael Lopez, Carolyn Porter, Lawrence Buell, Barbara Packer, and David Robinson—marks a significant critical turn in American literary historiography, which works to revise what critics like F. O. Matthiessen, Charles Feidelson, R. W. B. Lewis, Richard Chase, and Harold Bloom have understood to be the major theme of the Emersonian tradition: ahistoricism" (Cadava, 10).

10. A sense of history as that which has *already* been fulfilled, and is therefore a threat to a creative individual, is of course present in Bloom and Nietzsche as well. Hayden White sums up the sentiment in a more condensed fashion than it appears, to my knowledge, anywhere in Nietzsche's writing: "Nietzsche hated history even more than he hated religion. History promoted a debilitating voyeurism in men, made them feel that they were latecomers to a world in which everything worth doing had already been done" (White, *Tropics*, 32).

11. This sort of glib dismissal is part of what Bloom, following Nietzsche in *Twilight of the Idols*, calls Emerson's "cheerfulness" (Bloom, *Agon*, 156). "Cheerfulness" connotes for both Bloom and Nietzsche a moment in which individual freedom is expressed through a mechanism of repression, the nonconscious rejection of a knowledge of one's influences. Hence "cheerfulness" is more than a mere mood; rather, it is a psychological cathexis. Its presence signifies that, for instance, Emerson's statement of freedom is the result of a sublimation of negatively cathected reactions to influences that would otherwise have made the self precisely *unfree*. See also Bloom's chapter, "Emerson and Whitman: The American Sublime," in *Poetry*, 256–66.

12. This is an Emersonian term; the third essay of *First Series*, immediately following "Self-Reliance," is entitled "Compensation." Emerson at times characterizes "compensation" with an economic metaphor similar to the one in "Self-Reliance" that I shall discuss shortly: "It is as impossible for a man to be cheated by any one but himself as for a thing to be and not to be at the same time. If you serve an ungrateful master, serve him all the more. Put God in your debt. Every stroke shall be repaid. The longer the payment is withholden, the better for you; for compound interest on compound interest is the rate and usage of this exchequer" (*E*, 298).

13. Compare, for interest's sake, the anticitational practice of Bloom's *Anxiety of Influence*, *Map of Misreading*, and *Poetry and Repression*, none of which cites texts fully, if at all. De Man comments, "One senses Bloom's legitimate impatience with detail in a book that has much wider ambitions. . . . For the most part, the examples are *a priori* assertions of influence based on verbal and thematic echoes and stated as if they spoke for themselves. Bloom has no time to waste on technical refinements" ("Review of Harold Bloom," 268).

14. My argument relies in part upon Barbara Packer's discussion about what happens when the "Not-Me," that which opposes itself to my consciousness (potentially to be confronted, subsumed, categorized, and so forth), is another *text* (Packer, 110–20).

15. This quotation is from the essay "Plato; Or, the Philosopher" (*E*, 637).

16. From "Uses of Great Men" (*E*, 623).

17. In general, see Packer's chapter entitled "Portable Property," in *Emerson's Fall*, 85–147, for a comparable discussion of imitation and self-assertion in "The Divinity School Address," "The American Scholar," and "Self-Reliance."

18. Compare: "It is for want of self-culture that the superstition of Travelling . . . retains its fascination for all educated Americans" (*E*, 277).

19. Of course this can be read as a call not simply for individualism but for nationalism. These two meanings appear at first to be at odds with one another, since the individual as such is clearly in conflict with society, and presumably with the "nation" as well. But in a grandiose synecdoche Emerson also makes clear that the call for self-reliance is as applicable to the *individual nation* as it is to the individual him/herself. See especially the portions of the essay on traveling (*E*, 277–81). For instance: "Why need we copy the Doric or the Gothic model? Beauty, convenience, grandeur of thought, and quaint expression are as near to us as to any, and if the American artist will study with hope and love the precise thing to be done by him, considering the climate,

the soil, the length of the day, the wants of the people, the habit and form of the government, he will create a house in which all these will find themselves fitted, and taste and sentiment will be satisfied also" (E, 278).

20. Compare: "I much prefer that [my life] should be of a lower strain, so it be genuine and equal, than that it should be glittering and unsteady. I wish it to be sound and sweet, and not to need diet and bleeding" (E, 263).

21. "Manhood" is used similarly in work preceding "Self-Reliance," for instance in the "Divinity School Address" or "The American Scholar." For example: "Wherever a man comes, there comes revolution. The old is for slaves. When a man, comes, all books are legible, all things transparent, all religions are forms. He is religious. Man is the wonderworker . . . , etc." ("Divinity School Address," E, 88); or "Thank God for these good men, but say 'I also am a man.' Imitation cannot go above its model. The imitator dooms himself to hopeless mediocrity" (ibid., 89).

22. Emerson writes the following about public reception, likely an implicit reference to strong reactions to his "Divinity School Address": "The discontent of the multitude [is] more formidable than that of the senate and the college. It is easy enough for *a firm man* who knows the world to brook the rage of the cultivated classes. Their rage is decorous and prudent, for they are timid as being very vulnerable themselves. But when to their *feminine rage* the indignation of the people is added, when the ignorant and the poor are aroused, when the *unintelligent brute force* that lies at the bottom of society is made to growl and mow, it needs the habit of magnanimity and religion to treat it godlike as a trifle of no consequence" (E, 264–65, my emphasis).

23. Compare this apostrophe to what Matthiessen, following Emerson, identifies as "elegance": "Give me initiative, spermatic, prophesying, manmaking words" (quoted by Matthiesson, 35).

24. Compare this journal entry of Emerson's: "I have so little vital force that I could not stand the dissipation of a flowing and friendly life; I should die of consumption in three months. But now I husband all my strength in this bachelor life I lead; no doubt I shall be a well-preserved old gentleman" (quoted by Moon, 60).

25. Cavell writes the following in relation to Emerson's "Experience" (from the *Second Series*, 1844) and its potential reader: "An Emersonian essay is a finite object that yields an infinite response. The phrase 'obey one will' harks back, to my ear, to what I call the theory of reading in 'Self-Reliance', the part of it that is epitomized in Emerson's formula, 'Who has more obedience than I masters me', a statement of mastery as listening that pictures mas-

tery as of a text. From which it follows that what the essay is remembering, or membering, the one will it creates itself to obey, and creates in order to obey, is that which puts it in motion, the will of a listening, persisting reader. That would be, would so to speak give birth to, experience" (Cavell, *This New*, 101).

26. Kracauer, 7.

27. Compare: "Every new mind is a new classification. If it prove a mind of uncommon activity and power, a Locke, a Lavoisier, a Hutton, a Bentham, a Fourier, it imposes its classification on other men, and lo! a new system" (*E*, 276–77).

28. See Chai's chapter, "Emerson: The Divinity of the Self," 279–88. Also see Bloom's "Emerson: The American Religion," in *Agon*, 145–78, and "Emerson and Influence," *MM*, 160–76.

29. Compare: "Abide in the simple and noble regions of thy life, obey thy heart, and thou shalt reproduce the foreworld again" (*E*, 279).

30. Bloom cites the following entry in Emerson's journal, from May 26, 1937: "Who shall define to me an Individual? I behold with awe and delight many illustrations of the One Universal Mind. I see my being imbedded in it. As a plant in the earth so I grow in God. I am only a form of him. He is the soul of Me. I can even with a mountainous aspiring say, *I am God*, but transferring my *Me* out of the flimsy & unclean precinct of my body, my fortunes, my private will . . ." (*MM*, 164).

31. *Ecce Homo*, 326; *S*, 6:365. The whole passage, which is the opening of the section "Why I am a Destiny [*Schicksal*]," reads: "I know my fate. Someday there will be associated with my name the memory of something tremendous—a crisis such has there has never been on earth, the most profound collision of conscience, a decision that was conjured up *against* everything that had been previously believed. I am no man, I am dynamite."

32. Kierkegaard, *Authority and Revelation*, 109–10.

CHAPTER 7

1. *Ecce Homo*, 259; *S*, 6:298.

2. The entire passage is cited below.

3. *Ereignis* has been rendered by translators as "event," "occurrence," "appropriation," "appropriating event," "propriating event," "event of appropriation," "disclosure of appropriation," or, as often as not, left in the German. The latter two English terms attempt to capture the German's sense of "to appropriate, to make one's own [*ereignen*]" as well as "to occur, to come to pass

[*sich ereignen*]." The root *eigen* means "proper" or "own," as in "*eigentlich*" (proper, authentic) or "*Eigentum*" (property, characteristic). During the period of the *Nietzsche* lectures, Heidegger glosses *Ereignis* as "*Er-eignung*," a word more aptly suited to "Ap[-]propriation" (See Heidegger, *Beiträge*, 8). He later relates it also to *Eräugnis* ("insight," root *Auge*) (Heidegger, *Die Technik*, 44).

4. See Heidegger's discussion of the "essence" and "possibility" of a *metaphysische Grundstellung*, and of Nietzsche's particularly, in the final two sections of the second lecture course (*Ne*, 2:184f; *Ng*, 1:448f).

5. Heidegger also refers to "*die ewige Wieder*kehr des Gleichen," translated by Krell and others as "the eternal *recurrence* of the same." For the purposes of the present discussion, I do not note any pressing distinction between these terms.

6. At the time of the lectures, Heidegger clearly considers this description of eternal return a corrective to the run of Nietzsche scholarship: "In opposition to all the various kinds of unclearness and embarrassment [*Unklarheit und Verlegenheit*] with regard to Nietzsche's doctrine of return, it must be said at the outset, and can initially be said only in the form of an assertion, that the doctrine of the eternal return of the same is the fundamental doctrine in Nietzsche's philosophy. Without this teaching as a ground, Nietzsche's philosophy is like a tree without roots" (*Ne*, 2:6; *Ng*, 1:256).

7. Heidegger initially presents a four-part scheme for his second lecture course: "A. The preliminary presentation of the doctrine of eternal return of the same in terms of its genesis [*Entstehung*], its configurations [*Gestalten*], and its domain [*Bereich*]. B. The essence of a fundamental metaphysical position. The possibility of such positions previously within the collective history of Western philosophy. C. The interpretation of the doctrine of return as the *last* fundamental 'metaphysical' position in Western thought. D. The end of Western philosophy and its *other* beginning [*Anfang*]" (*Ne*, 2:8; *Ng*, 1:258–59). In the 1961 edition Heidegger adds, in brackets: "The discussion of C comprises the conclusion of the lecture [course] 'Will to Power as Knowledge'; the discussion of D is attempted under the title 'Nihilism as Determined by the History of Being' ['*Die seinsgeschichtliche Bestimmung des Nihilismus*']" (*Ne*, 2:8 n; *Ng*, 1:259). Thus, as Krell notes, only A and B are discussed within the second lecture course, although the last sections briefly address C. Nor are C and D laid out in the final two lecture courses as neatly as Heidegger's scheme and his notation of 1961 would suggest. See Krell's discussion in his analysis of the second volume (*Ne*, 2:241–59).

8. For a comparable discussion of the clash or "paradox" entailed when a

thought about "the eternal" originates in a particular moment of "history," see Kierkegaard, *Philosophical Fragments*, 89–110.

9. *Ecce Homo*, 295; *S*, 6:335. I have followed, with some alterations, Krell's translation in *Ne*, 2:12, instead of Walter Kaufmann's in *Ecce Homo*. Note that much of the rhetorical force of this passage consists in the *extremity* of the contrast between the "eternality" of the thought of return itself and the particularity in time and space, even the mundanity, of its inception—a sublimity of magnitude.

10. For a more complex and useful discussion of the "scientific" aspect of eternal return, see Deleuze, *Nietzsche*, 44–49, 68–75. Deleuze criticizes both a "mechanistic" and a "thermodynamic" interpretation of return, but also argues strongly against the notion that return is simply a principle of "permanence" or "being." Nevertheless, his reading overlaps with Heidegger's in several ways, particularly in its analysis of the doctrine as a specific relation to the "principle" of will to power (49). Deleuze writes: "It is not being that returns but rather the returning itself that constitutes being insofar as it is affirmed of becoming and of that which passes" (48). In turn, one must consider return as a "selection" or "practical synthesis" which "produces becoming-active." The following summation suggests both the commonalities and the distinctions between Heidegger's and Deleuze's versions of return: "Eternal return, as a physical doctrine, affirms the being of becoming. But, as selective ontology, it affirms this being of becoming as the 'self-affirming' of becoming-active. . . . The complete formula of affirmation is: the whole, yes, universal being, yes, but universal being ought to belong to a single becoming, the whole ought to belong to a single moment" (72).

11. The entire passage is instructive with regard to Heidegger's attitude toward Nietzsche's view of his own procedure, as well as toward Heidegger's hyperbolic opinion of his own interpretive task: "[Indeed] Nietzsche falls back upon the natural-scientific, physical, chemical, and biological writings of that time, and in letters written during these years speaks of plans to study natural sciences and mathematics at one of the major universities. All this demonstrates clearly enough that Nietzsche himself also pursued a 'scientific side' to the doctrine of return. In any case, the appearance [*Augenschein*] speaks for [such] facts. Of course the question is whether appearances, even when they are conjured by Nietzsche himself, ought to serve as a standard of measure [*Leitmaß*] for the interpretation of the thought of thoughts in his philosophy. Such a question becomes necessary the moment we have grasped Nietzsche's philosophy and the confrontation with it—that is, with all of Western philos-

ophy—as a matter for this century and the century to come" (*Ne*, 2:83; *Ng*, 1:340).

12. The whole passage cited by Heidegger reads: "And so the human being outgrows everything that once surrounded [*umschlang*] him. He does not need to break the fetters; unexpectedly, when a god beckons, they fall away. And where is the ring [*Ring*] that ultimately encircles him? Is it the world? Is it god?" (*Ne*, 2:10; *Ng*, 1:260). Heidegger cites the first edition of this text, *Mein Leben. Autobiographische Skizze des jungen Nietzsche*, which he was partly responsible for publishing (in quoting the following passage I will remark that the date is 1937): "This autobiographical sketch [or, self-presentation—*Selbstdarstellung*] was first discovered in 1936 by an examination of the posthumous papers [in the possession] of Nietzsche's sister, and upon my recommendation was published specially by the Nietzsche Archive. My intention [in making the recommendation] was to give present and future German nineteen-year-olds something essential to think about" (*Ne*, 2:10; *Ng*, 1:260–61). Krell notes that the version of Nietzsche's text to which Heidegger refers here is available in the *Werke in drei Bänden*, 3:107–10.

13. Such disdain is apparent in the two earliest sections of the first lecture course, where Heidegger introduces Nietzsche as his topic. Here, for instance, Heidegger is commenting on the Nietzsche Archive's "*historisch-kritische Gesamtausgabe*," then still in preparation: "1. As a historical-critical complete edition [*Gesamtausgabe*], which brings out each and every thing it can find, and is guided by the fundamental principle of completeness, it belongs among the ranks of nineteenth-century undertakings. 2. In the manner of its biographical-psychological commentary and its similarly thorough tracking down [*Aufspüren*] of all 'data' on Nietzsche's 'life,' and of the opinions of his contemporaries about [this data], it is a product of the psychological-biological addiction of our times" (*Ne*, 1:10; *Ng*, 1:18).

14. *Zarathustra*, 268–70; *S*, 4:198–200. During my discussion of Heidegger's reading of eternal return in *Thus Spoke Zarathustra* I will cite passages directly from the Colli-Montinari *Studienausgabe* rather than through Heidegger's own citations. The section entitled "On the Vision and the Riddle [*Vom Gesicht und Rätsel*]" is in *Zarathustra*, Part 3/2, 267–72; *S*, 4:197–202. Heidegger's interpretation of this section appears primarily in three sections of his lectures: 1. "'On the Vision and the Riddle'" (*Ne*, 2:37–44; *Ng*, 1:289–97); 2. "'The Convalescent [*Genesende*],'" also following a Nietzschean subtitle (*Ne*, 2:49–62; *Ng*, 1:302–17); 3. "Moment and Eternal Recurrence" (*Ne*, 2:176–83; *Ng*, 1:438–47).

15. The passage up to this point reads as follows: "'Stop, dwarf!' I said. 'It is I or you! But I am the stronger of us two! You do not know my abysmal [*abgründlichen*] thought; *that* you could not bear!'

"Then something happened that made me lighter, for the dwarf jumped from my shoulder, being curious. And he crouched on a stone before me. But just there was a gateway, where we had stopped" (*Zarathustra*, 269; *S*, 4:199).

16. *Zarathustra*, 269–70; *S*, 4:199–200.

17. *Zarathustra*, 270; *S*, 4:200.

18. This is Krell's coinage, from Heidegger's "[*Wer Nietzsches schärfsten Gedanken*] *wie der Zwerg denkt . . .*" (*Ng*, 1:295).

19. *Zarathustra*, 270; *S*, 4:200.

20. Heidegger writes in a section entitled "The Thought of Return and Freedom," glossing the significance of the "Moment": "[If] you shape something supreme [*einen höchsten*] out of the next moment, [just] as out of every moment, and if you note well and retain [*festhältst*] the consequences, then this moment will come again and will have been what already was: 'eternity suits it.' But this will be decided only in your *moments*, and only out of what you yourself hold concerning beings, and how you hold yourself in their midst—out of what you will and are able to will of yourself" (*Ne*, 2:136; *Ng*, 1:398).

21. The point Heidegger makes here is supported by his comparison of the dwarf's answer to the description of return given by "Zarathustra's animals, the eagle and the snake" (see *Ne*, 2:54; *Ng*, 1:308–9).

22. See my discussion in Chapter 3.

23. The whole passage is instructive for its acknowledgment of the "danger" of perspectivism: "We do not remedy the supposed and feared damage and danger of philosophy's locatedness [*Standortcharakter*]—such location being the essential and indispensable legacy of every philosophy—by denying and repudiating the fact; but only by thinking through and grasping the locatedness of philosophy in terms of its original essence and its necessity, that is to say, by posing anew the question about the essence of truth and of human *Dasein*, and by radically [*vom Grund*] re-posing and answering that question" (*Ne*, 2:118; *Ng*, 1:379–80).

24. "Who is Nietzsche's Zarathustra?" in *Ne*, 2:211–33 (*VA* 101–26).

25. The main "qualification" is that the question "Who is Nietzsche's Zarathustra" is "answered" in the essay only through a series of riddles: "He is the advocate [*Fürsprecher*] of the proposition that all being is will to power" (*Ne* 2:213; *VA*, 103); "He is the teacher of eternal return . . . and of the overman"

(*Ne*, 2:214–15; *VA*, 105); "He is the advocate of Dionysus" (*Ne*, 2:230; *VA*, 123), and so on—all metonyms for Nietzsche himself, although this is never explicitly declared. Thus "Nietzsche" is not a direct "answer" to the question except by association; or in other words, the "answer" *is* that the *question* of the essay can be phrased: "Who is Nietzsche?"

26. *Ecce Homo*, 256; *S*, 6:295–96.

27. Bahti, 110–11. In general see Bahti's discussion in his third and fourth chapters, of the role of digestion in Hegel's *Phenomenology* and *Aesthetics*.

28. Ibid., 111.

29. *Ecce Homo*, 237; *S*, 6:279, Nietzsche's emphasis.

30. Such asceticism Nietzsche contrasts with the profligacy of his own "spiritual diet" while he lived and taught in Basel: "During my time in Basel my whole spiritual diet, including the way I divided up my day, was a completely senseless abuse [*Mißbrauch*] of extraordinary powers, without any [re]supply of power to cover this consumption [*Verbrauch*] in any way, without even a thought about consumption and replenishment" (*Ecce Homo*, 241; *S*, 6:283).

31. *Ecce Homo*, 239; *S*, 6:281. The passage containing this assertion is useful for its utter ambiguity between ostensible figural and literal references to food; it gives a good sense of the general polemically mundane tone of the section "Why I am so Clever," and of the book overall (note that Kaufmann's English translation separates into paragraphs what in the German text is less severely distinguished by dashes, while Hollingdale's version of *Ecce Homo* [53–54] more scrupulously retains the punctuation): "A few hints more from my morality. A hearty [*starke*] meal is easier to digest than one that is too small. That the stomach as whole becomes active: the first presupposition of a good digestion. One must *know* the size of one's stomach. For the same reason one ought to be advised against those long-drawn-out meals which I call interrupted sacrificial feasts, those at a *table d'hote*—No meals between meals, no coffee: coffee spreads darkness [*verdüstert*]. *Tea* is wholesome only in the morning. A little, but strong: tea is very unwholesome and sicklying o'er the whole day if it is too weak by a single degree. Everybody has his own measure here, often between the narrowest and most delicate limits. In a climate that is very *agaçant*, tea is not advisable for a beginning: one should begin an hour earlier with a cup of thick, oil-free cocoa" (*Ecce Homo*, 239; *S*, 6:281).

32. *Ecce Homo*, 238; *S*, 6:279–80.

33. This reading of Nietzsche's literalistic polemic goes directly against Arthur Danto, whose view I also take to be typical with respect to "figures" in

Nietzsche's text. For Danto, "[Nietzsche's] great misfortune has been the literalness with which even his more sympathetic critics have interpreted him" (200). Danto is aware that "much in [Nietzsche's] writing is merely personal," or "biograph[ical]," but he concludes that this has "nothing to do with philosophy at all," and is rather the result of Nietzsche's lack of "discipline to write for a true public" (ibid.).

34. Alexander Nehamas's interpretation of eternal return, both with respect to the passage now under discussion and to *Thus Spoke Zarathustra*, is basically limited to a view of the doctrine as just this sort of an "ethical" suggestion, despite the fact that Nehamas is fully aware of Nietzsche's "cosmological" pretensions for his *Lehre*. Nehamas initially states, plausibly enough, that "it is clear that this passage, in which the demon plays the role Zarathustra plays in 'On the Vision and the Riddle,' does not presuppose the truth of the view that the world, or even that one's own life, eternally repeats itself; it does not even presuppose that this idea is at all credible" (151). However, Nehamas also asserts, implausibly, that "Nietzsche is simply not interested in this question" (151), and furthermore, categorically, that "the eternal recurrence is not a theory of the world but a view of the self" (150). Nehamas assumes that the "world" is sufficiently separable from the "self" so as to make the meaning of eternal return decidable as a choice between these two domains, an assumption which contradicts even his own quite sophisticated view of "perspectivism" in Nietzsche. For Heidegger, by contrast, eternal return is an (at least) implicit strong criticism of precisely the distinction between theoretical (cosmological) thinking and practical (ethical) thinking that Nehamas must invoke in order to declare the doctrine to be one and not the other.

35. *Ecce Homo*, 238; *S*, 6:280.

36. Nietzsche makes at least one complimentary reference to Feuerbach, by contrast with Richard Wagner, and albeit not directly related to the issue of food discussed here: see Nietzsche, *On the Genealogy*, 100. Ida Overbeck, whose husband was Nietzsche's friend Franz, reports that Nietzsche often quoted "ideas of Ludwig Feuerbach" during the 1880s (Gilman, 114).

37. See Derrida's essay "White Mythology" in *Margins*, 225–26.

38. Krell's *Daimon Life* contains some discussion of Heidegger's ambivalent relation both to the concept of "life" and to *Lebensphilosophie*. See especially pp. 33f with respect to *Being and Time*.

39. Compare this paraliptical description of *Lebensphilosophie*: "In any serious and scientifically-minded 'philosophy of life' (this expression says about as

much as 'the botany of plants') there lies an unexpressed tendency, if rightly understood, towards an understanding of the Being of *Dasein*. What is striking in such a philosophy, and this is its principle defect [*grundsätzlicher Mangel*], is that 'life' itself as a kind of Being [*Seinsart*] does not become ontologically a problem" (*BT*, 43–44 [46]).

40. Schelling, 77.

41. The "difference" between figurative and nonfigurative, or between figurative and antifigurative, is close to that difference between the "literal" and the "rhetorical" analyzed by Paul de Man in his essay "Semiology and Rhetoric," 121–40. A "rhetorical question," like the figure of food I have been analyzing, suggests for itself two possible interpretations, "one which asserts and one which denies its illocutionary mode" (de Man, "Semiology," 129). De Man states that the only possible mediation between these interpretations would be "an extra-textual intention"; but such an "intention" is precisely what is provided, or imputed, by yet another *text*, that is, by a revision. De Man himself both points out this supplementary "other reading" and rather conventionally covers it up again by claiming that "the reading is not 'our' reading, since it uses only the linguistic elements provided by the text itself . . . [,] not something we have added to the text" (138). In a sense, this denial of responsibility may be both true and untrue, for the trope of the text's giving "us" its own terms to work with is paradigmatically that of the revision-encounter, an imputed *paralipsis* of truth, which depends on something like rhetorical persuasion for its truth-effect. Hence one gets de Man's peremptory refutation of the suggestion that he might be reading-into the text at hand: "We were only trying to come closer to being as rigorous a reader as the author [Proust] had to be in order to write the sentence in the first place" (139).

42. *Zarathustra*, 271; *S*, 4:201–2. Heidegger's discussion occurs in *Ne*, 2:176–83; *Ng*, 1:438–47.

43. *Zarathustra*, 272; *S*, 4:202. The biting and spitting of the snake's head is itself a specific parody of a canonical Christian metaphorics concerning the metaphysical hierarchy of the eaten body, and its relation to the "consumption" of texts. Werner Hamacher, in his lengthy discussion of the metaphorics of eating, biting, and nausea in Hegel's early work, notes: "On the interpretation [*Deutung*]—which was, incidentally, current amongst the church fathers—of the lamb of Passover in the Lord's Supper as holy scripture and of the holy scripture as the lamb of Passover, Origen writes (in Joan lib. 10, 18)—'In eating, one should begin with the head, that is to say with the most

important and most fundamental doctrines about heavenly matters'" (*Pleroma*, 111).

44. The passage reads: "The shepherd, however, bit as my cry had advised him; he bit with a good bite. Far away he spit the head of the snake—and he jumped up. No longer shepherd, no longer human—one transformed, one made radiant, one who *laughs*! Never yet on earth has a human being laughed as he laughed! O my brothers, I heard a laughter that was no longer human laughter . . ." (*Zarathustra*, 272; *S*, 4:202).

45. Compare Hamacher, *Pleroma*, 103–10.

46. Heidegger first makes this point in *Ne*, 2:47; *Ng*, 1:299. See also *Ne*, 2:179; *Ng*, 1:442, where Heidegger calls the black snake the "counter-image [*Gegenbild*]" of Zarathustra's own snake.

47. Compare Klossowski's discussion of the "difference between eternal return and traditional fatalism" (71–73).

EPILOGUE

1. Genette, 2.
2. Lacoue-Labarthe, *Subject*, 1.
3. Fish, *Is There a Text*, 342.
4. Ibid., 349.
5. Ibid., 347.
6. Ibid., 349.
7. Ibid., 354.
8. Rorty, "Historiography," 51–52.
9. Ibid., 52.
10. Ibid.
11. Rorty, *Contingency*, 97. This view of irony is traceable to Kierkegaard's vital theorization of the "ethical" aspects of irony and humor, ultimately derived from Hegel's interpretations of romantic literature in the *Aesthetics*. See Kierkegaard, *Concept of Irony*, 282–88, and *Concluding Unscientific Postscript*, 251–300, 499–525. Rorty takes such a view of philosophy-as-irony to characterize post-Kantian philosophy at least through Derrida. His advocacy of such "ironist theory" for philosophical writers remains of limited usefulness, because although it adopts a simplistic quasi-Kierkegaardian notion of irony as a subjective position—"the generic trait of ironists is that they do not hope to have their doubts about their final vocabularies settled by something larger than themselves" (*Contingency*, 97)—it lacks the complex dialectical ambiva-

lence that makes irony, for Kierkegaard, a fundamentally incoherent position. Irony's essentially productive incoherence consists in the impossibility of maintaining, in the mode of pure self-relation, a relation to another—which the text inherently must be. Rorty's own position on irony rapidly ends in just the sort of unproductive incoherence one might expect, following Kierkegaard too simply. For instance, in describing Coleridge, Rorty proposes a pair of suggestions that are clearly paradoxical when one considers that poetry is necessarily related to an audience: "The generic task of the ironist is the one Coleridge recommended to the great and original poet: to create the taste by which he will be judged. But the judge the ironist has in mind is himself" (ibid.). It would be fascinating to consider why the poet, according to Rorty, would need to "create" his own taste in order to judge himself, unless one radicalizes, more than Rorty is willing to do, the sense in which the "self" is precisely not a self-relation but the abysmal reflection-of-reflection of that self in others via the self's production, the anticipatory creation of what the "self," to others, will have *appeared* to be.

12. Rorty, "Historiography," 54.

13. Ibid., 63.

14. Rorty, *Contingency*, 73.

15. Ibid., 74.

Works Cited

Note: I have retranslated many of the passages I cite from Heidegger, Nietzsche, Hegel, and others. I wish to express my gratitude to the earlier translators of these writers into English, to whom I have referred often in my research and whose publications I cite below and in the Notes. Where I have altered or replaced their translations, it is usually in order to opt for literalism over elegance in a close reading and implies no criticism of their versions of these texts.

Adorno, Theodor W. *The Jargon of Authenticity*. Trans. Knut Tanowski and Frederic Will. Evanston, Ill.: Northwestern University Press, 1973.

Allen, Graham. *Harold Bloom: A Poetics of Conflict*. New York: Harvester Wheatsheaf, 1994.

Aristotle. *Metaphysics*. Trans. W. D. Ross. In *The Basic Works of Aristotle*, ed. Richard McKeon. New York: Random House, 1941.

Baeumler, Alfred. *Nietzsche der Philosoph und Politiker*. Leipzig: Reclam, 1931.

Bahti, Timothy. *Allegories of History: Literary Historiography after Hegel*. Baltimore, Md.: Johns Hopkins University Press, 1992.

Bernasconi, Robert. *The Question of Language in Heidegger's History of Being*. Atlantic Highlands, N.J.: Humanities Press, 1985.

Blanchot, Maurice. "From Dread to Language." In *The Gaze of Orpheus*, trans. Lydia Davis; ed. P. Adams Sitney, 3–20. New York: Station Hill, 1981.

Bloom, Harold. *Agon: Towards a Theory of Revisionism*. Oxford: Oxford University Press, 1981.

———. *The Anxiety of Influence: A Theory of Poetry*. Oxford: Oxford University Press, 1973.

————. *The Breaking of the Vessels*. Chicago: University of Chicago Press, 1982.

————. *Figures of Capable Imagination*. New York: Seabury, 1976.

————. *The Flight to Lucifer*. New York: Farrar, Straus, Giroux, 1979.

————. "The Internalization of Quest-Romance." *The Yale Review* 58, no. 4 (summer 1969). Reprinted in Bloom, *The Ringers in the Tower*, 13–35.

————. *Kabbalah and Criticism*. New York: Continuum, 1975.

————. *A Map of Misreading*. Oxford: Oxford University Press, 1975.

————. *Poetry and Repression: Revisionism from Blake to Stevens*. New Haven, Conn.: Yale University Press, 1976.

————. *The Ringers in the Tower: Studies in Romantic Tradition*. Chicago: University of Chicago Press, 1971.

————. *Shakespeare: The Invention of the Human*. New York: Riverhead, 1998.

————. *Wallace Stevens: The Poems of our Climate*. Ithaca, N.Y.: Cornell University Press, 1976.

————. *The Western Canon: The Books and Schools of the Ages*. New York: Riverhead, 1994.

————. *Yeats*. New York: Oxford University Press, 1970.

Bloom, Harold, Paul de Man, Jacques Derrida, Geoffrey Hartman, and J. Hillis Miller. *Deconstruction and Criticism*. New York: Continuum, 1979.

Cadava, Eduardo. *Emerson and the Climates of History*. Stanford, Calif.: Stanford University Press, 1997.

Cavell, Stanley. *Conditions Handsome and Unhandsome: The Constitution of Emersonian Perfectionism*. Chicago: University of Chicago Press, 1990.

————. *This New Yet Unapproachable America: Lectures after Emerson after Wittgenstein*. Albuquerque, N.M.: Living Batch, 1989.

Chai, Leonard. *The Romantic Foundations of the American Renaissance*. Ithaca, N.Y.: Cornell University Press, 1987.

Cicero. *Ad Herennium*. Trans. Harry Caplan. Cambridge, Mass.: Harvard University (Loeb) Press, 1954.

Danto, Arthur. *Nietzsche as Philosopher*. New York: Columbia University Press, 1965.

de Bolla, Peter. *Harold Bloom: Towards Historical Rhetorics*. London: Routledge, 1988.

Deleuze, Gilles. *Cinema I: The Movement-Image*. Trans. Hugh Tomlinson. Minneapolis: University of Minnesota Press, 1986.

————. *Nietzsche*. Paris: Presses Universitaires, 1965.

————. *Nietzsche and Philosophy*. Trans. Hugh Tomlinson. 1962. Reprint, New York: Columbia University Press, 1983.

de Man, Paul. *Blindness and Insight*. Minneapolis: University of Minnesota Press, 1973.

———. *The Resistance to Theory*. Minneapolis: University of Minnesota Press, 1986.

———. "Review of Harold Bloom's *Anxiety of Influence*." Appendix to *Blindness and Insight*, 267–76.

———. "Semiology and Rhetoric." In *Textual Strategies*, ed. Josué Harari, 121–40. Ithaca, N.Y.: Cornell University Press, 1979.

Derrida, Jacques. *Dissemination*. Trans. Barbara Johnson. Chicago: University of Chicago Press, 1981.

———. "Heidegger's Silence: Excerpts from a talk given on 5 February 1988." In *Questions and Answers*, ed. Günther Neske and Emil Kettering, 145–48. 1988. Reprint, New York: Paragon, 1990.

———. *Margins of Philosophy*. Trans. Alan Bass. Chicago: University of Chicago Press, 1986.

———. *Of Spirit*. Trans. Goeffrey Bennington. Chicago: University of Chicago Press, 1989.

———. *Speech and Phenomena*. Trans. David B. Allison. Evanston, Ill.: Northwestern University Press, 1973.

Descombes, Vincent. *The Barometer of Modern Reason*. Trans. Stephen Adam Schwartz. New York: Oxford University Press, 1993.

Emerson, Ralph Waldo. *Essays and Lectures*. Ed. Joel Porte. New York: Literary Classics of the United States, 1983.

Farias, Victor. *Heidegger and Nazism*. Trans. Paul Burrell. Ed. Joseph Margolis and Tom Rockmore. Philadelphia, Pa.: Temple University Press, 1989.

———. *Heidegger et le Nazisme*. Trans. into French by Myriam Benarroch and Jean-Baptiste Grasset. LaGrasse: Verdier, 1987.

———. *Heidegger und der Nationalsozialismus*. Frankfurt am Main: Fischer, 1989.

Fish, Stanley. *Is There a Text in this Class?: The Authority of Interpretive Communities*. Cambridge, Mass.: Harvard University Press, 1980.

———. "Literature in the Reader: Affective Stylistics." In *Reader-Response Criticism*, ed. Jane P. Thompkins. Baltimore, Md.: Johns Hopkins University Press, 1980.

———. *Surprised by Sin*. London: Macmillan, 1967.

———. "What Makes an Interpretation Acceptable?" In *Is There a Text in this Class*, 388–55.

Fynsk, Christopher. *Heidegger: Thought and Historicity.* 1986. Expanded ed., Ithaca, N.Y.: Cornell University Press, 1993.

Gadamer, Hans-Georg. "The Political Incompetence of Philosophy." In *The Heidegger Case*, ed. Tom Rockmore and Joseph Margolis, 364–69. Philadelphia, Pa.: Temple University Press, 1992.

———. *Truth and Method.* 1960. 2d rev. ed. Trans. and rev. Joel Weinsheimer and Donald G. Marshall. New York: Crossroad, 1989.

Gasché, Rodolphe. *The Tain of the Mirror: Derrida and the Philosophy of Reflection.* Cambridge, Mass.: Harvard University Press, 1986.

Genette, Gerard. *Paratexts: Thresholds of Interpretation.* Trans. Jane E. Lewin. New York: Cambridge University Press, 1997.

Gilbert, Sandra M., and Gubar, Susan. *The Madwoman in the Attic: The Woman Writer and the Nineteenth-Century Imagination.* New Haven, Conn.: Yale University Press, 1979.

Gilman, Sander, ed. *Conversations with Nietzsche.* Trans. David J. Parent. New York: Oxford University Press, 1987.

Hamacher, Werner. *Pleroma: Reading in Hegel.* Trans. Nicholas Walker and Simon Jarvis. Stanford, Calif.: Stanford University Press, 1998.

———. "Pleroma." In Introduction to Hegel, *Der Geist des Christentums*, ed. Werner Hamacher. Frankfurt am Main: Ullstein, 1978.

Hegel, G. W. F. *Aesthetics: Lectures on Fine Art.* Vols. 1–2. Trans. T. M. Knox. New York: Clarendon, 1998.

———. *The Difference Between Fichte's and Schelling's System of Philosophy.* Trans. H. S. Harris. Albany: State University of New York Press, 1977.

———. *Differenz des Fichte'schen und Shelling'schen Systems der Philosophie.* In *Werke*, vol. 2, (*Jenaer Shriften*), ed. Eva Moldenhauer and Karl Markus Michel. Frankfurt am Main: Suhrkamp, 1970.

———. *Enzyklopädie der philosophischen Wissenschaften im Grundrisse: (Erster Teil: Die Wissenschaft der Logik).* In *Werke*, vol. 8, ed. Eva Moldenhauer and Karl Markus Michel. Frankfurt am Main: Suhrkamp, 1970.

———. *Logic.* Trans. J. N. Findlay. Oxford: Oxford University Press, 1975.

———. *Phänomenologie des Geistes.* Hamburg: Felix Meiner, 1988.

———. *Phenomenology of Spirit.* Trans. A. V. Miller. Oxford: Oxford University Press, 1977.

Heidegger, Martin. *Being and Time.* Trans. John Macquarrie and Edward Robinson. New York: Harper and Row, 1962.

———. *Beiträge zur Philosophie (Gesamtausgabe 65).* Frankfurt am Main: Vittorio Klostermann, 1989.

————. *Einführung in die Metaphysik*. Frankfurt am Main: Vittorio Klostermann, 1983.

————. *The End of Philosophy*. Trans. and ed. Joan Stambaugh. New York: Harper and Row, 1973.

————. *Gesamtausgabe*. Vol. 1–65. Frankfurt am Main: Vittorio Klostermann, 1976–1994.

————. *Hegel's Phenomenology of Spirit*. Trans. Parvis Emad and Kenneth Maly. Indianapolis: Indiana University Press, 1980.

————. *History of the Concept of Time*. Trans. Theodore Kisiel. Bloomington: Indiana University Press, 1992.

————. *Identität und Differenz*. Pfullingen: Günther Neske, 1957.

————. *Identity and Difference*. Trans. Joan Stambaugh. New York: Harper and Row, 1969.

————. *Introduction to Metaphysics*. Trans. Ralph Mannheim. New Haven, Conn.: Yale University Press, 1959.

————. "Letter to the Rector of Freiburg University, November 4, 1945." In *The Heidegger Controversy*, ed. Richard Wolin, 61–66. Cambridge, Mass.: MIT Press, 1991.

————. *Nietzsche*: Vol. 1 and 2. Pfullingen: Günther Neske, 1961.

————. *Nietzsche*. Vol. 1: *The Will to Power as Art*. Ed. and trans. David Farrell Krell. New York: Harper Collins, 1979.

————. *Nietzsche*. Vol. 2: *The Eternal Recurrence of the Same*. Ed. and trans. David Farrell Krell. New York: Harper Collins, 1991.

————. *Nietzsche*. Vol. 3: *The Will to Power as Knowledge and as Metaphysics*. Ed. David Farrell Krell. Trans. Joan Stambaugh, David Farrell Krell, and Frank A. Capuzzi. New York: Harper Collins, 1987.

————. *Nietzsche*. Vol. 4: *Nihilism*. Ed. David Farrell Krell. Trans. Frank A. Capuzzi. New York: Harper Collins, 1987.

————. *Nietzsche: der europäische Nihilismus* (*Gesamtausgabe*, vol. 48). Frankfurt am Main: Vittorio Klostermann, 1986.

————. *Nietzsches Lehre von Willen zur Macht als Erkenntnis* (*Gesamtausgabe*, vol. 47). Frankfurt am Main: Vittorio Klostermann, 1989.

————. *Nietzsches Metaphysik* and *Einleitung in die Philosophie—Denken und Dichten* (*Gesamatausgabe*, vol. 50). Frankfurt am Main: Vittorio Klostermann, 1990.

————. *Nietzsches metaphysische Grundstellung in abendländischen Denken: Die ewige Wiederkehr des Gleichen* (*Gesamtausgabe*, vol. 44). Frankfurt am Main: Vittorio Klostermann, 1986.

————. *Nietzsches 2d Unzeitgemäße Betrachtung* (*Gesamtausgabe*, vol. 46). Frankfurt am Main: Vittorio Klostermann, in preparation.

————. *Nietzsche: Der Wille zur Macht als Kunst* (*Gesamtausgabe*, vol. 43). Frankfurt am Main: Vittorio Klostermann, 1985.

————. "Nur noch ein Gott kann uns retten." *Der Spiegel* 30, no. 23 (May 31, 1976): 193–219.

————. *Sein und Zeit*. Tübingen: Max Niemeyer, 1977.

————. *Die Technik und die Kehre*. Pfulligen: Günther Neske, 1962.

————. *Vorträge und Aufsätze*. Pfullingen: Günther Neske, 1954.

Husserl, Edmund. *Ideas Pertaining to a Pure Phenomenology and to a Phenomenological Philosophy*. Trans. F. Kersten. The Hague: Martinus Nijhoff, 1983.

Hyppolite, Jean. *Genesis and Structure of Hegel's Phenomenology of Spirit*. Trans. Samuel Cherniak and John Heckman. Evanston, Ill.: Northwestern University Press, 1974.

Ingarden, Roman. *The Cognition of the Literary Work of Art*. Trans. Ruth Ann Crowley and Kenneth R. Olson. Evanston, Ill.: Northwestern University Press, 1973.

————. *The Literary Work of Art*. Trans. George G. Grabowicz. Evanston, Ill.: Northwestern University Press, 1973.

Irigaray, Luce. *Speculum of the Other Woman*. Trans. Gillian C. Gill. Ithaca, N.Y.: Cornell University Press, 1985.

Iser, Wolfgang. *The Act of Reading*. Baltimore, Md.: Johns Hopkins University Press, 1978.

————. *The Implied Reader*. Baltimore, Md.: Johns Hopkins University Press, 1974.

Jaspers, Karl. *Nietzsche: An Introduction to the Understanding of his Philosophical Activity*. Trans. Charles F. Wallraff and Frederick J. Schmitz. 1936. Reprint, Chicago: Henry Regnery, 1965.

Jauss, Hans Robert. *Aesthetic Experience and Literary Hermeneutics*. Trans. Michael Shaw. Minneapolis: University of Minnesota Press, 1982.

————. *Toward an Aesthetic of Reception*. Trans. Timothy Bahti. Minneapolis: University of Minnesota Press, 1982.

Kant, Emmanuel. *Critique of Pure Reason*. Trans. Norman Kemp Smith. New York: St. Martin's Press, 1965.

————. *Prolegomena to Any Future Metaphysics*. Trans. Paul Carus. Rev. James W. Ellington. Indianapolis, Ind.: Hackett, 1977.

Kierkegaard, Søren. *Authority and Revelation.* Trans. Walter Lowrie. Princeton, N.J.: Princeton University Press, 1985.

——. *The Concept of Irony.* Trans. Lee Capel. Bloomington: Indiana University Press, 1965.

——. *Concluding Unscientific Postscript to Philosophical Fragments.* Ed. and trans. Howard V. Hong and Edna H. Hong. Princeton, N.J.: Princeton University Press, 1992.

——. *Fear and Trembling.* Ed. and trans. Howard V. Hong and Edna H. Hong. Princeton, N.J.: Princeton University Press, 1983.

——. *Philosophical Fragments.* Trans. David Swenson. Rev. Howard V. Hong. Princeton, N.J.: Princeton University Press, 1962.

Klossowski, Pierre. *Nietzsche and the Vicious Circle.* Trans. Daniel W. Smith. Chicago: University of Chicago Press, 1997.

Kosík, Karel. *Die Dialektik des Konkreten: Eine Studie zur Problematik des Menschen und der Welt.* Frankfurt am Main: Suhrkamp, 1967.

Krell, David Farrell. *Daimon Life.* Indianapolis: Indiana University Press, 1992.

——. "Introduction to the Paperback Edition: Heidegger Nietzsche Nazism." In Heidegger, *Nietzsche.* Vols. 1–2, ed. and trans. David Farrell Krell, ix–xxvii. New York: Harper Collins, 1991.

Kracauer, Siegfried. *The Mass Ornament: Weimar Essays.* Trans. and ed. David Y. Levin. Cambridge, Mass.: Harvard University Press, 1995.

Kripke, Saul. *On Rules and Private Language.* Cambridge, Mass.: Harvard University Press, 1982.

Kuhn, Thomas. *The Structure of Scientific Revolutions.* Chicago: University of Chicago Press, 1970.

Lacoue-Labarthe, Philippe. *Heidegger, Art and Politics.* Trans. Chris Turner. Cambridge, Eng.: Blackwell, 1990.

——. *The Subject of Philosophy.* Trans. Thomas Trezise, Hugh J. Silverman, Gary M. Cole, Timothy D. Bent, Karen McPherson, and Claudette Sartiliot. Minneapolis: University of Minnesota Press, 1993.

——. *Typography.* Trans. Christopher Fynsk. Stanford, Calif.: Stanford University Press, 1998.

Lovejoy, Arthur O. *The Great Chain of Being.* Cambridge, Mass.: Harvard University Press, 1936.

Löwith, Karl. *Martin Heidegger and European Nihilism.* Trans. Gary Steiner. Ed. Richard Wolin. New York: Columbia University Press, 1995.

Lyotard, Jean-François. *Heidegger and "the jews."* Trans. Andreas Michel and Mark Roberts. Minneapolis: University of Minnesota Press, 1990.

Matthiessen, F. O. *American Renaissance.* London: Oxford University Press, 1941.

Moon, Michael. *Disseminating Whitman: Revision and Corporeality in* Leaves of Grass. Cambridge, Mass.: Harvard University Press, 1991.

Moynihan, Robert. *A Recent Imagining: Interviews with Harold Bloom, Geoffrey Hartman, J. Hillis Miller, Paul de Man.* Hamden, Conn.: Archon, 1986.

Nehamas, Alexander. *Nietzsche: Life as Literature.* Cambridge, Mass.: Harvard University Press, 1985.

Neske, Günther, and Kettering, Emil, eds. *Martin Heidegger and National Socialism: Questions and Answers.* Trans. Lisa Harries. 1988. Reprint, New York: Paragon, 1990.

Nietzsche, Friedrich. *The Birth of Tragedy and The Case of Wagner.* Trans. Walter Kaufmann. New York: Vintage, 1967.

———. *Ecce Homo.* Trans. Walter Kaufmann. In *On the Genealogy of Morals and Ecce Homo,* ed. and trans. Walter Kaufmann. New York: Vintage, 1967.

———. *Ecce Homo.* Trans. R. J. Hollingdale. New York: Penguin, 1979.

———. *The Gay Science.* Trans. Walter Kaufmann. New York: Vintage, 1974.

———. *On the Genealogy of Morals and Ecce Homo.* Ed. and trans. Walter Kaufmann. New York: Vintage, 1967.

———. *Großoktavausgabe.* Leipzig, 1905.

———. *Mein Leben. Autobiographische Skizze des jungen Nietzsche.* Frankfurt am Main: n.p., 1936.

———. *The Portable Nietzsche.* Ed. Walter Kaufmann. New York: Viking, 1982.

———. *Sämtliche Werke: Kritische Studienausgabe.* Vols. 1–15. Ed. Giorgio Colli and Mazzino Montinari. Berlin: Walter de Gruyter, 1967–1977.

———. *Thus Spoke Zarathustra.* Trans. Walter Kaufmann. In *The Portable Nietzsche,* ed. Walter Kaufmann, 103–439. New York: Viking, 1982.

———. *Twilight of the Idols.* Trans. Walter Kaufmann. In *The Portable Nietzsche,* ed. Walter Kaufmann, 463–564. New York: Viking, 1982.

———. *The Will to Power.* Trans. Walter Kaufmann and R. J. Hollingdale. Ed. Walter Kaufmann. New York: Vintage, 1967.

———. *Der Wille zur Macht.* Leipzig: Alfred Kröner Verlag, 1930.

———. *Werke in drei Bänden.* Munich: Carl Hanser, 1956.

Ott, Hugo. *Martin Heidegger: Unterwegs zu seiner Biographie*. Frankfurt am Main: Campus, 1988.

Packer, Barbara. *Emerson's Fall: A New Interpretation of the Major Essays*. New York: Continuum, 1982.

Plato. *Republic*. Trans. Paul Shorey. *Plato: The Collected Dialogues*. Ed. Edith Hamilton. Princeton, N.J.: Princeton University Press, 1961.

Pöggeler, Otto. "Being as Appropriation [*Ereignis*]." In *Heidegger and Modern Philosophy*, ed. Michael Murray, 84–115. New Haven, Conn.: Yale University Press, 1978.

———. *Martin Heidegger's Path of Thinking*. Trans. Daniel Magurshak and Sigmund Barber. Atlantic Highlands, N.J.: Humanities Press, 1987.

Preminger, A., and Brogan, T. V. F., eds. *The New Princeton Encyclopedia of Poetry and Poetics*. Princeton, N.J.: Princeton University Press, 1993.

Quintilian. *Institutio Oratoria*. Vol. 3. Trans. H. E. Butler. Cambridge, Mass.: Harvard University (Loeb) Press, 1986.

Rorty, Richard. *Contingency, Irony, and Solidarity*. New York: Cambridge University Press, 1989.

———. "The Historiography of Philosophy: Four Genres." In *Philosophy in History*, ed. Richard Rorty, J. B. Schneewind, and Quentin Skinner, 49–75. New York: Cambridge University Press, 1984.

Safranski, Rüdiger. *Martin Heidegger: Between Good and Evil*. Trans. Ewald Osers. 1994. Reprint, Cambridge, Mass.: Harvard University Press, 1998.

Salusinszky, Imre. "Interview with Harold Bloom." In *Criticism in Society*, ed. Imre Salusinszky, 44–73. New York: Methuen, 1987.

Sartre, Jean Paul. *The Transcendence of the Ego*. Trans. Forrest Williams and Robert Kirkpatrick. New York: Farrar, Straus, Giroux, n.d.

Schelling, Friedrich. *The Philosophy of Art*. Ed. and trans. Douglas W. Scott. Minneapolis: University of Minnesota Press, 1989.

Schneeberger, Guido. *Nachlese zu Heidegger: Dokumente zu seinem Leben und Denken*. Bern: n.p., 1962.

Schürmann, Reiner. *Heidegger on Being and Acting: From Principles to Anarchy*. Trans. Christine-Marie Gros. Bloomington: Indiana University Press, 1987.

Sluga, Hans. *Heidegger's Crisis*. Cambridge, Mass.: Harvard University Press, 1993.

Stevens, Wallace. *The Palm at the End of the Mind: Selected Poems and a Play*. Ed. Holly Stevens. New York: Vintage, 1972.

Suleiman, Susan R. "Introduction: Varieties of Audience-Oriented Criticism." In *The Reader in the Text*, ed. Suleiman and Inge Crosman, 3–45. Princeton, N.J.: Princeton University Press, 1980.

Szilasi, Wilhelm. *Martin Heidegger's Einfluß auf die Wissenschaften*. Bern: n.p., 1949.

Szondi, Peter. *Introduction to Literary Hermeneutics*. Trans. Martha Woodmansee. New York: Cambridge University Press, 1995.

Warminski, Andrzej. *Readings in Interpretation*. Minneapolis: University of Minnesota Press, 1987.

White, Hayden. *Metahistory: The Historical Imagination in Nineteenth-Century Europe*. Baltimore, Md.: Johns Hopkins University Press, 1973.

———. *Tropics of Discourse: Essays in Cultural Criticism*. Baltimore, Md.: Johns Hopkins University Press, 1978.

Wittgenstein, Ludwig. *Philosophical Investigations*. Trans. G. E. M. Anscombe. Oxford, Eng.: Blackwell, 1982.

Wolin, Richard, ed. *The Heidegger Controversy: A Critical Reader*. Cambridge, Mass.: MIT Press, 1991.

———. *The Politics of Being*. New York: Columbia University Press, 1990.

Index

Adorno, Theodor, 215n12
aesthetics, 50, 105, 107, 122, 225n20, 231n4; of the act of reading, 13ff, 102, 109ff, 120, 125, 211n19; of reception, 9, 13f, 103–11, 120, 211n19. *See also* art
allegory, 121–24, 128, 140f, 144, 224n14, 235n17
antinomianism, 238n8
antiphrasis, 68, 224n13–14
anxiety, 127ff, 232n4, 235n17–18
a priori (and *apriority*), 85–88, 138, 141, 237–38n7, 239n13
Aristotle, 53, 74, 200, 227n3
art, 12, 215–16n14, 220n5; as against nihilism, 36, 44–49, 58, 213n1, 215–16n14; and idealization, 45–48, 58, 216–17n17, 218nn22,24; in Plato, 27, 34f, 37ff, 53, 216–17n17, 217–18nn22–24; and truth, 22–30, 35–39, 42–54, 58f, 213nn1,2, 214–15nn11,13. *See also* aesthetics; discordance
as, and as-structure, 26, 29f, 40, 44, 51, 60, 67ff, 83ff, 91ff, 109, 122, 149, 214n8
Austen, Jane, 197ff, 202

Bahti, Timothy, 173, 246n27
basic word (*Grundwort*), 54–58, 221n10
Baudelaire, Charles, 109ff
Being (*Sein*), and becoming, 28, 70–75,

79, 97, 220n8; concealment or presence of, 58f, 72–75, 78f, 82–98, 131, 158f, 162, 222n13, 227n2, 228n9; history of, 79, 90–93, 96ff, 131, 158f, 229–30nn15,18; Platonic conception of, 31, 33–37, 72ff, 86–89, 214n10, 217n17, 218–19nn24,27; question of, 7, 24, 50, 59f, 68f, 72, 81–93, 96, 155, 170, 195, 215n13, 225n19, 227nn1,2. *See also* ontology
Bercovitch, Sacvan, 238n9
Bernasconi, Robert, 230n19
Blake, William, 197ff, 202
Bloom, Harold, 8f, 112–33, 137, 142ff, 149, 155, 200, 202, 211n22, 224n15, 232–33nn1–11, 234–36nn15–19,20–32, 238n11, 239n13, 241n30
Buell, Lawrence, 238n9

Cadava, Eduardo, 236–37n1, 238n9
canons, formation of, 1f, 8f, 104, 112, 114, 119–28, 132, 143, 194–99, 202; philosophical, 6, 96, 194–99
catachresis, 173ff, 179ff, 186, 190, 192
Cavell, Stanley, 236n1, 240–41n25
Chase, Richard, 238n9
Christianity, 41, 43, 148, 153, 173ff, 186, 248n43; and Platonism, 31, 33, 47, 88, 161, 179f
chronology, 59f, 97, 101, 116, 128, 135, 197, 230–31n20